Theatre Planning

Theatre Planning

edited by
Roderick Ham AADipl RIBA

University of Toronto Press

© Association of British Theatre Technicians
First published in North America
by University of Toronto Press
Toronto and Buffalo
ISBN 0–8020–1938–2
ISBN microfiche 0–8020–0278–1

(cuo)
oversize
NA
6821
T45
1972 b

WITHDRAWN

Printed in Great Britain by Balding + Mansell, Wisbech, Cambs.

Contents

Introduction

The Association of British Theatre Technicians was formed in March 1961 by a group of enthusiasts, all professionally connected with the theatre, who believed that it was time to improve technical standards.

There had scarcely been any theatre building in Britain for twenty years, continuity was broken and it was no longer just a question of starting again from where the matter had been left in the 'thirties. The war had accelerated the changes in society, technology was advancing rapidly and a reassessment of the problems of theatre planning and design was clearly necessary before a new generation of building arose. It was already apparent that mistakes were being made out of ignorance of the needs of the performing arts and the ABTT saw that probably its most important task was to examine these needs and make recommendations based upon the wide experience of its members in every branch of the theatre. The Association was a forum where ideas were exchanged and tested in discussion. Specialist committees were formed dealing with Architecture and Planning, Materials, Publications, Safety, Sound and Stage Lighting. Each of these committees embarked on technical studies and when the *Architects' Journal* proposed to publish a series of articles on theatres in its programme of design guides and information sheets, the ABTT took on the task of preparing the texts and diagrams. The first supplements were published at weekly intervals in the *Architects' Journal* in 1964 and a later series was added in 1967. Two thousand additional sets of articles were bound into paperback volumes and published as *Theatre Planning* and *Theatre Planning II*. The subject had not been covered as comprehensively before and there is little doubt that the work had a profound influence on those concerned with projects for new theatres. The original issues are now out of print and the ABTT decided that a new and completely revised edition should be prepared for publication in book form. The Arts Council was approached by Norman Marshall, the ABTT's chairman, and contributed a generous grant towards the cost of research and rewriting of the text and the Architectural Press undertook to publish the book.

The shortcomings of the original publications were mostly due to the magazine form they had to follow. There was no index and a good deal of repetition was inevitable. Some of the articles were only of passing interest and others have been superseded. Much of the basic information in the original work remains the same but all of it has been carefully scrutinised and much of it re-written. The book sets out to describe the principles and practical considerations which influence the design of the layout and equipment of buildings to house live performances. The information has been gathered from the experience of those who have to work in such buildings and who have to try to use them efficiently. As more is known about the workings of the proscenium theatre than about open forms it is inevitable that there are more references to it than to the less orthodox types of theatre but this does not indicate an editorial bias in favour of the proscenium. We have described what there is to describe and many of the problems examined are common to all forms of theatre. There remain entertainments and dramatic activities from tattoos to television which neither need nor ask for the kind of facilities here examined.

One subject not covered in this book is the multi-purpose hall. We have been concerned throughout to describe the optimum conditions for housing live performances, and these remain the same whether the building is labelled 'theatre' or 'multi-purpose hall'. If the process of making a hall multi-purpose forces compromises and prevents proper conditions from being obtained, that is not a valid excuse for applying lower standards. A great deal of ingenuity has been lavished on schemes of adaptability and much time and sometimes money spent on mechanical methods of achieving them. The fascination of the gadgetry should not be allowed to obscure the shortcomings of the results. In any one conformation or arrangement an objective assessment of the result usually shows that it is less satisfactory than a building specially designed to serve that particular purpose.

Flexibility of use remains an important virtue in any scheme but it is not synonymous with machinery as some would have us think. While it is very simple to phrase a brief which calls for a building to house banquets, dances, professional theatre, amateur operatics, film shows and jumble sales all in the same space, if not at the same time, it is virtually impossible to translate such words into a satisfactory solution in terms of building. It has never yet been done successfully though the quest has been as obsessive as for the philosopher's stone or the elixir of life.

Another school of thought which has ample coverage elsewhere especially in architectural magazines, is the one which demands a covered space and a kit of parts which in theory enable it to keep its options open until the last moment. Schemes of this nature usually rely heavily on rather speculative technological solutions to the problems encountered along the way and it would not be possible to do justice to them in a book of this nature.

In a work devoted to the study of the design of buildings for housing the performing arts it is well to sound a note of humility and remember that it is people and not buildings which make theatre. Dramatic magic can be created in the most unlikely places and in utterly unpromising surroundings. Nevertheless, good buildings can give full rein to the creativity of those who use them and can enhance the experience of those who come to watch and listen.

Acknowledgements   The original *Architects' Journal* series was edited by Leslie Fairweather, the principal authors were Peter Moro, Ian Appleton, Peter Jay and the present editor and this work has provided a sound foundation for the present volume. The editor is indebted to Peter Moro and Frederick Bentham for their continual advice and encouragement on matters both technical and syntactical during the two years over which the task of compiling and editing has been spread.

The chapter on acoustics was originally written by Henry Humphreys; safety, regulations and legislation are largely the work of Eric Jordan who also contributed the section on the comparison of theatres and all the drawings in that chapter. Stage scenery is adapted from the study by the ABTT Materials Committee first published by the *Architects' Journal*. The members of the committee of which the editor was chairman were: Ian Albery, Dorothea Alexander, Alan Cohen, Frederick Crooke, Richard Greenough, Bertram Harrison, Joseph McDougall, Harry Pegg and Edward Tietjen.

The Materials Committee joined by Peter Angier, Ethel Langstreth, Ken Smalley, Peter White-Gaze and Peter Woodham, gave invaluable assistance with the chapter on stage planning and with the glossary. Richard Brett contributed a note on powered flying. The ABTT Lighting Committee drew up the original recommendations for stage lighting installations, published in the *Architects' Journal*. The members at that time were: Eric Baker, Frederick Bentham, Charles Bristow, Bill Bruce, John Bury, Martin Carr, Peter Coe, Elidir Davies, Joe Davis, David Furse, Barry Griffiths, Cyril Griffiths, Robert Hall, Margaret Harris, Edward Hitchman, Peter Jay, Brian Legge, Robert Ornbo, Richard Pilbrow, Francis Reid, Peter Rice and John Wyckham.

That document has been completely revised by the committee now joined by: Brian Benn, Bill Besant, E. E. Faraday, Robert Fox and R. G. S. Anderson, who contributed the section on providing for television broadcasts from theatres, and Derek Gilbert whose notes on memory systems have been included. Requirements for control rooms were taken from the ABTT Information Sheet on the subject by Martin Carr. Sound installation and communications is adapted from the ABTT Sound Committee's studies on permanent equipment for theatres, permanent wiring for theatres and stage management by sound control. The members of the committee were: David Ayliff who, in conjunction with the West End Stage Management Association prepared the material on prompt corners, Bernard Bibby, Sylvia Carter, David Collison, Barry Griffiths, Shirley Matthews, Peter Moore, Roger Spence, Dorothy Tenham and Colin Wootton.

The basis of the chapter on film projection was the series of articles by Leslie Knopp and Anthony Wylson which appeared in the *Architects' Journal* in March, April and May, 1967 and the section on heating and ventilating is adapted from an Information Sheet by Paul Hanson published in the *Architects' Journal's* first series of design guides on theatres.

The editor is very conscious of how much he has learned from taking part in the deliberations of the ABTT Architecture and Planning Committee, chaired by Peter Moro, which over the last ten years has examined over a hundred schemes for new theatres or for the improvement of old ones.

The other members of the Architecture and Planning Committee were: Ian Albery, David Ayliff, Frederick Bentham, John Bury, Martin Carr, Douglas Cornelisson, Elidir Davies, Tony Easterbrook, John English, Michael Elliott, Eric Jordan, Iain Mackintosh, Richard Pilbrow, Ken Smalley and John Wyckham. In the editor's office, Ronald Bayliss, George Finch and David Hancock assisted with research, the text and the drawings, and Sheila Brenchley handled mountains of typing and duplicating.

1   Type and size of theatre

The word theatre has a diversity of meanings for different people and while it is neither possible nor even desirable to fit all theatre buildings into rigid categories, it will help to consider the various types of building at present existing and the way in which they differ from or are similar to one another.

Seating capacity   Usually the first characteristic which comes to mind is the seating capacity, especially in relation to the economics of the building.

It is misleading to relate the capital cost of a theatre to the number of seats without taking into account the many different standards of space, technical equipment and amenity which different buildings require for their particular purpose. For purely economic reasons it would seem that the maximum capacity possible should be aimed at but for every form of audience to stage relationship, there is a limit beyond which the view of the performance begins to deteriorate and people will no longer be prepared to buy seats from which they cannot see enough to enjoy what is going on. When live theatre was the only form of mass entertainment the public would put up with discomfort and a poor view for want of an alternative, but in these days of television and wide-screen cinema this is no longer true.

The capacity should be derived from the visual and acoustic limits for a particular kind of performance and the form of auditorium to stage relationship. These factors will be discussed later in more detail.

There will be times when there is a demand for seats which outstrips the capacity, for instance on Saturday evenings. It would be a mistake, however, to provide a couple of hundred seats for these occasions if they remain empty on most other days. Both capital and running costs would be increased and the effect of empty seats is depressing to both performers and audience. Full houses and difficulty in getting tickets are the best possible advertisement and are an incentive for the public to go on the less popular days.

It has been suggested that seating capacity should be related to the size of the town or catchment area in which the theatre is to be situated, but this is an unreliable guide. The success of a particular enterprise depends far more on the vigour of the management than the statistics of possible theatregoers. Some large towns have the greatest difficulty in filling a theatre whereas other quite small ones are very successful. Management policy plays the greatest part in the success or failure of a theatre but there are many cases where, however good the management, a shabby old building or a new one with an unwelcoming atmosphere will deter the public from coming.

In the case of teaching theatres and drama studios, seating capacity is of secondary importance. The main purpose is to provide the drama student with the feeling of an audience and seating for between 100 and 300 is usually sufficient.

The universities are building theatres which may be connected with a drama department, but are more often used for amateur productions by students. Professional companies may visit the theatre if it has suitable facilities, in which case a capacity of 400 or 500 would be appropriate. Schemes for university theatres vary a great deal due partly to the many purposes they have to serve, but also to a vagueness of intent leading to ill-considered briefs for their architects.

When a theatre is for amateur use, the seating capacity should be considered from a slightly different point of view. Most amateur groups can count on a limited audience of friends, relations and others who share their interest in amateur dramatics. If the total potential audience is, say, 900 (way above the average for most amateur societies) it will be of little satisfaction to them to go to all the trouble of rehearsing and preparing a play for one solitary performance. They would be much happier to fill a 300-seat theatre for three performances or even a 150-seater for six.

The situation of amateur opera is rather different. There is much greater expense involved in hiring scenery and costumes and few amateur societies can operate without engaging some professional orchestral players and principal singers. With a following which is often more numerous than that for straight drama (perhaps because the larger cast, the chorus and musicians have more relations and friends), amateur opera companies look for a large-capacity auditorium because the cost and organization of a series of performances is prohibitive. Their needs are difficult to meet and they are often obliged to play in very unsuitable premises. The danger is that their insistence on a larger capacity which will be used perhaps three or four times a year, will distort the brief for a building which will be used all the rest of the time for straight drama.

There are rare occasions when the total audience is known within fairly close limits, such as in a school or similar institution, but usually the number of people who can be persuaded to come is a matter of intelligent guesswork and hope.

The seating capacity is not the only measure of the size of a theatre. The size of the stage, the production facilities to support it and the scale on which the public areas are provided may have more effect. As a rough guide and to define terms used elsewhere in this book, the following definitions are adopted.

Very large	1500 or more seats
large	900–1500 seats
medium	500–900 seats
small	under 500 seats

Types of production

There is a wide range of types of production which may have to be provided for in a theatre. The brief may call for many different activities to be housed within the same space and a measure of flexibility will be essential. However there is a limit to the degree of adaptability which is possible without seriously compromising the success of the primary purpose of the building. A list of priorities of use will have to be made at an early stage. The detailed recommendations for the provision of accommodation for the cast for the various types of production are given in Chapter 15, p. 175 et seq.

Drama
The average straight play seldom has a cast of more than 12, but it can be from 2 to 20.

Drama (large scale)
Some plays, such as the Shakespeare histories, have large casts with many extras.

Grand opera, full-scale ballet, musicals, pantomime
These activities often involve singers, dancers and chorus. The style of production and scenery is usually spectacular and generally implies a proscenium stage form.

Chamber opera, chamber ballet, music hall and variety, cabaret, plays with music
The cast is not likely to be more numerous than for straight drama, but proper arrangements must be made for musicians.

Concerts
A symphony orchestra averages about 90 players, but may be 120 or more.

Chamber concerts including jazz, pop and folk music will normally be limited to ten or twelve musicians but occasionally they may number forty or fifty.

Recitals are the smallest scale of musical performance where solo singers and instrumentalists with an accompanist are concerned. The number of performers is seldom more than four or five.

Choral concerts may require space for 200–400 singers, or even more on special occasions, in addition to a large orchestra.

Size of orchestra   Most theatres should make provision for a small orchestra of about ten to twelve players, though when the principal use is for drama, there will seldom be more than two or three musicians.

A medium orchestra would be up to about forty players which would be sufficient for most operas and ballets. A full orchestra may number 120 which is needed for some operas (e.g. Wagner).

Films   This book is mainly concerned with provisions for live performances, but most theatres should make proper provision for projecting films. A building designed first and foremost as a cinema will not be suitable for live performances, but films can be shown successfully in buildings whose main purpose is to provide for live performances.

Pattern of use   Having decided the range of activities to be housed, the next factor to be considered is the pattern of use. The more intensive this is the more space will be required.

Multiple use   This occurs when more than one company has to be accommodated simultaneously, for example a children's matinee in the afternoon, a play in the evening followed by a late-night review. There is an increasing tendency for theatres to be used in this way, interspersing plays with films and concerts. It is economically sound to make full use of the building and where the theatre serves a community it is socially sound to provide a wide range of activities.

Repertoire   Theatres used by a company which maintains a repertoire of several productions which it may change every night and between matinee and evening performances. Almost all opera houses and other major enterprises, such as the National Theatre and the Royal Shakespeare Company, play in this way. Such theatres initiate their own productions and should have their own production organisation preferably on the same site. They need space to store the sets for the repertoire and mechanical aids to help them move them about.

Repertory   The so-called 'repertory' theatres present a new production at frequent intervals, usually fortnightly or three-weekly and rarely revive a production. They require production facilities for making sets, properties and costumes. Note the distinction between repertory and repertoire.

Touring theatres   These theatres take in touring productions at weekly or sometimes longer intervals, but only rarely initiate a production. The pattern of touring has changed very much in recent years. There is still a need for theatres to house the metropolitan-based national opera, ballet and theatre companies, but the viability of commercial tours of plays has declined.

Long run   Shows run for as long as box office takings permit, which may be for several months or even years. This is the characteristic of the West End Theatre in London. Like touring theatres, such buildings do not usually require elaborate production facilities on site. If they operate profitably, their workshops would be idle most of the time.

Intermittent use   Some university theatres and theatres belonging to amateurs are only used intermittently. In this case it is unlikely that skilled theatre technicians will be employed and the equipment must necessarily be simple to use and maintain. There should at least be a resident engineer to guide the part time voluntary staff.

2 Design of auditorium

The maximum distance from the effective centre of the acting area to the furthest seat in the auditorium has visual and acoustic limits. It varies according to the kind of activity and differs for concerts, ballet, opera, plays, etc.

Visual limits

Given a full view of the performer, there is still a limit to the distance at which he can project his performance and 'hold' his audience. This depends partly on his skill and partly upon the eyesight and acuteness of hearing of the audience. For most plays, it is essential that the audience should be close enough to discern facial expressions. The usually accepted maximum is 20 m from the geometrical centre for an open stage or from the setting line of a proscenium stage. For musicals and opera, in which facial expressions are less important, the distance can be increased up to 30 m. If it is necessary most of the time for performers to be seen against a background of special scenery, as in the conventional proscenium theatre, the sight lines and maximum distance from the performer restrict the number of audience it is possible to fit in. The number of people required to be accommodated in the auditorium should not be the sole criterion for selecting the width of proscenium opening.

Acoustic limits

The acoustic characteristics of a space, in simplified terms, are dependent upon the behaviour of sound reflections and on the period of reverberation. The period of reverberation must be short for clarity of speech; it is usually preferred longer for music, and longer still for choral singing. It depends mainly upon two factors: the amount of sound absorbed and reflected by the surfaces of the auditorium and the volume of the auditorium and stage. Design of reflecting and absorbing surfaces can assist acoustics but there is a limit to the size of a space in which sufficient clarity of unaided speech can be maintained. For different functions acoustic characteristics can be altered physically to a limited extent by covering or uncovering sound absorbing surfaces and by use of sound reflectors.

Artificial amplification of the sound is possible, but not usually desirable.

Forms of auditorium to stage relationship

In the live theatre there has been a strong reaction against the separation of the play from the audience, which is characteristic of the typical proscenium theatre of the recent past and this has encouraged a search for new actor to audience relationship or rather a revival of past forms. Essentially the aim has been to bring auditorium and acting area into the same architectural space and to get as close as possible a relation between the action of the play and the spectators watching it. The focus of the audience's attention is on the centre of the drama and members of that audience tend to group themselves round this focus. Controversy arises over how far round they should stretch or in other words what degree of encirclement of the stage is desirable.

The term 'open stage' is used for an arrangement in which performance and audience are contained within the same space. This is to distinguish it from the proscenium or picture-frame stage where the whole or a substantial part of the acting area is in a space separated from the audience by a wall with an opening, the proscenium, through which the performance is seen. These terms are not as mutually exclusive as they at first appear. The quality of an open-stage performance can be obtained within a theatre which, nevertheless has the means to shut off the acting area, or part of it, from the audience for the purpose of deploying scenery.

So many terms have been applied to the various forms, that it has been decided to classify them firstly by the degree of encirclement of the stage by the audience.

360° encirclement

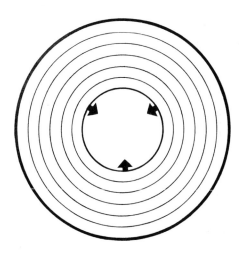

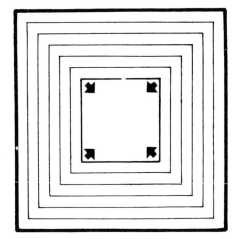

No. 2:1   *No. 2:2*

The acting area is surrounded on all sides by the audience. This form is also called theatre-in-the-round, island stage, arena or centre stage.

Entrances are made through the audience or from under the stage. There is no scenic background to the acting area and no problem of horizontal sight lines.

A variation of this form is the transverse stage where most of the audience sit on two opposite sides and face one another across the stage.

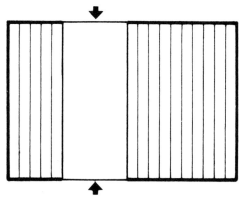

No. 2:3

Transverse stage

This type is rare at present in this country though interest may be stimulated by the theory that the English popular playhouse from Elizabethan times till the Commonwealth, was of this form. (Leslie Hotson: *Shakespeares Wooden O.*) This view is not generally accepted, the more common theory being that Shakespeare's theatre was 180° encirclement with a back wall containing doors, balconies, etc, from which entrances were made on to a large apron stage. Probably many variations and combinations of forms and methods were used.

No. 2:4   *Gulbenkian Centre, Hull, arranged for a theatre-in-the-round performance.*

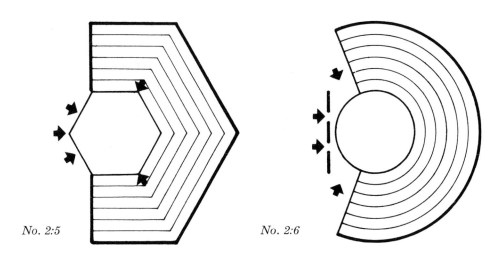

No. 2:5   No. 2:6

210°-220°   The classical Greek and Hellenistic theatres were of this type.
encirclement Entrances to the acting area can be made from a vertical wall or
platform on the open side, but the principal acting area is at the
focus of the seating. The essential feature of the original Greek
theatre was that it was always in the open air.

No. 2:7   *The thrust stage at the Crucible Theatre, Sheffield.*

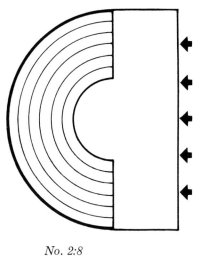

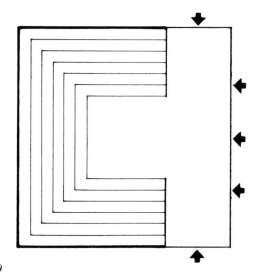

No. 2:8   *No. 2:9*

180° encirclement   The Roman theatre was of this type and the first Renaissance theatres copied the pattern. The emphasis has moved towards the back wall which now forms the boundary of the acting area. Extreme sight lines exclude any action behind the back wall.

More recent versions of this form are usually called 'thrust' stages, though the terms 'peninsular' or 'three-sided' stage are sometimes used. The Elizabethan public theatres are usually believed to have been in this form. Modern thrust stages vary the degree of encirclement and seldom bear much similarity to the ancient theatres.

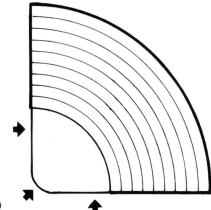

No. 2:10

90° encirclement   This 'wide fan' arrangement allows most of the action to be seen against stage walls or a scenic background rather than against members of the audience. It is a form with many possible variations allowing more extensive use of scenery than on thrust stages but still limited by the extreme sight lines. The technique of performance does not differ radically from that of the proscenium theatre.

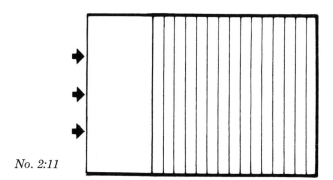

No. 2:11

Zero encirclement

End stage, as this is usually called, is only an open stage in as much as the acting area and the audience are within the same space. It is not sight lines which limit the use of scenery but the physical limitations of the structure. The end stage condition comes about because of the restrictions imposed by an existing shell or by a consciously chosen structure. It is basically a proscenium theatre without a proscenium arch and without the working areas needed to deploy scenery.

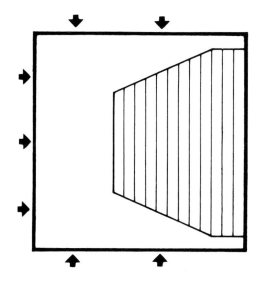

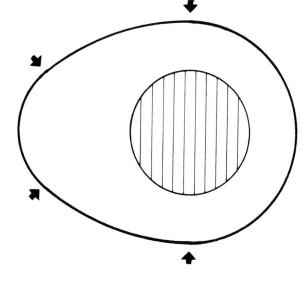

No. 2:12   *No. 2:13*

Space stage

The term used when the stage is carried partly round the audience (also called the wrap-round stage and calliper stage). The useful acting area is not really enlarged and the sides of the stage are not clearly defined but merge into the auditorium. Extreme side stages cannot have ideal sight lines from all seats.

The effects of the choice of the degree of encirclement

The advantages claimed by advocates of the open stage forms are that there is a much closer involvement of the audience in the action and a greater emphasis on the three-dimensional qualities of a live performance than can be achieved in traditional proscenium theatres. The essential differences between live performances and the two-dimensional media of film and television are thereby exploited.

With degrees of encirclement over about 120° performers mask each other and are often seen against the background of members of the audience on the other side of the stage. Voices and musical instruments are partly directional and so are facial expressions and gestures. Their effect is, therefore, different, depending upon what part of the auditorium each spectator sees or hears them from. Unless kept to a minimum, scenery and props will obstruct lines of sight. Lighting the actors without at the same time illuminating or causing discomfort to the audience, becomes increasingly difficult. Entrances for actors are not easy to manage and provision must be made for access to the stage through the audience or from below the stage. If these entrances are also used by the public, confusion can arise and some authorities may not even allow it. Actors' entrances should preferably be at acting area level and steps should be avoided.

Those who work on the more surrounded types of stage believe that skilful production techniques overcome these limitations and that the closeness of audience to performer relation enhances the intensity of the dramatic experience. The audience does not see the actors against pictorial scenery but bathed in light against a background of dimly lit rows of people similarly concentrating on the actors. From the artistic point of view the distinction between a performance on a surrounded stage and one on a confrontation type, is probably more important than that between a closed and an open stage. The latter distinction is more the product of safety regulations. Scenery is a fire hazard and the necessary protection of a safety curtain imposes physical restrictions on the building which are difficult to comply with in open stages. Without the orthodox protective devices, the restrictions placed by licensing authorities on the amount of materials for construction of scenery on open stages are likely to be severe.

The proscenium or picture frame stage

In discussing the various open stage forms, the essentials of the proscenium type have already been described. In its most blatant form there is an actual picture frame all round the proscenium opening. Used in this manner it is the embodiment of the 'fourth wall' convention where the action takes place within a room from which the fourth wall has been removed for the convenience of an audience of voyeurs.

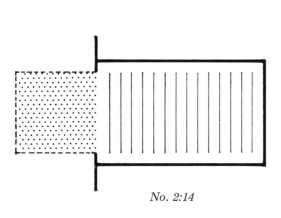

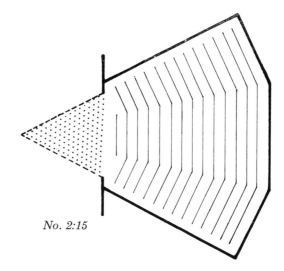

No. 2:14   *No. 2:15*

What we call the proscenium theatre is usually called the Italian type of theatre in Europe because of its origin in the Renaissance theatres of that country where the greatest flights of Baroque architectural imagination appeared not in the form of masonry but in canvas and paint on the stage. Originally developed to give scope for scenic extravagances, it later deteriorated in the search for extremes of naturalism and archaeological exactitude. Its main advantage remains in its ability to contrive elaborate scenic effects and transformations (provided that enough space and facilities are allowed) the mechanics of which can be concealed from the audience. Because of the geometry of sight lines it is difficult to arrange large audiences close to a picture-frame stage as the width of the auditorium is largely determined by the width of the proscenium opening. If the opening is made very large the expense of filling it with scenery becomes a very great burden on the company using it and if the sight lines are designed for the wide opening, masking the sides in will interfere with the view from side seats.

Forestage and apron stage

Scenery cannot be brought right to the back surface of the proscenium wall or it would foul the safety curtain and the house curtain. The line beyond which scenery cannot be set is called the setting line and is usually about 1m back from the face of the proscenium.

That part of the stage between the setting line and the stage riser, or edge of the stage if there is no riser, is called the forestage. When it is extended right out into the auditorium it is called an apron stage and it can give an open-stage effect by bringing the acting area into the same space as the audience. It is difficult to get satisfactory sight lines for both the apron and the area behind the proscenium arch, especially from balconies. Any scenery used in front of the safety curtain may have to be incombustible. The apron can be fixed or movable and is often lowered to form an orchestra pit.

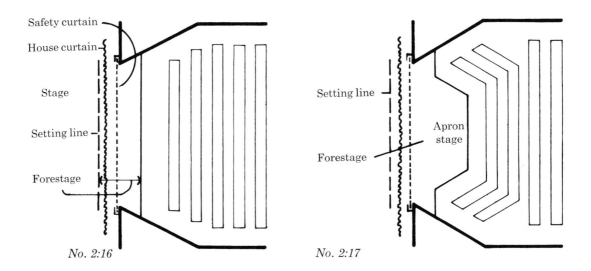

Safety curtain

House curtain

Stage

Setting line

Forestage

No. 2:16

Setting line

Apron stage

Forestage

No. 2:17

Performers' entrances

In the picture-frame theatre almost all performers' entrances are made behind the proscenium. In Restoration and Georgian plays it was common practice to enter the forestage by doors on either side of the proscenium arch, and this method of entry is again in favour, not only for productions in past styles but also for new plays. Regulations require fireproof doors and a fire check lobby.

Adaptability

Adaptability from one form to another is often demanded. If this merely means some slight alteration to forestage or false proscenium it does not pose insuperable problems of sight lines. A greater degree of adaptability, say from a proscenium to a 180° encircle-ment, or peninsular stage, means a major alteration to the seating. On a small scale this may be possible with mechanically or manually operated rostra but beyond four or five rows of seats the problems become immense, both technically and economically, if the audi-torium is to remain a satisfactory space in both forms. If entirely incompatible forms are wanted two separate auditoria should be considered. Certain theatres, however, used for teaching can be given a fairly high degree of adaptability as they exist primarily for the benefit of the actors and need make few concessions to the comfort and convenience of an audience. In such theatres changes which would, in professional conditions, be mechanized and there-fore extremely expensive can, with far less capital expenditure be arranged for manual alteration by making use of the plentiful supply of unpaid labour. Adaptability may be multi-form, giving a changeable relationship of performance to spectator or listener, for example from picture frame to open stage, or it may be multi-pur-pose allowing a change in the nature of the activities, for instance from drama to music.

No. 2:18   *The end stage in use at the Phoenix Theatre, Leicester.*

No. 2:19   *The full forestage and apron in use at the Nottingham Playhouse.*

The auditorium in section

It is not only by increasing the degree of encirclement that the number of audience within the optimum range of distances from the acting area can be increased. The auditorium must be considered in section as well as in plan. A greater concentration can be achieved in the vertical plane by adding one or more tiers. The view down on the performance emphasises its three dimensional qualities.

The various levels of the auditorium have been given many different names, e.g. stalls, orchestra stalls, amphitheatre, balcony, pit, circle, dress circle, upper circle, gallery, slips, grand tier. These terms by combinations and qualifications, have conveyed many subtle distinctions of luxury and prestige. In the past they had some validity when at the play or the opera it was just as important to be seen as to see. Such a profusion of nomenclature is becoming steadily less appropriate in present-day society. In the opinion of some the very presence of a circle is an indication of class distinction and, therefore, suspect, but this doctrinaire approach could have a sad effect on the atmosphere of the auditorium. Besides which, it is not unreasonable to give people the opportunity to pay more for a better view. The most important advantage of a multi-tier auditorium is that the number of seats can be increased without increasing unduly their distance from the stage. It also has the effect of surrounding the acting area with audience in section as distinct from extending it in plan, which is achieved by open stage methods. Most actors like to feel themselves the focus of the audience in both plan and section, which implies either a multi-level or steeply raked auditorium. One of the disadvantages of a multi-level auditorium is that it is more difficult to get good sight lines. The rake of the stalls has to be reduced so as not to push the gallery too high. The rake of the tiers is limited by safety regulations and by sight lines to the front of the acting area. A tier must not be allowed to interfere with the sight lines from the back row of the level below or with the acoustics of these seats. Several shallow tiers may be easier to handle in these respects than one or two deep ones. Access and escape may be complicated and space consuming and may get more so as the number of tiers increases.

Auditorium atmosphere

The quality of an individual's experience of a live performance depends partly on the fact that it is an experience shared with others. Audience and performers react upon one another. The audience becomes a community and its combined reactions stimulate and intensify the experience of the individual. While auditorium atmosphere is dependent on the quality of the design, there are practical as well as aesthetic factors involved. From the actors' point of view the audience should not be split into parts visually separated from one another, for example a large, high balcony may divide an audience into two. There should not be any visual obstacle or other distracting feature between audience and performance such as

No. 2:20

The auditorium at the Coliseum, London, built in 1904. One of Frank Matcham's many designs. Originally a large commercial theatre, after some years as a cinema it has recently been converted to its present use as an opera house. It is a good example of Edwardian theatrical atmosphere.

might be caused by a structural projection from the wall near the stage or by a balcony coming too low over the lower level back seats. Materials, textures and colour have an effect on auditorium atmosphere. They should help to create a receptive frame of mind in the audience before the performance begins but must not obtrude after it has started. During a performance they should have a negative quality so that for instance reflections of light do not distract the attention of spectators.

Audience seating   The decision on the practicable degree of comfort depends on the purpose of the theatre and the money available. The minimum requirements laid down by safety regulations afford a very low standard of comfort. On the other hand a close-packed audience has a better atmosphere than one that is spread too thinly and it should be remembered that while comfort is important, seats too widely spaced may destroy the atmosphere in an auditorium. These conflicting requirements have to be balanced and a compromise reached.

Loges and slips are shallow tiers at the sides which are not divided off like boxes. Large areas of blank, unpopulated auditorium wall can spoil auditorium atmosphere. In some cases this is greatly improved by boxes, loges and slips, but in proscenium theatres the sight lines from these are normally poor.

An open stage can have balconies probably without any sight-line problems. One of the drawbacks of the single-floor auditorium is that it looks half empty when it is, in fact, half full. A sparse audience in a multi-tier theatre is less obvious. The top balcony can be shut off for instance and the audience concentrated in the other levels.

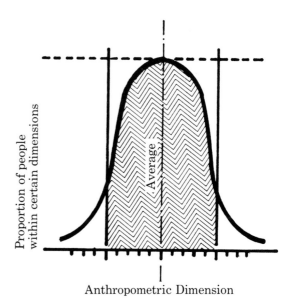

No. 3:1   *This is a typical curve obtained when a body dimension of a sample of people is taken and the number of people with similar measurements is plotted against the varying dimension.*
The proportion of people included within certain dimensional limits can be assessed and conversely the percentage of people excluded by a dimensional limitation can be estimated.

3 Sight lines

The importance of establishing visual limits which are acceptable for various types of performance has already been discussed. Having decided how much of the stage and the back and sides of the acting area must be seen by every member of the audience it is possible to construct a geometrical volume within which all the sight lines must be contained.

The planning of seating within this volume involves the adjustment of a number of variables some, but not all of which are within the power of the designer to control. The most important of these variables is one which cannot be regulated: the individual human being.

Anthropometrics Not only do anthropometric dimensions vary amongst individuals but the sitting postures adopted by each one are not susceptible to a discipline which would be convenient for mathematicians. In other words, the problem of the large lady with a hat sitting in front of a small shy gent will still remain. The key dimensions upon which sight line calculations depend are the height of the eye above the ground in a sitting position and the height of the top of the head above the eyes. If measurements of a sample of the population are taken these can be plotted on a curve which will show their distribution. From this curve the proportion of the population whose dimensions lie within certain limits can be calculated. Different curves could be plotted for children of certain ages and the data could be further refined by dividing the statistics for males and females and for different races.

Thus the proportion of the population whose dimensions lie within certain limits can be determined. In the case of the large person sitting in front of the small one, the probability of this occurring could be worked out mathematically.

Seat spacing   The architect does have control over the design of the seats and their spacing within limits laid down by safety regulations. His concern will be for comfort and the circulation of the audience to and from each seat. For comfort, wide spacing of rows is desirable but this may reduce the capacity of the auditorium to an uneconomic extent or push the rear rows beyond the acceptable distance from the stage. In a live theatre over-generous seat spacing may also spoil the atmosphere of concentration which intensifies the theatrical experience. While the seating should be comfortable enough for a two- or three-hour session it should help to keep the theatregoer alert rather than lull him to sleep. In cinemas the situation is not quite the same because the audience cannot play any positive part in the proceedings. The film reels on whatever the reactions of the watchers individually or collectively. Cinema managements are often more concerned with the effect of seat spacing on the sale of ice-cream in the interval than on the dramatic atmosphere of the auditorium.

Design of chairs   The quoting of row spaces without considering the detail design of the seats is very misleading. It is at least unwise to attempt to design an auditorium without first deciding the individual chair that is to be used. Most people's instinctive notion of comfort is judged by depth of upholstery, but a bulky and grossly padded chair may, in fact, be less comfortable than an apparently spartan one because it reduces the leg room between rows. It is also important for the seat to allow the audience to sit easily in a position which is natural for seeing the stage. In the live theatre the spectator is generally looking down on the stage while in the cinema he looks up and naturally takes a more reclining position.

With this data assembled and the critical dimensions assumed, the vertical sight lines can be worked out graphically by the following method and a satisfactory floor profile arrived at.

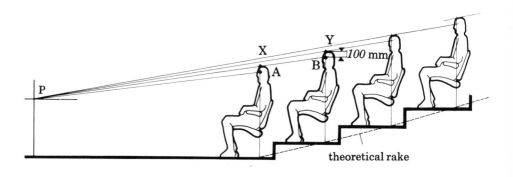

No. 3:2   *Method of calculating sightline with low P.*

The lowest and nearest point which the whole audience should be able to see clearly must be decided (P). If this is the edge of a horizontal stage, the nearest eye level should be above the horizontal plane. Verticals are then drawn through the eye positions for each row of seats. The point X, 100 mm above A on the first vertical, represents the top of the head of the person in the first row. When PX is produced through X, the point B at which it cuts the second vertical gives the eye position for the second row. 100 mm above B lies the point Y through which the next sight line is produced to cut the next vertical, and so on. When the eye positions for every row of seats have been determined, the floor line can be found by measuring 1120 mm below each on the verticals: this theoretical line is a shallow curve. (For these calculations 1120 mm is a reasonable floor to eye height, but a more accurate figure can be obtained by using anthropometric data related to the actual seat chosen.)

It should be noted that where this method of establishing the floor slope is strictly applied, the rake will usually be very steep. If the audience is to be on one level only this may not matter, especially with an open stage where the encirclement of the stage allows for a large audience. With a proscenium stage, however, the width of the audience is limited by horizontal sight lines and, in order to get more spectators into a given width it is necessary to introduce another tier or tiers and this may lead to a compromise on vertical sight lines. The rake must be reduced to make room for another level. Point P is taken 600 mm or 900 mm above the edge of the stage on the assumption that the actual edge may be seen between heads only and an unrestricted view of the performers from the knees upwards is all that is necessary.

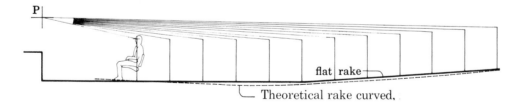

No. 3:3   *Theoretical rake curved. Maximum gradient of aisles without steps: 1 in 10.*

The situation is improved by staggering seats. The arbitrary choice of a position for point P and the variations in the dimensions of the individual members of the audience do not justify the refinement of a subtly curved rake. A varying rake may also introduce the complication of different heights of risers which are uncomfortable and sometimes dangerous to the public. The maximum gradient for an aisle without steps is 1 in 10 and the maximum slope for stepped seating is 35° (GLC).

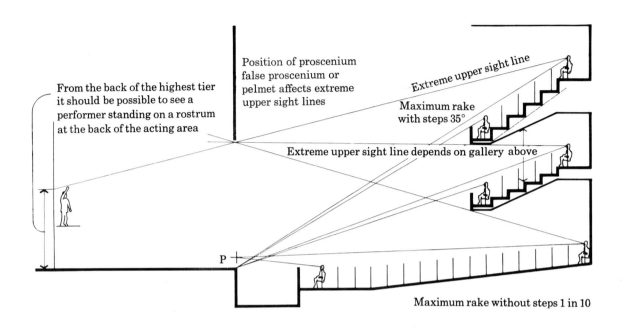

From the back of the highest tier it should be possible to see a performer standing on a rostrum at the back of the acting area

Position of proscenium false proscenium or pelmet affects extreme upper sight lines

Extreme upper sight line

Maximum rake with steps 35°

Extreme upper sight line depends on gallery above

P

Maximum rake without steps 1 in 10

No. 3:4   *Vertical sight lines.*

Vertical sight lines must be checked on several sections as well as the centre line through stage and auditorium.

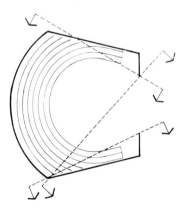

No. 3:5   *Check several sections.*

The section through stage and auditorium at any point is dictated by vertical sight lines which will be affected by the following factors:

1   Maximum distance desirable for the spectator farthest from the performance.

2   Depth of acting area and the vertical height above it essential to the type of performance.

3   Nearest and lowest part of the stage which must be within the unrestricted view of all spectators.

4   Highest point in acting area which must be visible to the spectators farthest from the stage. Balcony fronts, or soffits, proscenium or false proscenium pelmet or border must not obstruct sight lines through these extreme points.

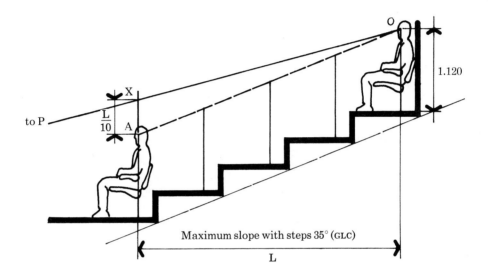

No. 3:6   *Graphical method for finding balcony rake.*

Vertical sightlines from tiers   The following is an approximate method of determining the slope of a tier. It does not replace the more meticulous method described above which can be applied to tiers as well as to main banks of seating.

First fix the eye position for the front row of seats (A) and the depth (L) to the eye position of the back row. Vertically above A find point X so that $AX = \dfrac{L}{10}$. Next draw a line from P (on stage) through X to cut the vertical through the eye position of the back row at O.

The rake of the tier will then be parallel to AO, but 1120 mm below (see note above on eye height of a seated person).

Note that the maximum slope with steps is 35° (GLC).

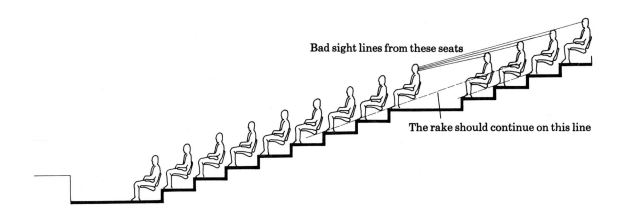

No. 3:7   *The line of the auditorium rake must be continuous over cross aisles.*
To start the rake again after the cross aisle, as shown above,
results in bad sight lines for the seats immediately behind the aisle.

Horizontal sight lines   Horizontal sight lines are most critical in theatres with a proscenium stage. Given a desired acting area, sight lines will limit the width of seating which can be provided in the auditorium.

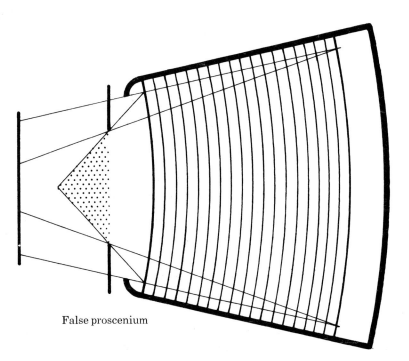

False proscenium

No. 3:8

Note that sight lines from side seats restrict the amount of the stage that can be used as acting area. The addition of a false proscenium will limit the acting area still further.

Staggered seating

In the calculations for determining vertical sight lines described above it has been assumed that it is necessary for the spectators in each row to see over the heads of the spectators in the row immediately in front of them. This is the ideal situation, but it is not always possible. One solution is to stagger the rows of seats. It is then possible to calculate sight lines based on each spectator seeing over the head of the person two rows in front. But it must be remembered that the heads of spectators in the row immediately in front will restrict the width of uninterrupted stage that can be seen.

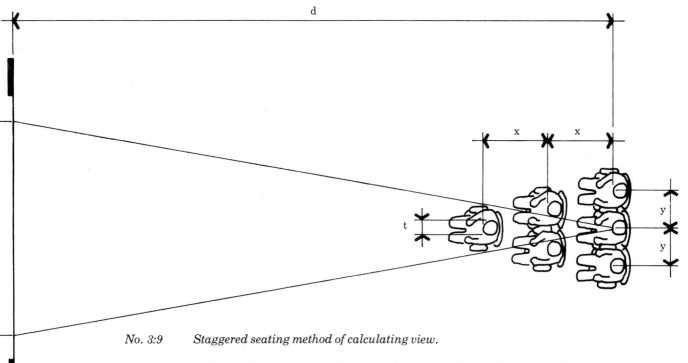

No. 3:9   *Staggered seating method of calculating view.*

For a given row spacing x and seat spacing y the unrestricted width of view of the stage (a) seen from any seat is proportional to the distance (d) of that seat from the stage, i.e., $a = kd$ where k is a constant $\dfrac{y-t}{x}$, t being the thickness of one head:

eg if $x = 900, y = 500$ and $t = 200$

then $k = 0.33$

thus at 9m from the front of the stage:

$a = 0.33 \times 9$

$= 3m$

i.e., 3m width of the stage can be seen without interruption which is one-third of the average 9m proscenium opening.

The value of staggering becomes progressively less the more oblique is the seat to the line of sight through the focus of the stage. If rows are straight heads in front will be more obstructive and it is uncomfortable to sit for any length of time at an angle to the focus of attention.

Viewing is more comfortable if the seat is on the line of sight through the focus of the stage. This can be achieved by curving the rows or setting side banks at an angle. Using the constant k the uninterrupted view can be found for any seat in the auditorium assuming that seats are directly facing the focus of attention.

No. 3:10   *Staggered seating may obscure a vital part of stage.*

Other methods of determining sight lines

As it is possible to work out the mathematical relationships of the variables involved in determining floor profiles, it follows that it is possible to programme a computer to produce either a series of levels or a direct visual representation. However, the method is rather out of scale for most theatre schemes even for architects who have a computer handy. It might be more appropriate for a vast seating capacity which would not be recommended here for other reasons.

There is another specialised machine, the Illustromat, which, given plans and sections will draw an accurate perspective view from any position in a matter of a few minutes. This could be used to check all the critical sight lines and would at once give a clear idea of the feel of the auditorium.

4   Acoustics

The acoustics of a theatre will affect every production in that theatre. Because of the extreme difficulty of making any noticeable change in the acoustic conditions by adjustments to the building itself (apart from some unavoidable variation resulting from the size of the audience) the architect in effect decides its acoustic characteristics at the outset.

Acoustic background

Some manipulation of the sound, if not of the acoustics, is possible by modern amplification systems, for example, special sound effects can be created and for some programme material, actors' or singers' voices may be amplified. This may go some way, but not all the way, towards creating good acoustic conditions for every one of the large number of different kinds of programme material which may be presented. Compromise appears inevitable; it is impossible for one auditorium to be equally suitable acoustically for a drawing-room comedy, a song and dance show, a Wagner opera and a symphony concert.

A theatre must be protected from all external noise and must have mechanical plant designed so that the total background noise level does not exceed certain criteria. The larger the auditorium the lower these criteria should be. For theatres with up to 500 seats a noise criterion of 25 dBA should not be exceeded and for theatres with more than 500 seats, this should be reduced to 20 dBA or less.

Particular attention must be paid to noise from flushing lavatories, talking in dressing rooms and rattling of cups in bars.

Seating rake and layout

The rake of seating is as important for sound as it is for sight. When sound passes at a low angle of incidence over an audience, it is strongly attenuated because of the highly absorptive properties of the audience. Reinforcement of sound by reflections from the ceiling makes it reasonable to provide a rake rather less steep than in ancient classical open-air theatres which had rakes of 35° or more.

Nevertheless a sight line clearance from one row to the next at any part of the house should never be less than 75 mm and in large theatres 100 mm or more is desirable.

If seats are set out on a circular or part circular plan there is a risk that the concave surface of the risers may cause focusing of sound.

The risers are shielded to some extent by the audience and the backs of seats which reduces the sound reflected from them, but as an added precaution they should be covered with a sound absorbing material. There are acoustic dangers in large areas of curved wall or curved balcony front with centres near the heads of the audience. The possible focus points of sound from the stage should be either outside the auditorium, in mid air or in a gangway. Concave areas of wall which may be troublesome should be absorbent or have a broken up surface to be sound diffusing.

Size and shape The smaller the average distance between the audience and the actor the better the acoustical result for normal drama, although for music or musical shows this is not necessarily true. In theatres for up to 200 or 300 people there should be no difficulty, but in larger theatres the acoustic design problems become more intractable. It is difficult to give precisely the largest practical audience size for good acoustics, assuming that sound amplification is not to be used, but it is probably about 1000. Because of the reduced average distance between stage and audience, open-stage theatres might be acoustically satisfactory with rather larger audiences. It must be remembered that the human voice has pronounced directional properties and at the higher sound frequencies, which are extremely important for intelligibility, the sound behind the speaker's head is at least 10 dB less than directly in front of his mouth. Members of the audience directly behind the speaking actor – and this could mean any member of the audience – are effectively up to four times the distance away in terms of the strength of sound compared with a member of the audience the same actual distance away in the direction the actor faces. This ignores the acoustic gain provided by reverberation and sound reflections from well positioned wall or ceiling surfaces. Although there may be some gain from these sources, the disadvantages of being behind the actor remain considerable. In proscenium theatres the stage house must be considered as an acoustical disadvantage because it represents a volume of enclosed space in which the sound can be lost. The larger the stage house the more the waste of acoustic energy and the more difficulty the actor has in projecting his voice through the proscenium opening unless he goes out into the auditorium onto a forestage.

The plan shape of the auditorium will be considerably influenced by the seating layout and for theatres (auditoria with low reverberation) almost any shape resulting from this influence is acoustically acceptable with the possible exceptions of circular or elliptical auditoria, unless special precautions are taken. Whatever the shape, simple plain surfaces, particularly anything approaching a sphere, cube or other regular solid polygon, should be avoided. Changes of surface level and modelling of the surfaces will provide acoustic diffusion which is advantageous. Projections with widths and depths of at least 100 mm are necessary to be effective and they are better arranged in a random pattern.

Balcony overhangs

In auditoria for natural sound, as distinct from cinemas, deeply overhung balconies should be avoided. It is best to restrict the depth from the front of the balcony to the rearmost row of seats under it to not more than twice the dimension from the audience head level (say 1150 mm from floor) to the balcony soffit, at the front line of the balcony.

Reverberation

Reverberation will improve acoustic conditions for the audience provided it is neither too much nor too little. For speech in auditoria of volumes between 300 and 12 000 m³ the average reverberation time with an audience present should not be more than 1 second or less than 0·5 second for highest intelligibility. Intelligibility begins to suffer, at first slowly, as reverberation is increased, but it deteriorates quite quickly at about 2 seconds and above. For music, longer reverberation times are required depending on the type of music. Values between 1 and 2 seconds are satisfactory for much programme material and thus the acoustics can be good for music without being unduly bad for speech.

Reverberation is directly proportional to the volume of the auditorium and inversely proportional to the amount of absorption in it. Allowing for the fact that common materials such as plaster or wood, however hard, will necessarily have some absorption, it is found that a volume of about 3 m³ per audience seat gives just about the right total absorption (audience plus surfaces) to provide a satisfactory reverberation time for ideal speech conditions. Therefore, if the auditorium can be designed on the basis of this calculation it will be unnecessary to introduce special sound absorbent materials on the room surfaces. Moreover, as the surfaces will be sound reflecting they can be disposed to promote useful reflections on to the audience and help compensate for the normal fall off of sound with distance from the sound source.

This approach to design is satisfactory for up to 300 seats. If about 0·6 m² is taken as the amount of floor area occupied by one person, including some allowance for circulation space, a room height of about 5 m is obtained. If the auditorium is a larger one (say exceeding 200 to 300 seats) the proportions will be poor with such a low ceiling height; a volume exceeding 3 m³ per seat therefore becomes unavoidable and it is then necessary to add absorbents to the room surfaces to obtain the optimum reverberation time.

In contrast to this, auditoria used primarily for music must be designed with a very much larger volume per seat (probably 9 m³) or it will be impossible to obtain long enough reverberation time however hard the surfaces. The closer together an audience can be seated the shorter will be the average distance to the stage and the easier it is to keep the volume per seat down to a low value. The densely packed audience in old theatres probably accounts for the reputation for acoustic excellence which many of them earned. However, modern regard for comfort has led to much more generous seat spacing than was common in the past. Continental seating, in which the row to row dimension is made large so that people may pass along a row without those already seated having to stand, reduces the number of gangways, but rarely produces a higher density of audience and tends slightly to increase the amount of absorption of each person because owing to their wider spacing they (or their clothes) are more exposed to the sound waves.

Reflectors

When the auditorium is large and the maximum distance to an audience seat is over 18 m, ceiling reflectors are a great help. They should be designed so that the reflections are concentrated more on the most distant seats. In designing reflectors it is necessary to decide on the positions of the sound sources, which will vary, particularly in a theatre with an adjustable stage. The aid provided by reflectors will be most necessary to an actor speaking from far up stage as in this position the stage house and proscenium arch have the greatest disabling effect. Other patterns of sound reflection resulting from sound sources in other positions must also be studied to ensure that generally satisfactory distribution of sound will be obtained. Materials for reflectors must be smooth and non-porous and should weigh not less than 5 kg/m² for speech only, or 25 kg/m² for music.

The same principles should be applied to an open-stage theatre, but the provision of a reflecting surface which will direct sound back over the actor's head from wherever he happens to be on the stage, is very difficult to achieve. One complication is that such reflectors will conflict with lighting positions.

Music

Music in a theatre adds to the design difficulties. The need may vary from an orchestra in a pit for musical shows or incidental music to that of presenting an orchestral or musical programme from the stage itself. The ideal acoustics suitable for light music, opera and symphonic music are all somewhat different and unless some means can be found to make a major change in the acoustic conditions of the auditorium, a compromise is unavoidable. The main need is to increase the reverberation time but this may be detrimental to intelligibility of speech and must therefore be done with caution. Possible solutions may be some form of electronic control of reverberation (assisted resonance) or physical variation by adjustment of the room surfaces or of the total volume.

Orchestra pit   The orchestra pit for a large opera house may need to accommodate up to 120 players while for other theatres not more than 10–12 may be needed. To avoid encroaching too much on auditorium seating area the orchestra pit sometimes extends under the front edge of the stage. This is not necessarily an acoustic disadvantage, especially with large orchestras, as it helps to improve the balance between orchestral sound and voices from the stage.

5 Safety

Theatre licensing was originally intended as a measure to preserve public order. In this century the grant of a theatre licence has become associated with safety requirements, and this legal basis explains why the procedure for obtaining local authority approval for a place of public entertainment is different from that required for other types of building.

There is a temptation for architects and theatre management to regard safety regulations as an irksome burden imposed from outside by uncomprehending officials. Unfortunately, there have been quite enough tragic experiences to prove that safety precautions dare not be neglected. However, since the introduction of safety regulations there have been remarkably few serious disasters in theatres in modern times, particularly in Britain, and those that have occurred can usually be traced to the neglect of their responsibility by somebody who should have known better.

The architect and the management of the theatre should understand the principles of a safe building and work together to achieve it. The technical staff of the local authority whose duty it is to administer the regulations should, on the other hand, have some appreciation of the workings of the theatre. Regulations can only be framed to deal with known building types. They cannot be expected to anticipate new ideas or forms of construction. Rigid application of the letter of the law may appear the easiest way out for an authority which wishes to relieve itself of any further moral responsibility, but this can bring the law into disrepute especially if a deviation from the written text is clearly as safe as the literal interpretation of it. Perhaps the best guarantee of public safety is the efficiency and integrity of the day-to-day management of the theatre, and this can be encouraged if those concerned have confidence and understanding of the safety arrangements. These should evolve in consultation between the architect and the authority's technical staff in such a way that while providing adequate protection, they are strictly related to the particular premises in question, and enforcible in practice by management and authority alike.

Hazards and safeguards

In the orthodox proscenium type of theatre the greatest hazards are those arising from fire on the stage. With all the care in the world the possibility of fire cannot be entirely eliminated when canvas and timber are used in scenic construction. Contrary to popular belief the so-called fire-proofing of scenic canvas does not make it non-combustible; it merely makes it less easy to ignite. Once it has caught alight it burns readily giving off a great deal of pungent smoke. Although a conflagration of scenery on stage will probably do a great deal of damage to the building it need not have disastrous consequence for the occupants provided panic is avoided. The strategy for dealing with an outbreak of fire on the stage is to confine it within the four walls of the stage tower and to use the powerful upward draught created by the chimney effect of the tower to draw heat and smoke away from the audience. The following arrangements, now generally in use all over the world, have been evolved from lessons learned in a number of spectacular theatre disasters in the past.

The proscenium wall

The proscenium wall is made to provide fire and smoke separation between the stage and the auditorium. The number of openings in it is restricted to essential pass doors, orchestra pit, access, etc, and each of these is carefully detailed to provide the necessary fire and smoke cut-off. The largest opening is the proscenium itself which is provided with a safety curtain.* The origins of the safety curtain are obscure but at least one was in existence long before the advent of regulations. In 1794 a safety curtain was provided at Drury Lane Theatre after its reconstruction. On the opening night this curtain, heralded by a verse oration, was lowered in the sight of the audience and its solidity demonstrated by blows with a hammer. It was then raised so that the audience could see cascades of water from a primitive drencher, fed by tanks in the roof, falling into an artificial lake, complete with boats and boatmen. Fourteen years later the theatre was again burned down and, as might be expected in this pre-regulation era, the tanks were empty. Brick proscenium walls and a safety curtain were first required by regulations towards the end of the nineteenth century.

---

*   The City of New York Building Code revised in November 1968 no longer insists on a safety curtain in all circumstances. It may be omitted provided various other conditions are complied with such as a water deluge on the curtain line, automatic safeguards controlling the auditorium and stage ventilation and the provision of more generous means of escape.

No. 5:1   *A lightweight framed safety curtain covered with asbestos cloth.*

The stage lantern

The automatic smoke vent or stage lantern is a most important fire safeguard introduced largely as a result of researches by Austrian engineers after the disastrous fire in the Ring Theatre, Vienna in 1881 when 450 persons were killed.

Auditorium ventilation

Ventilation of the auditorium is designed to maintain a flow of air towards the stage at all times. There should be a system of lobbies to prevent the sudden rush of air through exits from the stage. There is a prohibition on high-level natural ventilation over the gallery which is a complete reversal of earlier requirements. It was introduced following the fire at the Iroquois Theatre, Chicago in 1902. Nearly 600 persons were killed on this occasion. After scenery had caught fire, the safety curtain failed to complete its descent, smoke and flames were blown under the safety curtain by opening of the stage exits, and only a quarter of the persons seated in the gallery survived. The heavy death toll in other parts of the theatre was due largely to panic aggravated by serious breaches of regulations.

If a fire breaks out on the stage the stage lantern is opened either by manual release, automatic means (such as a fusible link), or in the last resort by the shattering under heat of the specially thin glazing. The safety curtain is lowered and the drencher turned on to prevent it buckling under heat. Automatic sprinklers above the stage also come into operation to reduce the scale of the fire as much as possible. When such a thing happens artists and backstage staff have only a very short time in which to make their escape and this should be borne in mind when planning the exits from the stage area including the flys, the grid and the stage basement. The layout and equipment of all the backstage areas must be designed to avoid outbreaks of fire and to make certain that if one does occur it is isolated so that no sign can reach the stage itself where a single puff of smoke could precipitate a panic. The individual dressing rooms, access corridors, property rooms, offices, workshops, stage basements, etc, should be separated from one another and from the stage.

All such compartments should be ventilated directly or by individual fire-resisting trunking to the open air. The dressing-room block and parts of the building where stage staff are employed should have alternative exit routes equipped with secondary lighting, appropriate door fastenings, etc. Such requirements are usually given in some detail in the licensing regulations, and they will also apply to some of the technical areas situated in the front of house such as lime boxes and projection rooms. The safety problem in each case is that of the very rapid evacuation of a relatively small number of people from premises with which they are familiar. Staff should have taken part in regular fire drill and the risk of panic is likely to be small. There may be cases where staff could suffer badly burned hands or damage to eyesight from potentially dangerous equipment. A person temporarily maimed in this way cannot negotiate ladders, catwalks, etc, and exit doors for them should be fitted with panic bolts only.

The stage is the special hazard but there are potential dangers for an audience both in the auditorium and the other parts of the building accessible to the public. These may be considered under two related, but distinct headings; fire and panic. Fire used in the strict sense of actual burns or injuries by falling debris is not a serious risk in the public portion of a modern theatre, if care is taken in the choice of materials. Precautions must be taken against the very rapid spread of flame; in some circumstances this can reach almost explosive proportions. A recent disaster of this type occurred in Liège during the early part of 1955. The auditorium of a cinema was lined with compressed paper acoustic material fixed on battens leaving an air space behind. The material was ignited near the screen by an unknown cause and flames spread with great rapidity over the whole auditorium, the ceiling collapsed 'within a few moments' and 49 out of 135 persons present died, all – or almost all – from asphyxiation. The use of highly flammable materials for wall and ceiling linings, curtains, light fittings, etc, must be avoided and sound absorbent materials, resonant panelling and other acoustic treatments must have a satisfactory degree of flame resistance.

Open stages   If no proscenium separation is provided the standard required on the stage or platform should be the same as that of the rest of the auditorium. All scenery, properties, etc, must be non-combustible or at least of low flammability, and restrictions are usually imposed on the use of a naked flame or similar potentially dangerous stage effects.

Panic   Panic in the audience is by far the most dangerous circumstance which can occur in any place of public entertainment. It is probably true to say that over 90% of many thousands killed in theatre disasters died from this cause and this cause alone. It is sudden and unpredictable and can happen in a wide variety of places to many types of audience and at many kinds of performance. It has often risen without any real physical danger being present. On more than one occasion in the early history of the Old Vic, before the introduction of safety regulations, the desperately overcrowded gallery was evacuated under near panic conditions. It has been pointed out that on these occasions, outright panic was averted by the social instincts of a local audience largely drawn from the criminal classes and among the few casualties which did occur, no women or children were included. Similar conditions prevailed in many old music halls and parallels drawn from other fields, shipwrecks, air-raid incidents etc, indicate that liability to panic is least common among groups of people having a common social background and an accepted position, however insignificant, within it. Further research might test the theory that present-day tendencies towards a highly competitive society lacking much of the social cohesion of an earlier period may increase the susceptibility to panic.

The borderline between a rapid, but orderly evacuation and a disastrous panic is dangerously narrow and every detail, however insignificant, may be important. Both the architect and the management should bear in mind that the problem is as much a psychological as a physical one. The actual form and layout of the premises is as vital as the presence of mind of staff or performers. Presence of mind is illustrated in the anecdote about Arthur Roberts who reacted to a cry of 'Fire!' in the old Surrey Theatre by standing calmly on the stage and telling his audience 'Stop where you are. There's no danger. Dammit – do you think I'd be here if there was?'.

Once a crowd of people is in the grip of panic it is doubtful whether any sort of control could ever be regained. Public safety therefore depends upon taking precautions to prevent its outbreak. All possible causes of alarm, fire, smoke or fumes, unusual sounds such as fire alarms and bells, photoflashes, the appearance of undue haste on the part of the staff, etc, must be avoided or reduced to the minimum. Measures which inspire confidence must be considered in every detail, such as maintained safety lighting, the regular lowering of the safety curtain and a clear view of exits and exit notices from all parts of the house. The staff must be trained to cope with emergencies in a calm and efficient manner.

Although the safety curtain as a fire and smoke barrier may well become obsolete, it would be unwise to disregard its psychological value. Audiences have grown used to its regular descent and the well-worn quotation 'For thine especial safety'. (Collins' Music Hall preferred Hamlet – 'What — has this thing appeared again tonight!' but it probably reassured the audience and, by a rather different association, the performers as well!)

Fire fighting appliances

The Fire Authority should be consulted on the scale of provision of fire appliances and where they should be placed in the building. Compliance with their requirements is a condition of the grant of an entertainment licence.

Fire-fighting equipment in the auditorium and public areas is generally in the form of permanently installed hydraulic hose reels. Stages in addition to sprinkler systems would have hydrants, hose reels and sand buckets. To deal with a performer's costume catching fire the stage and dressing-room areas should have blankets of heavy wool or asbestos strategically sited. The backstage areas will have water-type hand extinguishers. These are often placed in corridors where, if their presence has not been anticipated, they can be a dangerous obstruction. A fire extinguisher protruding from the wall can effectively reduce the width of a corridor and may even catch the costume of a performer hastening by. Recesses should be designed for extinguishers, buckets, blankets and for hose reels wherever there is a chance of these obstructing circulation space.

Different types of extinguisher are needed for particular hazards for instance carbon dioxide for electrical fires and foam for oil-fired boiler rooms.

Management responsibility

If the premises have to be evacuated the morale and training of the staff is vital; they must have confidence that proper safety measures are maintained at all times. The knowledge that some particular requirement is never enforced or that some piece of safety equipment, however small is not in working order could lead to disaster.

The management's problems of running the completed theatre must be considered. Periodic surveys and inspections should be made to check that the fabric and equipment is maintained in a safe condition.* From time to time alterations in the light of experience or to meet changing trends in entertainment are bound to be necessary, and they must be carried out to the same exacting standards as the original work. A theatre is old only because it has been a long time on the same site. The Old Vic for example was built at the end of the Napoleonic Wars, but it has been so altered, re-fitted and maintained that nothing beyond the massive brick-work of the main structure is recognisable as the original building.

---

*   The ABTT Information Sheet No. 5 *Safety Check Lists for Theatre Managements*, has been published to assist managements in drawing up their own list of duties and in allocating responsibility for carrying them out to various members of their staff.

6 Exits and means of escape

Amongst any audience there are bound to be some people visiting the building for the first time, and many others may not be particularly familiar with it. If an emergency arises and the premises have to be evacuated much depends upon the clarity of layout of the building. The alternatives open to members of the public should avoid creating a sense of uncertainty and indecision. For this reason the usual 'means of escape' principles which are applied to most other buildings or indeed to the staff portions of the theatre, do not strictly apply.

Escape routes   At least two exits should be provided from each tier or floor and they should be independent and remote from one another. Two exits close together would not in some circumstances provide an alternative means of escape, nor would they provide an alternative if they both joined into one common space such as a foyer. Exits from the auditorium must be distributed with safety in mind, but they should also be related to the normal circulation of the public. In an emergency it is easier for people to make their way out of the building in an orderly fashion if the route is already familiar to them. It is better to avoid special emergency exit routes if it is possible. If the building has to be evacuated because of an outbreak of fire on the stage, the public would not naturally go in the direction of a fire, even if the safety curtain had shut it off, and it is therefore inadvisable to place the only exits close to the proscenium. Another reason why it is better to have exits at the back of the auditorium is that in an emergency it is less dangerous to travel up steps than down. However, there are also hazards in the foyer area especially as now these often contain restaurants and coffee bars where cooking is done. The possibility of an emergency arising in this area will probably justify some exits near the front of the auditorium.

SR = The Building Standards (Scotland) (Consolidation) Regulations 1970

HO = The Manual of Safety Requirements in theatres and other places of public entertainment, issued by the Home Office

CSR = The Cinematograph Safety Regulations, for 1955, 1958 and 1965

GLC = GLC Places of Public Entertainment, Technical Regulations

Minimum number of exits from a room or storey

	SR	HO	CSR	GLC
Minimum No. of Persons	2	2		2
1–60	1		1	
Up to 500		2		2
61–600	2		2	
Up to 750		3		3
601–1000	3		3	
Up to 1000				4
Up to 1250		4		5
1001–1400	4		4	
Up to 1500		5		6
1401–1700	5		5	
Up to 1750				7
1701–2000	6		6	
Up to 2000		6		8
2001–2250	7		7	
Up to 2250				9
2251–2500	8		8	
Up to 2500		7		10
2501–2700	9		9	
Up to 2750	10	8		11
Up to 3600	12			15

In the case of the Home Office Manual the number and width of exits is calculated from a formula with a number of variables including the fire resistance of the construction and the height above ground level. Values have been assumed in order to arrive at the figures in the tables. Regulations are at present all in imperial measures which have been converted to the nearest millimetre. New regulations will be in metric but are not known at the date of writing.

Minimum total exit widths required (assuming a minimum of 2 exits)

(Min. per exit) No. of Persons	SR		HO		GLC	
	2′ 6″ to 3′ 6″	0·762 to 1·067	3′ 8″	1·118	—	—
200	7′ 0″	2·134	7′ 4″	2·236	7′ 0″	2·134
300	7′ 0″	2·134	7′ 4″	2·236	8′ 0″	2·438
400	7′ 0″	2·134	7′ 4″	2·236	9′ 0″	2·743
500	8′ 9″	2·667	9′ 2″	2·794	10′ 0″	3·048
750	13′ 3″	4·724	14′ 8″	4·470	15′ 0″	4·572
1000	17′ 6″	5·334	18′ 4″	5·588	20′ 0″	6·096
2000	35′ 0″	10·668	36′ 8″	11·176	40′ 0″	12·192
3000	52′ 6″	16·002	55′ 0″	16·764	60′ 0″	18·288

Exit widths   The widths of exits should be related to their use. Some licensing and other authorities have fixed minimum widths. A recommendation given in Ministry of Works *Post-War Building Study* No. 20 is to allow for a rate of movement in cinemas and theatres of 45 persons per minute per unit width of 520–530 mm. In new buildings exit doorways should not be narrower than two such units, 1070 mm, but in existing buildings not less than 960 mm in width is at present tolerated.

The number of exits and their widths should be such as to permit an audience to leave the auditorium in 2½ minutes. All exits should be through doorways or openings which are clearly indicated by notices illuminated by two systems of lighting and which are in themselves readily distinguishable from doors leading to bars, cloakrooms, etc. (Self-luminous signs are now being introduced, but they are not accepted by all authorities.) The whole of the exit route to the street should be properly lit from two independent systems and be provided where necessary with cut-off doors and smoke extract ventilation. Doors in escape routes should all open in the direction of escape. The only partial exception to this is in the case of doors used normally as entrances to the building which are permitted to swing both ways. Revolving doors or turnstiles do not count as exits; they can be very dangerous in case of panic and should never be used in theatres or cinemas. Intermediate doors in exit corridors and doors leading on to exit corridors should open in the direction of exit. Door handles and other fittings should not project into the exit way more than 75 mm. Exit routes wherever possible should be separate from those serving other tiers and lead as directly as possible to a place of safety. They should be enclosed by adequate fire-resisting construction and their possible use under panic conditions considered carefully. Bottlenecks, irregular surfaces or steppings and doors opening from the side into the line of exit should be avoided.

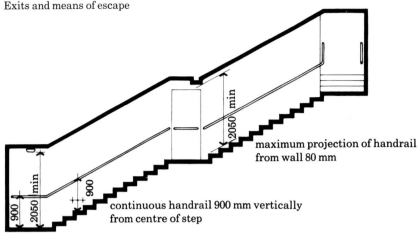

maximum projection of handrail
from wall 80 mm

continuous handrail 900 mm vertically
from centre of step

Section

No. 6:1

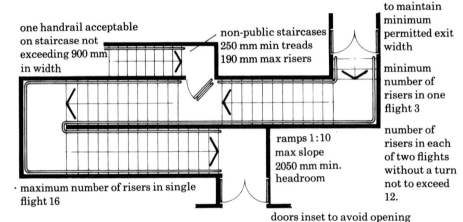

one handrail acceptable
on staircase not
exceeding 900 mm
in width

non-public staircases
250 mm min treads
190 mm max risers

doors recessed
to maintain
minimum
permitted exit
width

minimum
number of
risers in one
flight 3

ramps 1:10
max slope
2050 mm min.
headroom

number of
risers in each
of two flights
without a turn
not to exceed
12.

· maximum number of risers in single
flight 16

doors inset to avoid opening
onto public thoroughfare

door from non public areas
opening on to public escape
route to comply with opening
in direction of escape marked
PRIVATE and kept locked
handrail continues across door

Plan

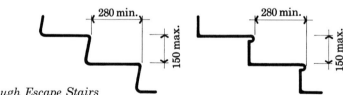

280 min.

150 max.

280 min.

150 max.

No. 6:2   *Section through Escape Stairs*

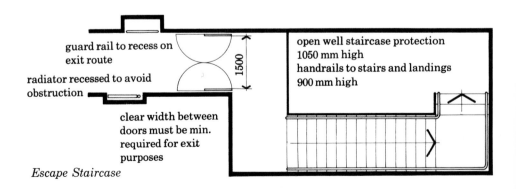

guard rail to recess on
exit route

radiator recessed to avoid
obstruction

1500

open well staircase protection
1050 mm high
handrails to stairs and landings
900 mm high

clear width between
doors must be min.
required for exit
purposes

Escape Staircase

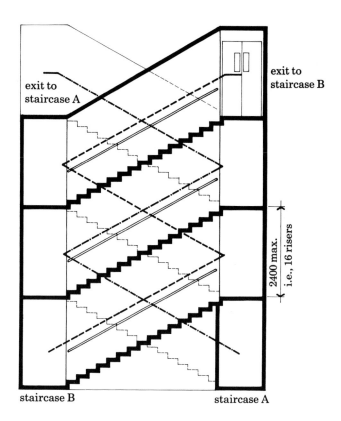

No. 6:3   *Scissors escape stairs* are an economic planning device which makes it possible to get two completely independent, fire separated staircases into one tower by using the maximum number of 16 permitted risers in each flight.

7 Seating layout and safety regulations

The minimum dimensions and gangway requirements which follow are based on those of the Greater London Council but it should be remembered that other licensing authorities have their own regulations which may differ from these considerably.

Minimum dimensions are shown below and in the diagrams.

Table 1 Distance of seats from gangways

Minimum seatway (measured between perpendiculars) E (mm)	Maximum distance of seat from gangway (510 mm seats) F (mm)	Maximum number of 510 mm wide seats per row	
		Gangway both sides	Gangway one side
305	3060	14	7
330	3570	16	8
355	4080	18	9
380	4590	20	10
405	5100	22	11

Table 1 shows the distance of seats from gangways. It should be noted that the width of individual seats is taken as 510 mm. The standard dimension at present is 1 ft 8 in (508 mm). While manufacturers' dimensions cannot be anticipated, 510 mm appears to be a sensible metric size. Dimensions given here may, therefore, be used for preliminary planning purposes, but exact sizes of seats must be checked with manufacturers.

55

tip up seats to be actuated
by weights

Plans—Seating with Arms

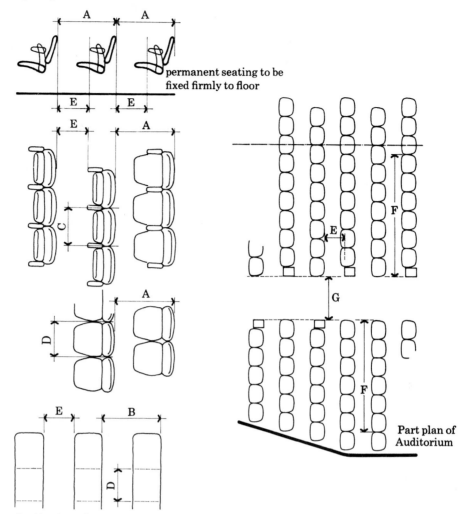

permanent seating to be
fixed firmly to floor

Seating without Arms

Seating without Backs

No. 7:1   *Auditorium Seating*   No. 7:2

Part plan of
Auditorium

Minimum dimensions:

A	Back-to-back distance between rows of seats with backs: 760 mm (minimum)	
B	Back-to-back distance between rows of seats without backs 610 mm (minimum)	
C	Width of seats with arms 510 mm (minimum)	
D	Width of seat without arms 460 mm (minimum)	
E	Unobstructed vertical space between rows (seatway) 305 mm. See table 1.	
F	For normal maximum distance of seat from gangway see table 1. But rows with more than twenty-two seats could be possible, provided that the audience was not imperilled.	
G	Minimum width of gangway 1070 mm.	

Balcony fronts   The top of the rester should be designed to discourage it from being used as a resting place for small articles such as binoculars and handbags and to prevent them from falling on people below. If it is too narrow some patrons may feel giddy, about 250 mm is an acceptable width. A guard rail must be provided opposite the full width of the end of each gangway.

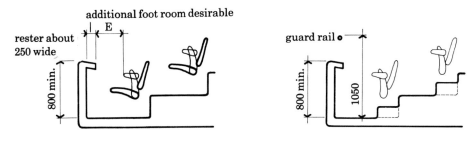

additional foot room desirable

rester about
250 wide

guard rail

No. 7:3   *Section through Balcony Front.*   *No. 7:4 Section through Balcony
Front opposite gangway.*

Continental seating

The term continental seating is now generally used to describe
seating in which each row extends virtually the full width of the
auditorium without any intersecting gangways. It has been used in
many theatres on the mainland of Europe, particularly in Germany,
but until recently it has not been permitted by the English licensing
authorities. The distance F in table 1 determines the length of rows
which are permitted in the GLC area and other authorities have
similar regulations. However, continental seating has been accepted in a few places in Britain and it is being introduced in several
more schemes which are in the design stage at the time of writing.
Its acceptance depends upon various other safety factors such as
the travel distance to an exit and may mean an increase in the
number of exits from the auditorium and wider gangways where
they do occur. The conditions have not yet been codified and permission depends upon the particular circumstances in each case.

The great advantage of continental seating is that none of the
best viewing positions are lost to gangways, and from the actor's
point of view the audience is undivided. As the space between the
rows has to be wider the audience has the added bonus of better
knee room and nobody has to pop up like a jack-in-the-box when
anyone else passes along the row. Seats are gained where gangways
would have been, but others are lost because of the wider spacing of
rows. Continental layouts are not a means of getting more seats into
a space than with conventional gangways, in fact the opposite may
occur. The critical dimension is the unobstructed seatway, dimension E in the table. The row spacing depends upon this dimension
and another variable, the front-to-back dimension of the seat. The
design of the seat is therefore of the first importance in the chain of
decisions which have to be taken in the process of designing an
auditorium. With a tip-up seat the arm rest would probably have the
furthest projection when the seat is up. If the back of the seat rakes
back it may overhang the seatway behind and reduce its width.
These problems can only be resolved by drawing a section of the

seats in relation to the various rakes or steppings of the auditorium.

The row spacing is wide enough for members of the audience to walk in and out quite easily, but not wide enough for more than single file. This in itself imposes a discipline on them and audience behaviour shows that they reach the exits from the auditorium more rapidly than with orthodox gangway layouts.

No. 7:5   Continental seating at the Thorndike Theatre, Leatherhead.

8   Legislation

Places of public entertainment are controlled under various enactments some general and some locally applied. Under the Theatres Act 1968 every house or other place of public resort kept for the public performance of stage plays must have either the authority of letters patent or a licence. Patent theatres were granted a royal charter by Charles II. They are The Theatre Royal Drury Lane, The Royal Opera House Covent Garden, The Theatre Royal Haymarket.

Licensing authorities

The County or County Borough Council has the authority to grant licences within its area. A County Council may delegate these powers to a District Council.

Cinematograph exhibitions

Under the Cinematograph Act of 1909 a licence is required for all cinematograph exhibitions where flammable film is used other than those in a private dwelling. Under the 1952 Act a licence is required whatever type of film is used, whether non-flammable or flammable, or television equipment. However, where only non-flammable film is used certain premises are exempt.

If the premises are used only occasionally and exceptionally for showing films to a paying public (which means not more than on six days in a year) a licence is not needed but the occupier must comply with the Secretary of State's regulations which are the Cinematograph Regulations of 1955 and 1958. He must also give the local licensing authority at least seven days' notice before the film show is due to take place and must comply with any conditions they may impose under cinematograph regulations.

No licence is required if the public are not admitted or if they are allowed in free. Institutions and non-profit-making organizations can ask the public to pay to see an occasional film without a licence for the premises. They can obtain exemption from the Commissioners of Customs and Excise, but only if the premises have not been used on more than three of the preceding seven days for a similar exhibition.

The uses of premises for music, dancing, singing, boxing and wrestling

These forms of public entertainment are controlled by authorities in a similar manner but not all under the same legislation. The Greater London Council has its own regulations as do certain parts of the Home Counties. The rest of England and Wales is different again.

Technical requirements, regulations and rules of management

The licensing authorities have power to make regulations affecting the construction and equipment of buildings used for public entertainment particularly on matters of protection from fire. They may also make rules and conditions which must be observed by the occupiers to ensure that the premises are maintained in a safe condition. Some authorities issue their regulations and rules of management separately while others combine them in one document.

Home Office manual

The Secretary of State makes regulations for cinemas, but not for other places of public entertainment. The Home Office *Manual of Safety Precautions in Theatres and other places of Public Entertainment* was issued in 1934 as a model code of requirements and conditions for the guidance of licensing authorities who would then make their own rules. Though it is rather out of date it still makes interesting reading and explains some of the background experience which has led to the safety measures it recommends.

The Greater London Council regulations and rules

The GLC has many more theatres within its area than any other licensing authority in the UK and its regulations for places of public entertainment in London are comprehensive covering the site, general arrangements, construction, electrical and mechanical services, lighting, heating and ventilation. It has a department with much experience of administering the regulations and it is sufficiently flexible to take account of new techniques, materials, methods of construction and of changing trends within the theatre such as the desire for open stages. The GLC issues separate *Rules of Management*.

Other authorities

Many authorities base their regulations and rules on the Home Office Manual while some use those of the GLC as a basis. This variation from place to place makes it essential to find out what the particular local authority's requirements are at an early stage in the design of any place of public entertainment.

The Fire Precautions Act 1971

This Act will apply to theatres and various other places of assembly and resort. Its purpose is to strengthen and rationalize the law relating to fire precautions in these places and in hotels, boarding houses and similar residential premises. It is also designed to control some places which have so far escaped the net, such as club theatres. Occupiers of premises used for such purposes will have to obtain a certificate of approval of means of escape from the fire authority to whom they will have to submit full particulars of the premises and its uses including plans. The building will be inspected where necessary and any work which must be carried out will be notified. This will have to be completed before a fire certificate is issued. The requirements may include conditions about providing and maintaining means of escape, employing enough staff and training them in what to do in case of fire. Records of fire drill and any incidents may have to be kept ready for inspection. If for a particular premises it is physically impossible to comply with the requirements then the fire authority may for instance limit the number of people who may be accommodated.

Building and other regulations about fire precautions

The fire certificate will be needed by the occupiers of existing buildings so that the fire authority can keep a check on their use. When it comes to new buildings the Department of Environment may make building regulations concerning means of escape under the Public Health Acts of 1961 and 1936 and the Secretary of State will have powers to amend local Acts such as the London Building Acts. He can make regulations to control means of escape, the internal construction of the building, and the other matters which are dealt with during the life of the building by the fire certificate.

The new Act will not introduce any additional regulations to the provisions of the Cinematograph Acts of 1909 and 1952 but this legislation will come under its wing and amendments may eventually be made.

Other general legislation

Theatres and other places of public entertainment are also subject to the various Acts which apply to most other types of building such as: The Town and Country Planning Acts; the national Building Regulations 1972 for England and Wales or in the case of the Inner London Boroughs, the London Building Acts 1930–1939 and the London Constructional By-Laws. (Theatres and other public places of assembly are defined in the 1939 Act as 'Public Buildings' and are therefore subject to special control by the District Surveyor.)

In Scotland the Building Standard (Scotland) Amendment Regulations 1965 will apply. Any offices and shops in places of entertainment will be required to conform to the Offices Shops and Railway Premises Act 1963. The Factories Act of 1961 may apply to the workshop and backstage areas of some theatres. The Factories Inspector may require machinery to be guarded in the interest of workers' safety and he may also have requirements for their health and welfare. The Fire Authority will see that there are proper means of escape for the staff.

9   Stage planning

The audience-to-actor relationship is the starting point round which the planning of a theatre evolves. For many reasons it is convenient in this chapter to consider the stage as a separate entity but the complexity of technical requirements must never be allowed to interfere with the vital relation of the auditorium to the acting area.

Provision for orchestra

The usual position for the orchestra is in a pit between audience and stage. This comes about because the conductor in opera and musical shows must be seen by both orchestral players and singers. Musicians can be placed in various alternative positions, usually above the main stage level, in the centre or at either side of the stage. This is practicable only for smaller groups of players and where it is not essential for the conductor to have control of singers or other parts of the performance. A musicians' gallery can be incorporated in the permanent structure of the building, for example, in a box at the side of the stage, but the needs of particular productions will differ and it is very unlikely that this will suit all purposes. It would be wrong to make permanent arrangements which would later become an unwanted obstruction.

By using closed-circuit television it is now possible for the conductor to control the performance from a remote position. He conducts the orchestra at the side of the stage while a camera trained on him relays his image to monitor screens in the traditional prompt box position or strategically placed in the wings to suit the production. Similarly, he can watch the progress of the performance on another screen relaying the show from a camera placed in the auditorium.

Size of orchestra

Orchestras vary greatly in size and in the space they require. A space allowance of 1 m² per player and for the conductor should be made and 5 m² for a piano and 5–6 m² for tympani. String players can usually share desks, but woodwind will probably each have different parts and must, therefore, have individual music stands taking up more room. Some modern works have a large percussion section which again demands more space. If the orchestra pit extends too far back under the stage the sound will be muffled unless special precautions are taken. The soffit of the covered portion should be designed to reflect sound out towards the audience. In opera houses, where Wagner or Richard Strauss are frequently performed, the orchestra has to be very large, up to 120 players, and unless the singers are to become unacceptably remote from the audience, the pit will have to extend some way under the stage. For other operas and musicals provision should be made for about forty players and their instruments.

The level of the floor of the orchestra pit should be adjustable between 2 and 3 m below stage to allow for the preferences of different directors and musicians. The walls of the orchestra pit should be dark and non-reflective to avoid picking up the inevitable light scatter.

Pit convertible to forestage

In most theatres whose use is mainly for drama a permanent orchestra pit can damage the audience to stage relation by leaving a gap between the two. The pit should be partly under the stage but it should not extend more than about 2 m back or it will interfere with traps in the stage. It is, therefore, common practice to cover over the orchestra pit and use it as a forestage. This can be done manually by assembling panels and framework, but the labour and time involved may well be an expensive embarrassment to the management and it is normally a great advantage to be able to make the change from orchestra pit to forestage mechanically by installing a lift or lifts. Even in quite small projects a lift in this position is one of the first pieces of mechanical equipment that should be installed.

The most usual provision is a single lift which can be stopped at various levels to act either as an orchestra pit, an extension to the auditorium seating or a forestage. The arrangements can be made more flexible by putting in two lifts which themselves could be further sub-divided.

Position of safety curtain

Normally the orchestra pit lift is placed on the audience side of the safety curtain. Some German theatres have brought the safety curtain forward to come down on the orchestra pit rail, the pit itself being taken out of the stage area. The advantage of this is that the auditorium seating remains unchanged and there is no question of removing seats to accommodate the orchestra. It seems more logical to maintain the capacity of the audience when a large-scale opera production is being staged rather than reduce it by removing seats to make way for the orchestra.

The vital audience to acting area relation is maintained for the

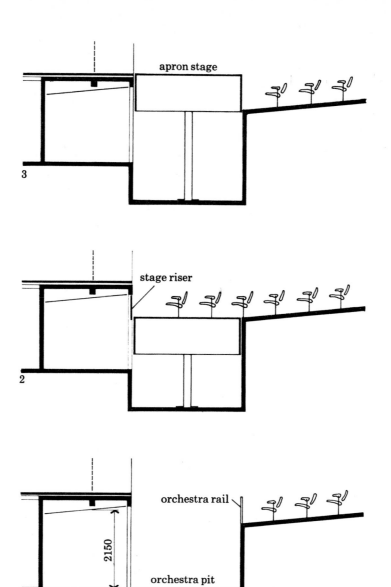

No. 9:1   Apron stage lift.

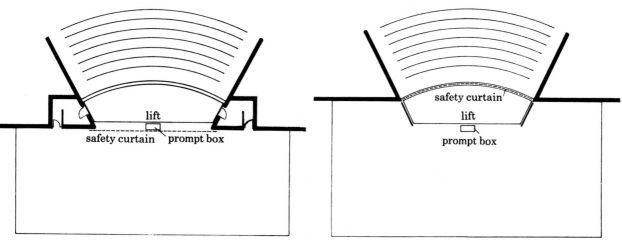

No. 9:2   Normal position of safety curtain.

No. 9:3   Safety curtain on the line of the
orchestra pit rail gives more flexibility.

straight drama and scenery can be set right down towards the front of the stage. For the large musical production it is inevitable that there will be an orchestral area between audience and singers and the relationship between stage and auditorium is not any different even if the acting area does have to be pushed back to accommodate the musicians. This arrangement does imply a larger stage area than would normally be allowed for a small theatre mainly intended for straight drama. It also implies greater width and flexibility in the arrangement of the proscenium.

Mechanical problems of lifts

The mechanical provisions required for lifts can impose severe limitations on their use. The most common method of operation is by electrical screw jacks which must be accommodated below the level of the pit in bore holes if this is below ground level. If this area underneath cannot be used, horizontal jacks working on a scissors principle are an alternative but the height of travel of this kind of lift is limited. Motive power can be provided by hydraulic rams. All lifts require guides somewhere round their edges to prevent them from moving from side to side under load. The screw jacks and hydraulic rams will provide the power and the support for a direct load but cannot provide much resistance to sideways movement. For economic reasons the guides are usually required at intervals all round the lift. This does not leave a completely clear floor area when the lift is in its lowest position. It is possible to eliminate the projecting guides provided that the lift platform is well braced and deep enough to be restrained by guides beneath the lowest level of the lift. This is expensive because the lift platform has to be made very much deeper and so does the pit into which it sinks. This pit will have to be at least the depth of travel of the lift plus sufficient additional depth to brace the lift through the guides when it is in its top position.

The authorities will require various safety devices to ensure that the lift is stopped if any person or thing is obstructing it.

The design of the front of the stage and of the covering of the lift will have to be carefully worked out to include any electrical points and traps. There may also have to be a float trap for footlights and a carpet cut.

Where fire separation of the stage risk is required the two-hour separation between auditorium and stage must be maintained and openings other than the main proscenium opening with its safety curtain must be protected by a fire check lobby with self-closing doors at each end. This applies to the entries to the orchestra pit under the stage and to doors onto the forestage.

Prompting

In the dramatic theatre, prompting is one of the duties of whoever is running the show from the control point which is called the 'prompt corner'. It should not be imagined that because this is most com-

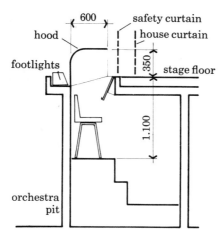

No. 9:4   Section through the prompter's box at the Royal Opera House, Covent Garden

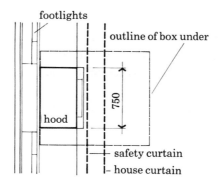

No. 9:5   Plan at stage level

monly called the prompt corner its main purpose is actually prompting. The full use and arrangement of the prompt corner is dealt with in Chapter 12. In a basically proscenium stage condition no special facilities are required but prompting as such in the case of thrust stages and theatre-in-the-round is sometimes a difficult problem. One solution which has been tried is the use of amplified prompting using a narrow beam directional loudspeaker.

With smaller open stages prompting can usually be done from behind or from a vomitory.

In the opera house the standard method of prompting is from a prompt box – a small enclosure covered on the audience side and open to the stage, sited on the front edge of the stage. The prompter sits in this box with his head just above stage level, with sufficient space around him to place his score on a sloping desk and raise his arms to stage level.

It is essential for the prompter to be able to see the conductor behind him, and to do this a mirror system is employed, arranged so that the image can be seen slightly above the prompter's normal eye level.

The hood covering the box should be kept as small as possible while still permitting the prompter some freedom of movement. Too large a box will obstruct the sight lines from the front row of seats and be a disfiguring element in any stage design. The hood must be painted matt black on the outside to avoid reflection, but internally should be white so that the light is reflected on the face of the prompter, whose visual expressions are valuable to the singers.

Some form of directional lighting, preferably low voltage, must be built in to illuminate the score without spilling light over the stage. A miniature spot is suitable and it should be possible for it to be dimmed and switched off remotely from the stage-lighting control position when the needs of the performance demand a complete blackout.

Height of proscenium

The minimum height of the proscenium opening is determined by sight lines from the highest seat in the auditorium. This is illustrated in diagram 3:4 page 32 (in Chapter 3 on sight lines).

An auditorium with more than one tier or with a very steep rake will need a higher proscenium than one with seating on a single tier with a gentle rake.

As there could be occasions when for some theatrical purpose a higher proscenium is needed, the building is more flexible if the structural proscenium is raised close to the height of the auditorium ceiling or even above it in some cases. Pelmets, the house tabs or the safety curtain can then be used to mask the upper part of the opening as required. It should be remembered that the higher the opening, the higher the fly tower will have to be.

To use the safety curtain for masking, the mechanism of the air buffer may have to be adjusted.

Proscenium arch

The tendency now in the theatre is to play down the picture frame and make the transition from stage to auditorium inconspicuous. Although there will be many productions which rely on the picture frame there will be others in which it is essential to avoid any emphasis on the proscenium arch.

Entrances to the stage

There should be entrances for performers from the dressing-room area to either side of the stage. It should be possible to reach either side without crossing the actual stage area. Performers crossing behind the set may often cause backcloths or cycloramas to shake either by actually touching them or by setting up a draught. This can be very distracting to the audience and can be avoided if there is a passageway outside the stage area. Nevertheless it is wrong to conclude that circulation space is not needed behind the acting and setting area because there are many occasions when an entrance for actors is required at the back of the set.

Escape from stage

Safety regulations will require that there is at least one fire-protected exit from the stage to the outside which has no other fastening but panic bolts. With larger stages an additional means of escape may be required by the authorities.

Fire hazard of stage scenery

Some sort of scenery and methods of changing it will be needed for almost all live performances. Even on open stages where sight lines prevent the use of orthodox sets there is a tendency to load what space there is with scenery. The traditional materials used to make it are wood and canvas because they are cheap and easy to handle, but their great disadvantage is the ease with which they catch fire. Theatres burned down so regularly in the nineteenth century that stringent safety regulations had to be imposed to protect audiences.

Traditionally constructed scenery is an obvious fire risk and most licensing authorities will not allow its use unless it is possible to seal it off from the audience with a fire barrier, in case of emergency. In the proscenium theatre with a fly tower, this is done by the use of a safety curtain and drencher. But in other open-stage forms of theatre it is difficult though not necessarily impossible to arrange for some corresponding device.

If there is no means of shutting off the stage from the audience, the licensing authorities will probably impose restrictions on the materials that may be used for scenery. If it has to be non-combustible cost is increased and the designer's scope reduced.

The full safety equipment for a stage may also include an automatic smoke vent, sprinklers, hose reels, fire buckets, extinguishers, smoke detectors and so on, but the safety curtain is the most important because of the limitations it imposes on planning.

Safety curtain

There are various kinds of safety curtain. Maximum protection is given by the rigid type which is normally suspended in one piece. Two- and even three-piece rigid safety curtains have been installed where flying height is limited. Where the risk is considered smaller roller asbestos curtains and festooning asbestos can be used. In some cases a heavy wool fabric is considered sufficient.

The heaviest form of rigid curtain which has earned the name of 'the iron', as it is often called by people in the theatre, consists of a steel frame of angles or channels faced on the stage side in steel sheet not less than 16 swg thick and on the audience side in asbestos cloth with wire reinforcement woven in and sometimes another sheet of steel. This runs in steel guides which cover the edges of the curtain and are set back from the proscenium to give an overlap of at least 450 mm. The curtain is suspended on steel wire rope and counterweighted so that when released it will still be heavy enough to fall under its own weight. As it reaches the end of its travel it is slowed down by an air buffer which prevents it from crashing into the stage. When it is down it should completely seal the proscenium opening. Along its bottom edge it is provided with a pad of rolled asbestos cloth and at the top the seal is formed by an angle which closes down on another asbestos pad over the proscenium or by a steel channel and a sand trough. The curtain should descend at an average speed of not less than 300 mm per second and should close completely in 30 seconds.

The curtain can be raised by a hand winch or more usually by an electric or hydraulic hoist. Rules of management usually insist that it should be lowered in the presence of the audience at every performance and, of course, no obstruction must be allowed to interfere with its action.

The construction does not always have to be quite so heavy. Asbestos fabric stretched on a steel frame is sometimes acceptable, but the rest of the devices still have to be provided. Roller asbestos and heavy wool curtains are often allowed for smaller buildings without full flying facilities. These must have emergency release arrangements and a drencher. The purpose of the drencher in a rigid steel curtain is to keep the steel cool enough to prevent it buckling. In asbestos and wool curtains it also adds weight which prevents the curtain billowing out with draughts.

The releases for the safety curtain and the drencher are put on the working side of the stage near the prompt corner. A duplicate release for each is also required near the principal exit from the stage.

Automatic smoke vents   These are often called 'haystack lanterns' because the original and still the commonest kind were haystack shape.

Some kind of automatic smoke vent may be required over any stage in a theatre seating more than about 400 (the number varies according to the authority) whether there is a proper fly tower or not. If there is a stage which has to have a safety curtain, the automatic smoke vent is certain to be required. If a fire should occur on the stage their purpose is to draw the smoke and fumes rapidly away. The principle is that light panels are held leaning out so that when the fastening is released they will fall open under gravity.

A quick-release mechanism is operated by hand from the prompt corner and there is a fusible link which can release the panels automatically. If these means fail the panels should quickly shatter under the action of heat. Thin glass sheets in metal frames behave in this manner and it is for this reason and not to let in daylight that glass is used. The glass is painted black to exclude light.

Regulations require the cross-sectional area of the vent to be a proportion of the floor area of the stage. The GLC requires one-tenth, but the figure may vary elsewhere. An automatic smoke vent may be required in a scenery store within the building.

The stage floor   The floor of the stage is itself an important scenic element which can best be exploited when there is a stage basement solely for use in connection with a performance extending under the whole of the principal acting area. This basement should have at least headroom and preferably 2400 mm clear height. An alternative means of escape has to be provided.

The stage floor itself must have some flexibility in its construction. The most rigid and intractable form of construction is a reinforced concrete slab and this must be avoided. Timber, on the other hand, supported by bolted steel supports, can easily be adapted. Traps can be cut in the floor wherever they are wanted and if necessary the whole stage surface can be removed over the basement area.

A further step towards increasing adaptability is to make the whole stage in sections which can be removed separately. Still greater sophistication can be achieved by mechanizing the stage with lifts. If this sort of installation is contemplated, the height of the basement will have to be increased and if it is intended to bring sets or large pieces of scenery from below, it may be necessary to have 6–9 m clear and to extend the basement under the whole of the stage.

No. 9:6   *Underneath the demountable stage at the Crucible, Sheffield.*

Raked stage

Stage lifts are discussed in more detail later, but a word should be said here about raked stages which were once an accepted feature of our old theatres and still have strong supporters in the theatrical profession. The original purpose of a raked stage was to improve the perspective effects of scenery painted in the traditional manner on a series of wing flats all parallel to the proscenium. It also gives some marginal improvement in sight lines. Some performers feel that the raked stage assists their performance, whereas to others, particularly dancers, it is a hindrance. The great disadvantages are that scenery other than a series of parallel flats, becomes much more complicated to make and handle and to take on tour. Solid three-dimensional scenery cannot easily be moved about because verticals will not remain plumb. If the seating is properly designed the sight lines should be good without a rake on the stage. If a rake is wanted for a particular production it can be built on top of a flat stage, or the entire acting area can be tilted mechanically. Stages should, therefore, preferably be flat, especially if stage machinery is to be used, so that shallow lightweight revolves can be built on top when required. They should also be wide and deep enough for shallow wagons to be used on top if needed for a particular production.

Stage floor material

The selection of a material for the stage floor is governed by conflicting factors which cannot be entirely reconciled. One important consideration is fire resistance and this usually means that hardwood, not less than 32 mm finished thickness must be used. Some authorities include good quality tongued and grooved softwood such as Columbian Pine in this category. Others may require an extra thickness if softwood is used.

Other properties sought in a boarded floor are that it should not warp or shrink badly as a result of heat or moisture changes, it should be reasonably easy to screw into and should recover well after a screw has been removed; it should not tend to splinter or be brittle.

It is not easy to find either softwoods or hardwoods with these characteristics, but hardwoods have a much longer life and this is most often the deciding factor in Britain. Where straight drama is played the floor is much of the time covered with a stage cloth, but this is not so for dancing. Dancers always prefer the resilience of softwood and where the main use is for ballet, it will probably be necessary to accept the higher maintenance costs and a life of only five years which are the consequences of choosing softwood.

There are problems in the choice of finish for the floor. The timber should be stained to a dark colour to avoid unwanted reflections of stage lighting. It should not be slippery which would be dangerous particularly for dancers. Even matt sealers are unpopular with dancers, but it is very difficult to keep a floor clean if it is not sealed in some way.

There are many temporary coverings that can be laid on stage floors for special purposes or to provide a working surface, but it is not appropriate here to discuss them at length. Mention ought to be made of linoleum which, provided it is well laid and thick enough (6 mm) has proved to be a useful semi-permanent stage finish. It recovers quite well from being screwed into, is quiet, wears well and remains stable. Cleaning is not difficult, but the lino should neither be highly polished nor scrubbed with strong detergent which will remove the linseed oil and make it start to crack. Another finish which is often used is hardboard which can be ill-treated and then renewed without much expense.

Changing scenery   The stage must be designed for rapid changing of scenery during a performance. Lack of space will create difficulties and will limit the scope of productions.

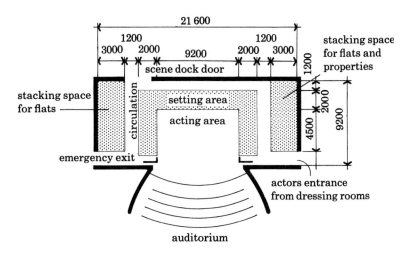

No. 9:7   *This diagram shows space requirements for a stage where sets are assembled and dismantled for each change. More width and more depth would be desirable.*

Stacking space for flats and storage space for properties and rostra could be provided along the back wall if the depth were increased, but this is much less convenient than storage in the wings. The depth should not be increased at the expense of wing space. If there is not enough room to provide even this amount of working space for a picture-frame stage, the question of whether it would be better to have some kind of open stage should be considered.

Methods of changing scenery   The elaboration of the methods of changing scenery depends upon the prospective use of the building. The more frequent the changes of production are likely to be, the more extensive should be the provision of facilities and space for handling scenery.

Mechanical aids to scene changing have two main purposes: first, to permit the scope of productions to be varied while making them economical to run by saving time and manpower. When each set has to be assembled piece by piece changes are virtually confined to intervals. If complete sets are ready to roll into position the minimum of time and manpower is needed to change them and there is no need for a break in continuity of a performance.

Second, in theatres and opera houses with a repertoire it is useful to have sets for more than one production built so that performances of different shows can be given on the same day or so that rehearsals can continue without interfering with the current production.

Some or all of the following methods can be used singly or in various combinations. Those that demand least space in plan are most commonly used but in general, extra space is more valuable than elaborate machinery. Scenery can be moved in and out of the view of the audience vertically above by using a flying system and vertically below by using lifts. It can be moved horizontally to the sides and the rear on movable stage sections or rotated on revolves.

Flying   Vertical movement by means of a flying system has the great advantage that scenery can be moved in or out very quickly and does not take up valuable floor space when it is stored in the fly tower. Even if for various reasons it is not possible to have a fly tower, it is still essential to be able to suspend things over the stage such as stage-lighting equipment, curtains, pelmets, legs and borders. All these can be suspended from tracks or pulley blocks attached to the structure of the roof.

In its earlier form all the suspension cables were ropes made from natural fibres such as hemp and manilla. Most suspension is now by steel wire rope, but 'hemps', as they are called, are still used for some purposes. A special piece of scenery which cannot be conveniently handled by the counterweight system could have a set of hemps fitted up to take it. Hemp lines are hauled up by the muscle power of flymen and tied off on cleats on the fly rail. They may have a sand bag or shot bag tied to them to act as an improvised counterweight.

If an efficient method of changing scenery is required a proper fly tower is necessary, high enough for the tallest flats and backcloths to be taken right up out of sight of the audience. This is the factor which has most bearing on the height of the grid which is the working platform of steel slats over the stage where alteration and maintenance of the fly system is carried out.

Height of grid   A desirable height for this grid is three times the height of the proscenium and the minimum for proper functioning is two-and-a-half times this height.

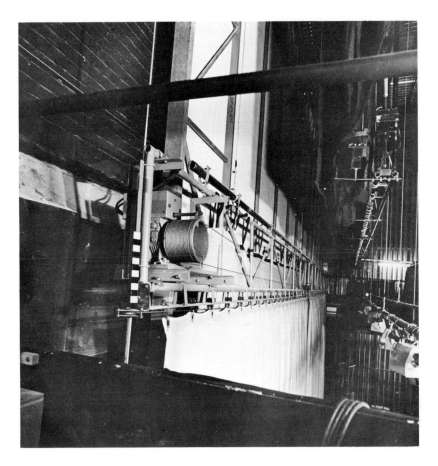

No. 9:8   The photograph shows the safety curtain in the 'up' position. The house
curtain is suspended on a beam track and can be used as a drop curtain
or drawn by a motor. Also shown is the bottom of the cinema screen
and the No. 1 spot bar.

No. 9:9   The grid in an installation where the loftblocks are attached to the
main structure of the roof, allowing unobstructed working space.

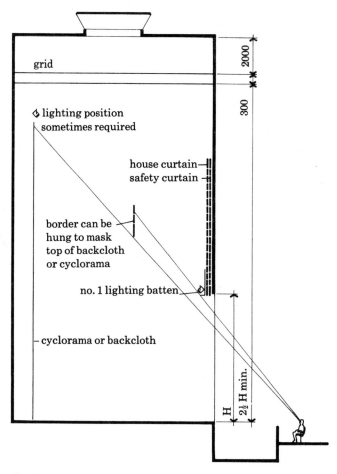

grid

◊ lighting position
  sometimes required

house curtain
safety curtain

border can be
hung to mask
top of backcloth
or cyclorama

no. 1 lighting batten

cyclorama or backcloth

2000

300

$2\frac{1}{2}$ H min.

H

No. 9:10   *Section*
Effect of front row sight lines on proscenium dimensions and masking.

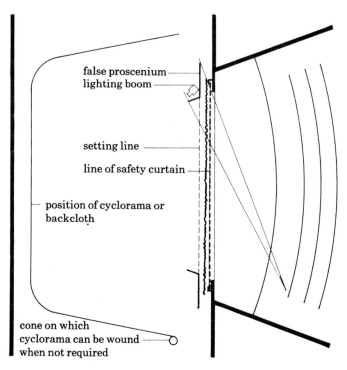

false proscenium
lighting boom

setting line

line of safety curtain

position of cyclorama or
backcloth

cone on which
cyclorama can be wound
when not required

No. 9:11   *Plan.*

The proscenium in this case is the working proscenium. The structural proscenium may be too high to mask sets of a reasonable height. The diagram shows how the sight lines from the lowest and closest seats in the auditorium affect the height of the grid. We have already seen how the furthest and highest seats in the auditorium determine the minimum height of the proscenium. The view of the flys from the front seats can be hidden by borders suspended from the grid. If these are too low or too many, the spacious effect of a setting with a cyclorama or a large backcloth is lost.

The higher the grid the less likely this is to happen.

The width of the area covered by the flying system should overlap the proscenium opening (W) by 2 m on either side. This width should not be interrupted for the full height of the tower to the grid.

The width of the fly tower itself is determined by adding a further 2 m to one side to allow for counterweights and the fly gallery from which they are operated. It is usual to add a further $1\frac{1}{2}$–2 m to the other side of the stage for another gallery.

The minimum internal width of the fly tower should, therefore, be W+8 m.

Counterweights

In a counterweight system scenery is suspended on steel cables which pass over pulley blocks on or above the grid and on the side wall of the fly tower and is balanced against counterweights which run in cradles up and down this wall.

The pieces of scenery are attached to a suspension barrel which must be capable of travelling from the stage floor to the underside of the grid. The distance of travel of the counterweights is equal to the height of the grid above the stage and a continuous vertical wall must be provided for the counterweight guides allowing extra height for the blocks at the top and bottom and for the length of the weight cradle. This system is the simplest and easiest to operate and is called a single purchase counterweight system.

For the actual operation of flying systems the total width between side walls of W+8 m is sufficient, but if counterweight guides come down to stage level they will take up about 750 mm including guard rails. This reduces the wing space of the counterweight side to 3250 mm which is rather cramped. If the flys were operated from the stage floor as they sometimes are instead of from a fly gallery, yet more space would be taken up reducing the wings still further to about 2 m. Usually, more wing space than this is necessary and with single purchase flying the whole fly tower must be widened to provide for greater width. This is reasonable up to a point, but with deep wing spaces needed the fly tower can become uneconomically large.

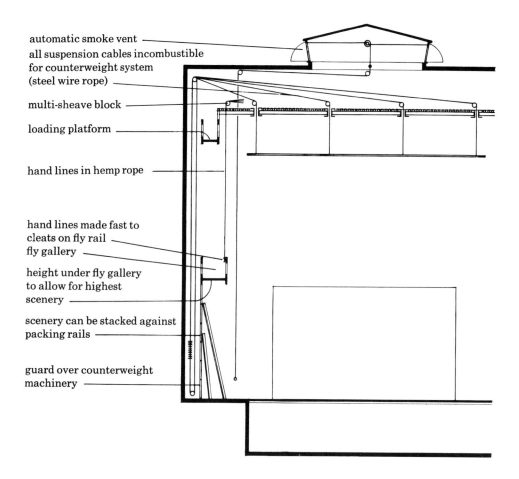

automatic smoke vent

all suspension cables incombustible
for counterweight system
(steel wire rope)

multi-sheave block

loading platform

hand lines in hemp rope

hand lines made fast to
cleats on fly rail
fly gallery

height under fly gallery
to allow for highest
scenery

scenery can be stacked against
packing rails

guard over counterweight
machinery

No. 9:12   Section through stage with single purchase counterweight system.

**Double purchase
counterweights**

The alternative is to free the stage floor of counterweights and raise
them so that the wings can be continued underneath the walls of
the fly tower. If single purchase counterweights were used the same
vertical height of the wall would be required and the fly tower
would become that much higher. In other words, if the counterweights were taken 7 m above the stage floor a further 7 m of height
would have to be added to the fly tower above the grid which is
clearly impracticable. A solution is to use double purchase counterweights where, by introducing two extra blocks, the length of travel
of the weights is halved in relation to the suspended scenery. This
correspondingly reduces the height of the wall required.

The disadvantage is that while the weights travel half as far they
have to be twice as heavy which increases the labour of loading and
unloading, lengthens the cradle required to hold the weights and
increases the friction and inertia in the system which have to be
overcome. It is also less easy to gauge the exact height to which a

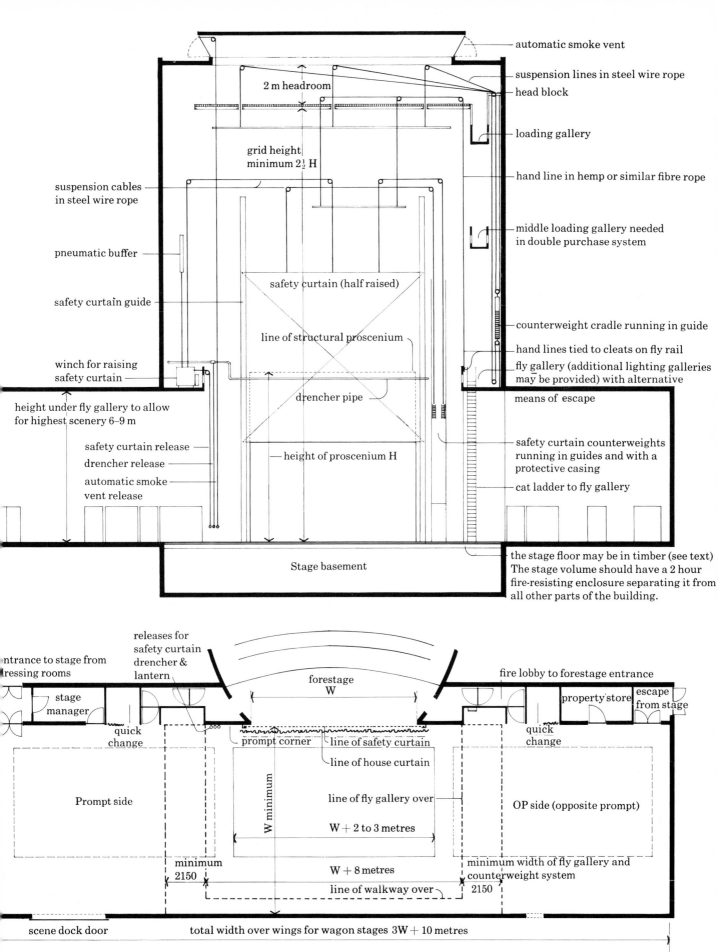

- automatic smoke vent
- suspension lines in steel wire rope
- head block
- loading gallery
- hand line in hemp or similar fibre rope
- middle loading gallery needed in double purchase system
- counterweight cradle running in guide
- hand lines tied to cleats on fly rail
- fly gallery (additional lighting galleries may be provided) with alternative means of escape
- safety curtain counterweights running in guides and with a protective casing
- cat ladder to fly gallery
- the stage floor may be in timber (see text) The stage volume should have a 2 hour fire-resisting enclosure separating it from all other parts of the building.

2 m headroom

grid height minimum 2½ H

suspension cables in steel wire rope

pneumatic buffer

safety curtain guide

safety curtain (half raised)

line of structural proscenium

drencher pipe

winch for raising safety curtain

height under fly gallery to allow for highest scenery 6–9 m

safety curtain release
drencher release
automatic smoke vent release

height of proscenium H

Stage basement

releases for safety curtain drencher & lantern

entrance to stage from dressing rooms

stage manager

quick change

fire lobby to forestage entrance

property store

escape from stage

forestage W

prompt corner
line of safety curtain
line of house curtain
line of fly gallery over

W + 2 to 3 metres

W minimum

Prompt side

OP side (opposite prompt)

quick change

minimum 2150

W + 8 metres

line of walkway over

minimum width of fly gallery and counterweight system 2150

scene dock door

total width over wings for wagon stages 3W + 10 metres

No. 9:13   Diagram showing the layout of a stage equipped with a double purchase flying system and wagon stages.

piece of scenery is raised or lowered than with a single purchase
system. As the counterweight cradle is longer it is difficult to reach
all of it from one level and an extra loading gallery should be provided beneath the main loading gallery. The handling ropes should
also be double purchase. It is understandable that in the theatre,
single purchase systems are greatly preferred because they are so
much easier to work.

One method of providing plenty of wing space without introducing double purchase counterweights is to concentrate the wing
space on the opposite side of the stage from the counterweight wall.
If, as they usually do, economics curb the amount of space which
can be allotted to the stage, it may well be better to concentrate a
large area on one side rather than distribute half shares on either
side.

*No. 9:14   Operating a counterweight line from the fly gallery. An outstation of
the stage management control system can be seen on the left.*

No. 9:15   *A loading gallery showing a weight being put into one of the cradles.*

No. 9:16   *Double purchase counterweight system allowing wing space to extend underneath.*

No. 9:17   *The head block of a counterweight system showing a cradle in the top position.*

Positions for operating flys

There is no mechanical reason why flys should not be operated from anywhere along the travel of the counterweights. In double-purchase systems the operator must, in any case, be on a gallery above the stage.

In single-purchase systems the operator can be on the stage floor. This takes up 1 m of valuable wing space and is a method of working which would be used only in smaller theatres where there is no separate fly operator and the job has to be done by someone who has other duties at stage level. The normal operating position is from a fly gallery above the stage, but it is possible to have a choice of positions by moving the rope lock. No line should have more than one rope lock if confusion is to be avoided.

The fly tower should usually extend for the full depth of the stage, but if this is very deep the flying system can be curtailed and the stage continued at lower height in the same manner as over the wings on either side. An indication of the extent of the stage which it is desirable to cover with the flying system is at least 3 m from the back of the acting area or $1\frac{1}{3}$ times the proscenium width back from the safety curtain.

Spacing of counterweight lines

Although spacings as close as 75 mm have been used, the recommended minimum is 100 mm and 150–200 mm is common. This minimum is dictated not only by the multi-sheave headblocks, but also by the practical use of the flys. If cloths or flats are suspended too close together there is a danger of their fouling one another as they are moved. Closely spaced lines allow more flexibility in positioning the scenery, but if they are so close that it is dangerous to hang pieces on adjacent lines the advantage of flexibility is lost. The position of the first line behind the safety curtain is dependent on the depth taken up by the safety curtain and the drencher. The house curtain immediately behind these must be far enough back to avoid the danger of its fouling the safety-curtain mechanism. The diagram shows an arrangement just behind the proscenium which is only one of many possible.

Some directors will not want a false proscenium at all, others may prefer to have more lighting between the house curtains and the first border. The diagrams show a return on the false proscenium to give the appearance of thickness, but some will prefer not to have this on the grounds that it can interfere with lighting or that it tends to push the setting too far upstage away from the audience.

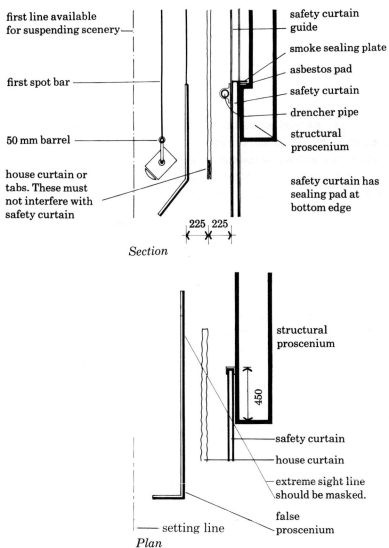

first line available for suspending scenery

first spot bar

50 mm barrel

house curtain or tabs. These must not interfere with safety curtain

safety curtain guide

smoke sealing plate

asbestos pad

safety curtain

drencher pipe

structural proscenium

safety curtain has sealing pad at bottom edge

225 | 225

Section

structural proscenium

450

safety curtain

house curtain

extreme sight line should be masked.

false proscenium

setting line

Plan

No. 9:18   *Typical layout of proscenium arch.*

Loftblocks

When loftblocks for the counterweight lines are suspended from beams above the grid, the grid itself is left clear for working. It is then easier to fix spot lines and sets of hand lines where they are wanted on the grid.

The spacing of lines should not exceed 4 m or the barrel will sag. Bridles can be used to prevent sagging, but they restrict flying height. With wide stages it is better to have four suspension lines to each counterweight set.

Power operated flying

It is obvious that mechanically operated flying installations must eventually supersede the traditional manually-operated counter-weights. Systems where a cable is wound on to a drum powered either electrically or hydraulically have been in use for many years in Germany, but until recently little work had been done on the problem in this country. The reasons were economic because a power-operated set is likely to cost several times as much as an orthodox, manually-operated counterweight set. The eventual saving in labour costs and the increase in efficiency will ultimately justify the capital expenditure, but it is only with the advent of large-scale schemes such as the National Theatre and the Barbican that this sort of sophistication has been contemplated.

Much of the expense lies in the sensitivity demanded of the mechanics which have to compete with human operators. If a flyman can feel some unexpected resistance he can make an instant correction and avoid an accident, but a machine, if it cannot sense that something is wrong may continue and cause a trail of damage before it is stopped. The motors must have a wide range of speeds up to about 2 m per second, and must stop at predetermined positions with great accuracy. A piece of scenery must not hit the stage floor with a crash. The motors have to be very quiet and hydraulic noises must be eliminated. It is clear that the specification is very demanding and although all the performance criteria can be met by mechanical engineers, the problem has been the expense of doing so.

The established British manufacturers of stage equipment have combined with electrical and hydraulic concerns to investigate the potential of developments in these branches of engineering. Particular attention has been given to bar and point flying and standard systems are being developed for both. Improved methods of control were originally produced for synchronising point suspensions and are now being applied to electrically powered bar flying. A hydraulic cylinder, using a nylon-coated wire rope in place of a piston rod, provides another prime-mover for flying which will save the labour of loading and unloading counterweights. Both these methods can be used in standard fly tower designs although specialist advice should be sought in the detail planning stage. One advantage is that the loading galleries can be dispensed with. Space has to be found for the pump and reservoir which serve the hydraulic system.

Theatres with open or space stages may wish to make provision for flying and suspension of three-dimensional settings. Specially designed control equipment is available to drive any number of individual hoists to the required relative heights. Once positioned these hoists can be locked in a group so that they always move together to 'deads' which can be set by pressing a button after they have been driven to the required height during a fit-up. All such equipment should include overload and slack-rope detectors and be fully protected against failures. There are two alternative methods of positioning the hoists in the grid: either individual mobile units can be carried into position, clamped down and plugged in, or the hoist can be fixed to the walls of the fly tower from where it drives a double-purchase load hook suspended beneath, and running on, a fixed track in a similar way to a hammerhead crane. This method has the advantage that the lateral position of the hooks can be adjusted from the stage. Specifications prepared for this type of flying equipment have called for a very close tolerance on relative hook positions and extremely low noise in operation. Rotating machinery and solid-state drive equipment is available.

Both systems use an electrical feedback loop to maintain the accuracy and control required. The rotating drive equipment would generally require a separate sound-insulated room while the solid-state equipment may be able to be accommodated in an enlarged dimmer room.

Stage lifts   Lifts, bridges or elevators in the stage itself have various uses which come within the following categories.

1   **Multi-level stage:** For raising, sinking or tilting parts of the stage to provide rostra, traps, ramps or to give a rake to part or the whole of the acting area. There is a well-established tradition of massive sets on several levels for opera and the action of many plays can be made much more interesting if the geography of the acting area can be altered in three dimensions. Lifts are not essential for this but an extensive system of rostra entails a great deal of carpentry and materials. For a long-run play this may not matter but in a repertoire the problem of finding storage for several sets with rostra may become acute. Lifts can help to solve the problem and in particular they can save on the labour of changing from one multi-level set to another.

2   **Special effects:** Lifts are used for special effects of scenery or characters rising from or sinking below the stage. These effects are likely to be needed for the more spectacular entertainments such as operas, ballets and pantomimes.

3   **Moving scenery:** Lifts can be used for moving pieces of scenery or whole sets from below the stage. It must be remembered that scene changes that depend on lifts will not be as rapid as those depending on flown scenery. Lifts move more slowly and, for safety reasons, should not be operated in the dark. With the exception

of special effects during performances lifts would be operated between shows or in intervals.

Safety of lifts   Some of the mechanical problems of lift design have been mentioned in connection with adaptable orchestra pits and forestages. It is not possible to provide complete safeguards in the use of lifts without rendering them useless from a practical point of view. This is one reason why they are designed to move rather slowly. Even so, great care has to be exercised in their operation.

Safety nets are sometimes placed between lifts when, for instance, they are used to provide an entrance from beneath the stage.

It may be necessary to install automatically rising safety barriers round the edge of the aperture left in the stage when the lifts descend.

The extensive system of lifts shown in the diagrams could be used

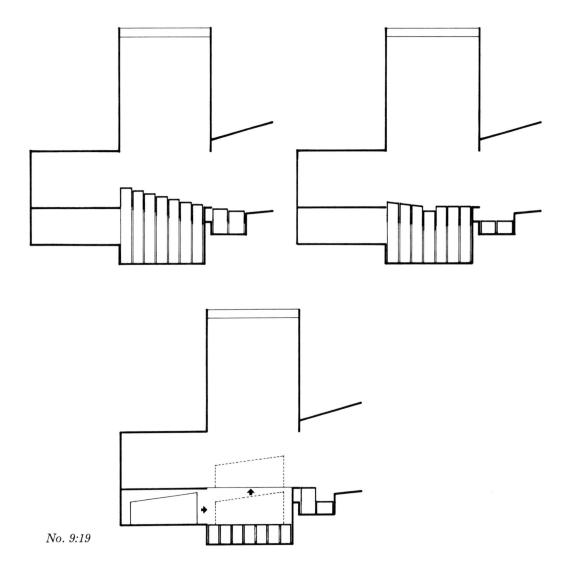

No. 9:19

in various ways. The first shows the system used to make a concert orchestra platform. Acoustics are not likely to be good unless the wings and the fly tower are masked. This could be done by suspending reflectors from the grid, or by introducing a band shell which is the practice in the United States.

The second diagram shows the lifts used to form different levels on the stage, including a rake. The forestage is lowered to form an orchestra pit. This sort of arrangement would be typical for operas. A cyclorama or backcloth with masking borders and wings would be suspended from the grid.

The third diagram illustrates how lifts may be used to bring a complete set on a wagon from beneath the stage. Used in conjunction with a wagon system at stage level it would be possible to have four or five complete sets in existence at one time.

This sort of elaborate mechanization has scarcely been attempted in this country. Experience of large-scale mechanical stages is mostly confined to Germany in the heavily subsidised state theatres. Lifts and wagons used in this way are rather cumbersome and slow. There are other operations that would have to be carried out at the same time such as rolling and unrolling the cyclorama and masking with borders and wings. To make full use of the wagons, sets would probably be designed to carry their own masking and for this reason wagons should be wider than the proscenium opening.

It must be remembered that stage-lighting systems probably cannot accommodate more than two complete lighting plots from the sheer physical difficulty of finding room for the number of lanterns unless the necessary discipline of standard lantern settings is accepted. A single production with two or three scene changes may make big demands on the total available lighting equipment. When it is one of a repertoire of elaborate productions the time taken to change the lighting, redirect lanterns and change colour filters may well be the limiting factor.

Sectional lifts   If the lifts can be broken down into a number of different sections which can be operated separately the system is much more flexible, particularly for forming rostra. The danger of providing a system of stage lifts is that their use may be very limited in relation to their cost. For this reason the system should be as flexible as possible within the budget allowed. However, it should be remembered that the greater the flexibility the greater will be the cost.

The distance of travel of a lift will probably be from 6 m below the stage to 4 m above. It would be a great advantage if the lift area could be broken up into a number of independent platforms rising the full height without the interruption of guides, counterweights, etc. Telescopic lifts of this kind can be made, but their use is limited to cases where the vertical travel is small in relation to the horizontal dimensions as in orchestra pit lifts. With the long travel usually required for stage lifts the mechanical problem of accurately aligning the various sections of floor becomes extremely difficult and safety becomes a greater consideration. It is more usual to find the arrangement shown in the diagram where the lifts are in the form of a series of bridges spanning right across the acting area. Sectionalisation is achieved by incorporating smaller lifts within each of the larger bridges.

Operation of lifts   Stage lifts can be operated by ropes, screw jacks or hydraulic rams.

The quickest moving lift is the rope and electric motor type. The diagram shows how one motor operates a set of ropes connected to each end of the bridge. The motor could be in a different position at the side in which case the far set of ropes would have to be longer than the near set to carry over the blocks and transfer the pull to the other side. This kind of rigging, with counterweights, takes up a good deal of space and limits access to the lift when it is under the stage.

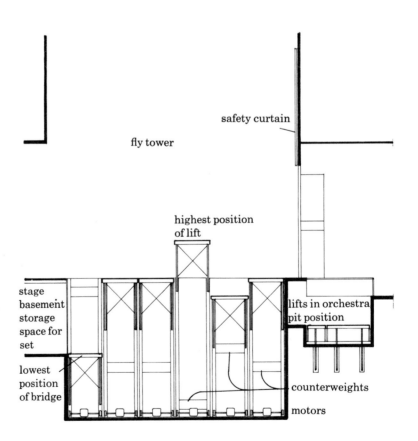

No. 9:20   *Section* AA.

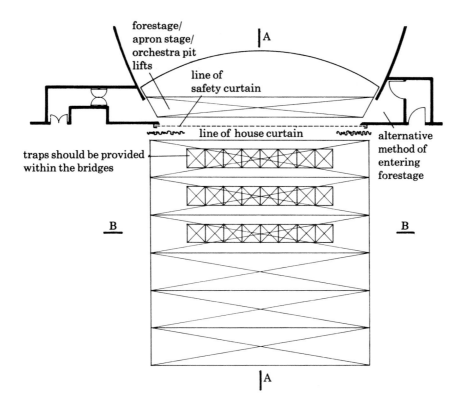

forestage/
apron stage/
orchestra pit
lifts

line of
safety curtain

traps should be provided
within the bridges

line of house curtain

alternative
method of
entering
forestage

B   B

A

Plan of stage with a system of bridges.

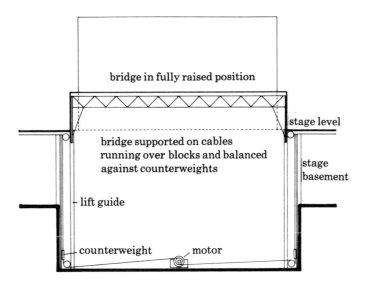

bridge in fully raised position

stage level

bridge supported on cables
running over blocks and balanced
against counterweights

stage
basement

lift guide

counterweight   motor

No. 9:20   *Section* BB.

Electrically operated screw jacks are more compact but very slow and have certain mechanical weaknesses. Hydraulic rams are slow but have the advantage of being very quiet and smooth in operation. Although they normally have guides at the end there are no ropes or blocks to get in the way. A compressor plant would have to be built at some expense unless there is a hydraulic main within reach.

Revolving stage

Three or four complete sets can be built on the revolve and scene changes can be effected smoothly without it being necessary to drop the curtain.

The revolve can be put to theatrical use for special moving effects, but it should be remembered that the novelty of this will wear off very quickly. The revolve cannot project beyond the house curtain unless a complicated and expensive curved safety curtain is used.

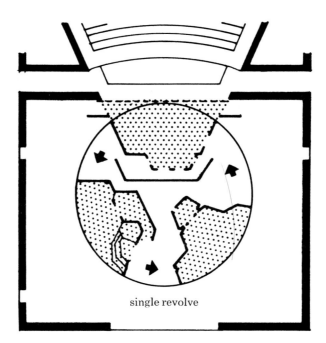

single revolve

No. 9:21

Twin revolves

Sets are built in two halves each half on a separate revolve. The junction between the two parts of the set needs very careful alignment and sets are limited to the same depth. It is unlikely and not recommended that this system be used for a permanent installation. It is quite usual for portable revolves to be made for a particular production.

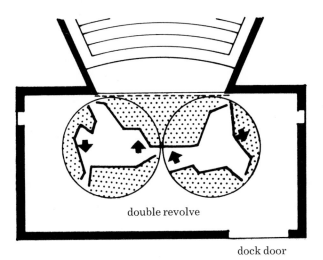

No. 9:22

double revolve

dock door

Wagon stages   Complete sets are built on shallow platforms which can be rolled into position. A full wagon system demands a great deal of space. Each wagon must be larger than the proscenium opening and deeper than the acting area required so that there is room for the supporting structure of the set which is built upon it and there must be sufficient space left round it for circulation. Permanent wagons flush with the stage floor demand an elaborate tramway system and leave part of the rest of the stage at a lower level. A more flexible arrangement is to build wagons which roll on the stage floor. The problem of the step up has to be solved for each production. One

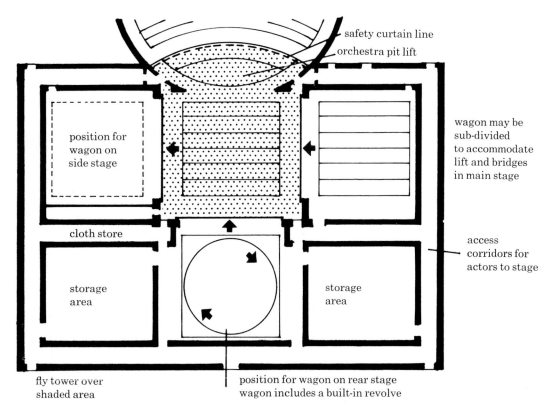

safety curtain line

orchestra pit lift

position for wagon on side stage

wagon may be sub-divided to accommodate lift and bridges in main stage

cloth store

access corridors for actors to stage

storage area

storage area

fly tower over shaded area

position for wagon on rear stage wagon includes a built-in revolve

No. 9:23   *The T-shaped stage with one wagon at the back is the standard layout of many German theatres. Another variation is split wagons in which each set is divided into two, one half being carried on each wagon.*

solution is to have a lift the same size as the wagon. When the wagon is correctly aligned the lift is lowered until the top of the wagon is flush with the rest of the stage floor. There must be provision for dismantling and storing the wagons when not in use.

There are many possible arrangements of wagon stages some of which are illustrated in the following diagrams.

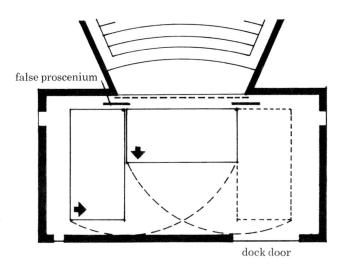

No. 9:24   This drawing shows two wagons, one on each side of the proscenium called 'jackknife' wagons, which can be pivoted into position alternately. This would not be a permanent installation.

No. 9:25   A portable revolve specially built for a production.

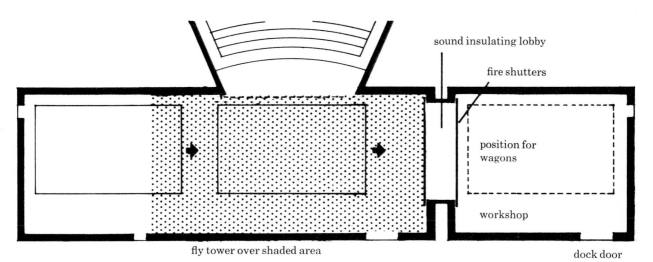

sound insulating lobby

fire shutters

position for wagons

workshop

fly tower over shaded area

dock door

No. 9:26   *This diagram shows the workshop used to house one of the wagons. Changes are slowed up by the opening and closing of the shutter between the workshop and the stage: this has to be fire-resisting, soundproof and noiseless.*

An ingenious form of combined lift and revolve shown in the diagram has been built in the USA at Birmingham Southern College, Alabama. The revolve is split along its diameter with a setting on each half. One change can be made by revolving at stage level and presenting the other half of the revolve to the audience. The rear half can now descend to the basement where it makes up the rear half of another revolve at basement level. This too can turn to bring another setting into position ready for raising to stage level. When this semi-circle has ascended to stage level and has been joined to the half revolve already there it can be pivoted into position facing the audience and the cycle can be continued.

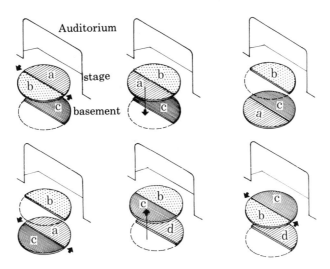

No. 9:27

10   Stage scenery

It is necessary to make a distinction between two types of performance. In the case of concerts and recitals the performance is purely aural and no visual make-believe is involved. For plays, opera and ballet, on the other hand, the audience are expected, according to convention, to suspend their disbelief of what they are told or what they see: however naturalistic the setting, everyone knows that it is all a pretence, and the spectator enters into the spirit of the deception.

It is often said that an illusion is created in the theatre, but this is true only in the sense that it is willingly connived at by each member of the audience. Each one knows that he is sitting in a theatre seat and, if he is a reasonable being, no amount of naturalism and verisimilitude can overcome his fundamental objectivity or remove the necessity for his conscious acceptance of the theatrical conventions.

The unwritten rules are very flexible, and there is nothing immutable about the conventions which are acceptable at any point in time. At the ballet we accept that a dancer is a princess bewitched and changed into a swan, while at the theatre we can accept that we are eavesdropping and peeping-in on a scene lifted out of everyday life. In both cases the setting is equally unreal.

The theatre is a place of fantasy which relies on the imaginative co-operation of the audience. For it to live and flourish, it cannot be tied down by a too-literally defined set of conventions.

Functions of stage scenery

The stage setting assists visual expression of the dramatic performance by providing a geography for the actor within the stage space, assisting the action and contributing to the atmosphere of the play and clarifying the time and place of the action. It also serves to screen other visual distractions from the audience.

The stage setting is made up of scenery, properties and costume. There are three kinds of properties; hand properties, i.e. things worn or handled by the actors, e.g. a sword or a fan; purely decorative properties which may be virtually part of the scenery, e.g. a vase of flowers or a picture on a wall; and large pieces, such as tables, chairs, bedsteads or other items used in the action which are known as 'stage properties' or 'props'. Often the dividing line between properties and scenery is hard to define. The stage setting is more than mere decoration or illustration; it is an integral part of a production. It should both present a visual stimulus to the imagination and emphasize the mood of the play.

History   In the classical Greek, Roman, early Spanish and Elizabethan public theatres the audience surrounded the greater part of the stage; there was usually a permanent architectural background to the stage and a permanent arrangement of different acting levels. In such theatres the plays themselves indicated the time and place of the action and little or no scenery was needed. Assistance of the action and the geography for the actor were provided by 'practical pieces'. It was in Renaissance Italy, where artists and architects were preoccupied with the newly discovered laws of perspective that elaborate scenery began to be developed. The theatres used were mainly court theatres which catered for much smaller audiences. The solid construction of permanent architectural settings gave way to flimsy timber frames covered with canvas. The greatest flights of baroque architectural imagination were not realized in masonry, but on painted cloth in the theatre. Such scenery was often more lavish and important than the play itself. It became the convention in the eighteenth and nineteenth century and still lingers on in traditional pantomime. Pollock's toy theatres, first produced in the Victorian era and still on sale today, illustrate the system very well.

Running parallel to the proscenium were wings which could be slid in and out to form the sides of a setting, and above were suspended borders to complete the top of the frame. The back of the scenic picture was filled in with a painted cloth. A scene change was made by sliding out one set of wings and sliding in another, raising and lowering the appropriate borders and dropping in a new back cloth. The classical Greek theatre used stage machinery, such as derricks for the *deus ex machina* and scenic effects have been used at all periods of history since. Elaborate feats of engineering were required for changes and effects of baroque and later scenery of the same kind.

It was in the latter part of the nineteenth century that, in order to meet the needs of the domestic scenes of the realistic drama, it became common to close in the sides of the acting area by turning the flats forming the wings to an angle of about 60°. The three-sided box set with its seemingly right-angled walls, was thus created, a form with which we are familiar today mainly for interior scenes. To simplify construction of scenery at an angle to the proscenium and

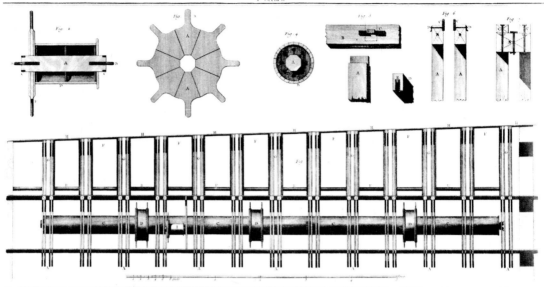

Machines de Théatres, *coupe des deux Planchers du dessous avec la pente du Theatre, et Construction des assemblages developpés garnies de leurs ferrures*

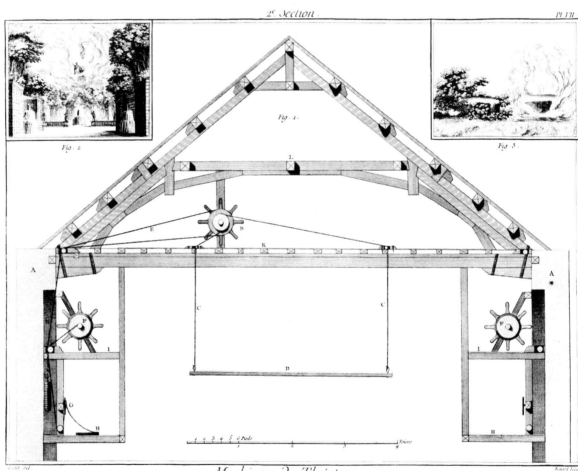

2.ᵉ *Section*.

Pl. VII.

Machines de Théatres,

Elévation en coupe avec le service des Treuils pour la descente d'une Machine d'aplomb, et idées ou esquisses de Décorations d'un Jardin avec une gloire de feu et banc de gazon de feu

No. 10:1   Illustrations of stage machinery taken from D'Alembert & Diderot's
           Encyclopédie ou Dictionaire Raisonné des Science, des Arts et Métiers
           (1751–1756).

to accommodate heavier furnishings, it was now better for the stage floor to be made flat, although many raked stages remained and some are still in use.

The beginning of the twentieth century brought new philosophical, historical and aesthetic considerations into theatrical thought. In a reaction against the excesses of archaeological realism in Shakespeare productions of the time, Poel introduced the adaptable curtain set, still much in use as a cheap way to furnish a stage but visually limited. One technological advance had a very powerful influence on scenic design and that was the use of lighting by electricity. The first to realize the revolutionary effect that precise control of lighting would make were Adolph Appia and Gordon Craig. The sculptured shape of the actors and their setting could be emphasized. The stage floor as an element in the design became more important. Scenery became more solid to cast real shadows instead of having shadows painted on a flat surface. Large set pieces made scene changes difficult, but many apparent changes could easily be effected by lighting; this opened new possibilities for the 'permanent' set.

All the various 'isms' of art have been reflected in scenic design, sometimes profoundly, often superficially. In this century Cubism, Expressionism, Surrealism, Constructivism have all had their effect. Many purists reject the use of scenery altogether because it is associated with the proscenium arch and 'bourgeois theatre', but in the open and thrust stages in use today there is very little sign of a diminution in the volume of scenery used.

At the present time, the wing set, the box set, the curtain set, the permanent set and the open set, and their various intermediate forms, can all be found in our theatres as policy or whim of management, designer or director may demand.

Considerations affecting stage setting

Whether a production is to be spectacular or intimate, the stage settings must be appropriate, not only to the play or opera itself, but also to the limitations of the particular stage on which they will appear.

Consideration must be given to:

(a)   requirements of the licensing authority;
(b)   size and form of the stage/auditorium;
(c)   what stage machinery, if any, is available;
(d)   the possibilities for stage lighting.

Requirements of licensing authorities

Where public performances are given, one of the principal factors which determine the quantity and nature of the scenery to be used in a production is the requirements of the licensing authority. They will not usually permit the unrestricted use of stage scenery unless the premises are equipped with a safety curtain and other fireprotection apparatus such as an automatic smoke vent and sprinklers over the stage. In premises without these safeguards restrictions are normally placed on either the quantity of scenery to be kept and used on the premises, or the materials from which the scenery may be constructed, or sometimes both. Even in premises equipped with a safety curtain, etc, there is usually a licensing condition requiring the scenery materials to be rendered and maintained non-flammable.

The licensing authorities arrange for the periodic inspection and on-site testing of scenery, drapes, etc, to ensure that their conditions are properly complied with, and it is probably thanks to this practice as much as to the increasing fire-consciousness of theatre technicians that in Great Britain in the last fifty years there has been no fire during a performance in a theatre on the scale of the theatre tragedies of the last century. In London, in premises without a safety curtain, the main house curtain is normally required to be of inherently non-flammable material, that is, material not requiring treatment to render it non-flammable.

Most licensing authorities will, of course, permit the use of scenery and stage drapes made from incombustible or inherently non-flammable materials in premises without a safety curtain, and those forms of stage where there is no proscenium or other separation between acting area and audiences.

At the time of writing (1971), a new act dealing with fire and safety in buildings has passed through the British Parliament. New national regulations will be brought in but these are at present still being drafted and it is not clear what form they will take. The principles will doubtless remain the same and it is to be hoped that some account will be taken of the unorthodox methods of staging which have become more popular since the Home Office *Manual of Safety Requirements in theatres and other places of public entertainment* was published in 1934. Regulations by definition are framed to regulate the situation as it exists at the time. They can only deal with the *status quo* and can not be expected to anticipate what will happen in the future. It is, therefore, important that they should not be so rigid that they prevent innovations and frustrate new means of artistic expression. The regulations are drawn up to protect persons and secondly property, not for the convenience of the administration whose job it is to enforce them.

Size and form of stage

All kinds of difficulties are likely to arise from trying to reproduce or imitate a stage setting designed for a stage quite different from that on which the play is to be presented.

A setting originally designed for, and artistically satisfying when used on, a large stage will almost certainly be out of scale and ineffective if reproduced in a cut-down form on a small stage. All stage settings should credibly suggest an environment that is appropriate in a theatrical sense.

'Suggest' is the keyword – realism is not essential. The form of actor-audience relation is a fundamental factor controlling the design of scenery. 'Adaptable' theatres in which the physical form of the stage can be altered at will to suit the producer's concept of a play, add to the problems of both designer and builder of the scenery.

In most theatres the form of stage is fixed and can be modified only within very narrow limits, so that the settings have to be tailored to the stage.

Obviously, where the whole or a substantial part of the acting area is behind a proscenium opening scenery can be in the form of painted flats and/or cloths which provide a background and sur-roundings for the action. This type of scenery can also be used in a much more limited way, on an open stage which has at least one side against a wall, although it becomes more difficult to merge the scenic setting into the décor of the auditorium. But flats and cloths cannot be used on the projecting portion of a thrust stage, nor upon an in-the-round stage, across which spectators need to have a virtually unobstructed view. In such open-stage settings any scenery must be kept low or 'transparent'.

Stage machinery

Another factor that will affect the scenery is the amount of stage machinery available. It may be either part of the permanent equip-ment or installed for the particular production. It can have two functions:

(a)   suspending and changing scenery;
(b)   creating illusions and special effects.

Most professional theatres with picture-frame stages have pro-vision for flying scenery, etc, either with or without a counterweight system and/or motorized handling equipment, but there is scope for certain items of flown scenery even on a completely open stage.

Other stage machinery may include revolves, trucks and lifts and mechanical devices for special effects, such as vertical rollers for traversing a long back-cloth to give the illusion of linear movement (e.g. along a street) or rockers to simulate the motion of a boat.

Stage lighting

The appearance of scenery on a stage depends very largely upon lighting, and it is hardly possible to design a set now without considering how it is to be lit. Optical projection is often an essen-tial part of a setting and can be the sole scenic device.

General requirements for scenery

Apart from any licensing requirements about non-flammability, etc, there are six practical requirements which stage scenery must fulfil:

1   It must be economical and materials must be carefully chosen to keep down costs and avoid waste.

2   It must be of the simplest and most efficient construction consistent with its purpose.

3   It must be strong enough to stand handling in the course of scene changes and in transport from one theatre to another.

4   It must be easy to store in the minimum space.

5   It must be suitable for quick and quiet scene changing by the minimum number of stage hands.

6   It must be easily assembled on stage when changes of setting are necessary during a performance.

Forms of scenery   Although there are almost unlimited possibilities of modification to suit the needs of a particular production and the inspiration of the designer, the arrangements and devices described below are commonly used in both professional and amateur productions.

House curtains   These are used to close off from the view of the audience the whole of the acting area except for any forestage or apron designed to project beyond them. They are placed immediately behind the proscenium if there is one. They may be either draw curtains, suspended from sliding or rolling carriers running in an overhead track and opened by being drawn off to the sides; or drop curtains, hung on a set of lines and closed by lowering vertically, or festoon curtains, fixed at the top and raised by drawing the meeting edges up to the top corners of the proscenium arch so that the fabric is gathered upwards and to the side; or they may be combinations or variations of these basic arrangements. All these types are weighted at the bottom with lengths of chain inserted in the hem. These curtains are also known as 'house tabs'.

Cyclorama   One of the main types of settings used in the theatre depends upon the use of a cyclorama.

This is basically a large plain surface used as a background to a setting. By varying the intensity and colour of light upon it many different effects can be obtained. If there is no mark on the surface on which the eye can focus, illusion of great depth can be created. Ideally the cyclorama should be self-masking, extending out of sight behind the proscenium. It should close round the sides of the acting area and eliminate the necessity for wings or legs to mask the sides. It should also stretch as high as possible to reduce the need for masking by borders hung above the stage. A permanent plaster cyclorama can be built into the back wall of the stage, but although very effective it takes up a great deal of room and limits the use of the rear stage area. An alternative is to have the back wall of the stage plastered and painted white. Although this might be a good idea in some circumstances it is very difficult to prevent the back wall from becoming damaged. There are many occasions when scenery and props will be stacked against it.

The more usual arrangement is a stretched fabric cyclorama which is erected for a particular performance. In its most usual form it is a large cloth attached at top and bottom to bars with curved or angled ends and stretched taut. To function properly the cyclorama must be very high (see diagram *9:10*). This usually means that it cannot be flown out of sight. A variation of the fabric cyclorama is the type that is rolled on and off a cone at the side of the stage and is suspended on a track round the acting area. This type allows much more scope for changing scenery than the fixed variety. It is more likely to be used in a large theatre or opera house where it will be big enough and far enough away from the audience for the inevitable wrinkles not to spoil the cyclorama effect of infinite depth. On a smaller stage the effect would be lost and it would be more accurately described as a curtain surround.

The usual colour of a cyclorama is off-white towards blue which is commonly used for sky effects and projection, but other colours and textures can be used for special purposes. Black velvet or velour can be used for dark nights or other special effects implying vast distances.

Permanent masking

This is placed just behind the proscenium arch to mask the offstage edges of pieces of scenery set further away from the audience, and comprises the tormentors and teaser, or false proscenium, or show portal. Frequently, other permanent maskings are placed at intervals between a false proscenium and a cyclorama; these are known as portals and together they provide a permanent masking so that offstage areas cannot be seen from any seat in the auditorium.

Other cloths, flown pieces and built sets can be set between the permanent maskings, and this is the frequent practice in revues and musicals.

Backcloth-and-wing sets

A backcloth or backdrop, is a large sheet of canvas, usually somewhat larger than the proscenium opening, battened at top and bottom and suspended on the upstage side of the acting area to form a general background to the setting; it is frequently painted to represent the sky or a distant view. It is made so as to be rolled up for storage, and, if large, a special roller is provided. Cut-cloths are cloths with voids cut in them to reveal another cloth set behind; frequently more than one is used, as in a woodland scene. In the sense used here, wings are painted and usually profiled flats of

No. 10:2   *Two sets at the Royal Opera House, Covent Garden, on this and the following pages, showing quite different approaches to set design on the same stage. Above: a good example of the traditional scene painters art, the set for Act 1 of the Zefferelli production of 'Tosca' in 1964, designed by Renzo Mongiardino.*

canvas on battens, which are set to stand out from the sides of the acting area approximately parallel to the proscenium, to add atmosphere to the setting, to cut off the spectators' view of the ends of the backcloth and to mask the offstage spaces at the sides of the acting area, the wings. They are normally used in pairs, one to 'stage right' and the other to 'stage left', and the offstage edges of each pair are masked by the pair in front or by the tormentors just behind the proscenium opening. Borders are similar to backcloths, but very much shorter from top to bottom, and are used above the acting area to mask the scenery suspension lines, lighting battens, etc. They may be painted to represent sky, overhead foliage, etc. The border furthest upstage masks the top edge of the backcloth, and the top edge of each border is masked by the one in front; the top edge of the foremost border is masked by the teaser just behind the proscenium arch.

Box sets   A box set is comprised of a series of canvas flats arranged in a more or less continuous line around three sides of the acting area; it is

No. 10:3   *The view from the wings shows how the illusion of solidity has been obtained.*

normally used for interior settings. Specially constructed flats incorporating doors, or windows or dummy fireplaces or other features, are inserted where required, and the view beyond 'practical' openings is masked by backings which may be single flats, a series of flats, drops or borders.

The top of a box set may be closed in by suitably painted borders, as used in backcloth-and-wing sets; or by a ceiling piece, which is a large horizontal canvas-covered frame hung on two sets of lines with the downstage edge higher than the upstage edge; or by a series of teasers, small ceiling pieces comprising rigid borders with horizontal extensions at the bottom. The last two methods leave gaps between adjacent units through which light may be projected. Recently, however, it has become the practice in some productions to leave the top of the set open and let the light source be seen.

Other scenery units   Other units, which can be used with any of the settings described above, include rostra, steps, groundrows, rocks and built-up ground, columns and trees (see glossary).

Curtains   In addition to the house curtains already described, fabric curtains may be used as part of stage settings. Curtains used to dress window openings, etc, in the scenery are included under the heading of stage properties.

Traverse curtains – known as 'tabs', are usually placed upstage of the false proscenium or tormentors and suspended on a tab-track which is normally manually operated; their purpose is to provide a backing for front scenes. They may be made from canvas, hessian,

No. 10:4   *The set for Michael Tippett's opera 'The Knot Garden' at the Royal*
Opera House, Covent Garden, designed by Timothy O'Brien, lighting
by John Bury, produced by Peter Hall and first presented in 1971.
Scenery was projected on to a surround of stretched cords. The two
concentric revolves had a series of vertical tubes set on them. Compare
with illustrations on pages 100 and 101.

gauze or other scenic material, or from plain-coloured fabrics such
as velours; they are frequently used in revues and similar presentations where front scenes alternate with full-stage scenes; they may
also be used in a half-way position when they are known as 'half-
way tabs'.

**Setting and changing
scenery**

Backcloth-and-wing sets of almost any form can be suspended from
above and, where height and equipment are provided for flying
scenery, the scene can be changed by pulling one setting up out of
sight and letting another down in its place. Even where provision is
not made for flying, this type of setting is convenient to erect and
strike and therefore can be changed easily. Where the wings cannot
be suspended from above, they can stand on the stage floor and be
held upright by braces; cloths can be rolled or tripped when not in
use.

No. 10:5   The 'Knot Garden' set from the wings.

With the backcloth-and-wing settings, however, the representation of any particular place involves considerable stylisation, especially interior scenes. An appearance of solidity at the sides can be obtained by substituting book flats for the ordinary wing pieces, but these are much heavier and more difficult to handle. For transformation scenes, common in pantomime and classical ballet, the change of setting can be made in sight of the audience by using gauzes which, when suitably lit, enable one setting to become visible through another. Striking effects can be achieved in this way.

Box sets, normally used for naturalistic interior settings, cannot be changed so easily. They have to be stylised to reconcile the size of the proscenium with the relatively small dimensions of a domestic interior. On a large stage, walls and windows have to be distorted in shape and size even when the intention is to convey an impression of realism. Box sets are normally built up flat by flat on the stage floor, which effectively limits major scene changes to the intervals of the performance unless they are made behind a cloth or curtain drawn downstage during the playing of a front scene. Neither of these types of setting is suited to fast-moving productions in which the scene changes rapidly. For productions of this kind, and particularly for Shakespeare, solid built-up settings are more often employed, which, with the addition of easily changed properties, can be made to represent any one of a number of different localities. In some cases, settings may consist of several large pieces which can be moved about and turned round to represent different objects; in other cases, the setting is permanent and may even be used for several different productions in the company's repertoire. In opera, there is an established tradition of massive sets, with the playing area on several levels.

Large rostra, ramps and steps are even more difficult to change than the pieces forming a box set, and this has led to the use of large revolves and lifts, where these exist or can be installed, and also to systems of wagons.

Materials for scenery

The general requirements for scenery materials may be summarised as follows. They must be relatively inexpensive, readily available, light in weight, easy to work with and durable. For flats and similar pieces, framing materials must have sufficient rigidity and should be easily jointed. Covering materials must be capable of being made taut on the frames and must have a surface that will take scenic paint. All scenery materials should be flame-resistant. In this respect, materials may be grouped under five headings.

1   **Non-combustible:** In normal circumstances these cannot be made to burn, examples: glass and asbestos.

2   **Inherently non-flammable:** These will burn away in a fire, but are difficult to ignite and do not continue burning unless kept in a flame, example: heavy woollen fabric.

3   **Self-extinguishing:** These take flame from a small source of ignition, but quickly cease burning when the source of ignition is removed or when the material immediately around that source has been consumed. Some plastics are of this type.

4   **Treated:** These take flame from a small source of ignition and would continue burning, but for the fact that they have been subjected to treatment to make them flame-resistant.

5   **Flammable:** These have not been and perhaps cannot be rendered

flame-resistant by treatment; they can be easily ignited by, and will continue burning after, contact with a small flame.

Most of the painted scenery used in the theatre, whether framed or unframed, is made from stout canvas, but other materials may be used. The canvas is commonly made from flax but, for cheapness, hessian is sometimes used.

Frames for scenery are almost universally made from timber which is soft enough for easy working, light enough for easy handling, yet strong enough to stand the stresses and strains to which scenery is subjected in use. The timber must be straight-grained, free from serious faults and well seasoned so as not to warp. Where an irregular profile is required, stout plywood is normally used. All these materials are of course combustible, and they are indeed flammable in their natural state and need treatment to render them flame-resistant. It is possible, of course, to construct scenery from non-combustible and/or inherently non-flammable materials, such as asbestos sheeting on light metal framing, but such scenery does not accord with the general requirements set out above and is resorted to only as an expedient to comply with the requirements of licensing authorities in certain premises where the more usual types of scenery cannot be permitted.

In recent years there has been an increasing use of plastics in the construction of scenery. All these are combustible and some are flammable. Only the flame-resistant or self-extinguishing grades of plastics should be used for scenery. Examples of these materials which have been used successfully include lightweight expanded polystyrene, unplasticised polyvinyl chloride, special cellulose acetate and polyester resin/glassfibre laminates.

Curtains and other draperies on a fully equipped stage may be of almost any fabric, treated, if necessary, to render it flame-resistant, but where a stage is not equipped with the usual safeguards the local licensing authority may insist that any curtains be of either non-combustible or inherently non-flammable materials. Until recently, these latter materials were limited to fabrics of natural mineral fibres, such as asbestos or glass cloth, or to fabrics of natural animal fibres, such as heavy woollen cloth. Advances, however, are being made with inherently non-flammable and self-extinguishing synthetic fibres, which should increase the range of fabrics available. All fabrics of vegetable fibres, e.g. cotton, flax, jute, etc, and many of the synthetic materials are flammable in their natural state, but most of them are responsive to treatment to remove the danger.

Mention should perhaps be made of the fabric known as 'silk noile' which has been used successfully for both curtains and painted scenery in premises where the licensing authority would not permit the use of treated materials. Among the synthetics, the guaranteed 'flare-free' nylon net should be borne in mind.

Experience and fire records indicate that the principal fire hazard in a properly constructed theatre is that associated with the use of traditional canvas scenery, especially when used in conjunction with a naked flame on the stage or unguarded or insufficiently guarded high-powered lighting units. Hence the requirement that canvas scenery should be treated to render it flame-resistant,* but it is accepted that the treatment does little more than render the scenery more difficult to ignite than if it were not treated. Nothing can make timber and flax canvas non-combustible, and such treated scenery will, in fact, burn if involved in a fire. There are various well-recognised methods of treating timber and fabrics to render them flame-resistant and, except in very exceptional circumstances, it is strongly advised that even where there is no licensing requirement to compel it, all scenery and hangings used on a stage should be so treated.

Timber, including plywood and hardboard, can best be rendered flame-resistant by thorough impregnation with a flame-retardant salt by an approved process, such as Oxylene or Pyrolith. A measure of protection can also be obtained by coating it with a flame-

---

*   Both the following solutions have been found suitable for scenery and for the coarser fabrics, and solution 2 has been found suitable for the more delicate fabrics.

Solution 1	Boracic acid	15 oz	450 grams
	Sodium phosphate	10 oz	300 grams
	water	1 gal	5 litre
Solution 2	Borax	10 oz	300 grams
	Boracic acid	8 oz	240 grams
	water	1 gal	5 litre

It is advisable to experiment with a small portion of the fabric before treating the whole, as the texture and colours of some materials are detrimentally affected. The fabrics should be dried without rinsing or wringing but may be mangled or ironed when dry.

A simple test for flame-resistance may be made thus:

A strip of the fabric, 25 mm wide and not less than 150 mm long, should be hung vertically in a draught-free position. A lighted match should then be applied for five seconds at the centre of the bottom edge. If less than 25 mm square in area has been consumed by the flame at the end of one minute, the material may be regarded as satisfactorily flame resistant. If the fabric has been claimed to be inherently non-flammable, it should be well washed in plain hot water and thoroughly dried before being tested. Where appropriate it is advisable to confer with the local licensing authority regarding methods of treatment and tests, as requirements may vary from place to place.

retardant paint, but this method is not acceptable to all licensing authorities. Generally speaking, the authorities do not require any particular method to be adopted to render scenery and curtain fabrics non-flammable so long as the fabrics have, in fact, been rendered satisfactorily flame-resistant. It must be remembered that most of the flame-retardant treatments are water-borne and consequently can be removed by any form of wet cleaning but some will stand a limited amount of dry-cleaning. It follows, therefore, that treated materials which have been washed or cleaned must be re-treated before they are used again.

During recent years, however, flame-resistant finishes have been developed which are durable and not affected by washing or cleaning. Among these are the Proban and Timonox processes.

Construction of scenery and painting

Flats and similar pieces are timber frames covered with tightly stretched canvas. Each frame is constructed from lengths of selected 74 mm × 25 mm prepared timber such as yellow deal. Sometimes 100 mm × 25 mm timber is used. The vertical members are called stiles and the horizontal members rails as in ordinary joinery. The frame must be perfectly square and rigid.

For jointing the members various methods may be used. These fall into two categories: fixed and temporary. Fixed joints are made at corners, traditionally by mortise-and-tenon, and dowelled or glued and screwed. Contrary to normal joinery practice, the mortise is cut in the rail and the tenon on the stile. This gives a very strong connection, but the time taken and expense incurred in making the joints often dictates the use of simpler and quicker methods such as glued and screwed half-lap joints and butt joints, both square and mitred. These latter joints are usually strengthened by adding corner plates of either thin plywood or hardboard, or even thin sheet metal; the reinforcing plates are fixed to the rear surface of the flats only and are kept clear of the outer edges of the frame. If necessary, the glue can be omitted. Connections can also be made with special metal fittings requiring only screws for fixing, or, to a more limited degree, with coachbolts. The rigidity of a frame is sometimes increased by fixing a bracing member at 45° across each corner. The in-between rails, known as toggle rails, are preferably fitted into the frames by temporary joints, each end being tenoned into a short piece of similar timber to form a T which can be attached to the inside edge of the stile with woodscrews; these members can be positioned as necessary to suit the attachment of other pieces of scenery.

The outer edges of stiles must be straight and true so as to avoid any possibility of gaps when flats are fitted together. The canvas, which should be on one side of the frame only, is cut slightly smaller than the overall frame size and is stretched across the frame by tacking with large-headed tacks to the wide surface of the outer frame members and then glued, but not to toggle rails or corner braces. The canvas must not be carried round the outer edges of the frame as the fabric would wear and the tautness of the fabric would be lost; furthermore the fabric would prevent the flats from fitting closely together.

Canvasing is a job which requires care and skill; a well-canvased flat has a smooth even surface without sagging or wrinkles. Unless the canvas is stretched tightly and evenly on the frame it will never give the illusion of solidity, however well it may be painted.

Other framed units are constructed in a similar manner. Door flats, window flats and fireplace flats have appropriate openings into which the door frames, window frames and fireplace surrounds can be fitted. These will not be the heavy sort of thing used in normal building construction. For realism, and to increase the illusion of solidity of the scenery, door and window openings are frequently formed with reveals of timber or other materials attached to the edges of the openings in the flats. Practical doors are made as light as possible consistent with realism; sometimes they have to be double-faced, constructed with plywood instead of canvas to retain solidity. Windows and 'glazed' doors are normally without glass to save weight and to avoid dazzle from reflected stage lighting. Real glass is never used, but where an infilling is necessary gauze or plastic material may be employed. After canvasing, the canvas is primed with a mixture of glue size and whiting. This gives the final tightening to the canvas as well as preparing the surface for scenic painting.

Cloths, borders, etc, are formed with similar canvas, the lengths being stitched together with flat seams where necessary; they do not have frames, but stout timber battens are fixed along their top and bottom edges. They are similarly prepared for painting.

Scene paint is prepared by mixing dry powder colour into a thick paste with cold water and then mixing in a hot solution of glue size until the required consistency for working is achieved. Whiting is often added to give body to the colour. All scenic paint dries much lighter than it appears when wet, and to check that the required tint has been achieved, a small piece of scrap canvas or other material is coated with the mixed paint and quickly dried near a radiator. When the paint/size mixture has cooled it can be applied to the canvas. If it is not allowed to cool down, previously applied colour will lift under the hot mixture. On no account should dry powder colour mixtures be used without adding size; the colour would either flake off or rub off on to costumes brushing against it, resulting in ruin of both sets and costumes.

As an alternative to the traditional scene paint, plastic (pva) emulsion paint may be used for scenic painting, but the two cannot be mixed or used together on the same piece of scenery. No glue size is needed; the paint is thinned, if necessary with cold water. A wide range of tints is now obtainable in this type of paint.

Should the canvas sag with use, a coat of glue size on the back will help to restore its tautness.

Storage of scenery   Scenic flats need to be stored in pairs, face to face, resting on the bottom rail to prevent warping. Their size depends upon the scale of the stage, but average dimensions would be 1·2 m × 5 m. Flats are best stored in packs – the number of flats required for one setting – and racks should be provided for each pack. These racks should be situated in the scenery store adjacent to the stage or workshop or both. It is desirable that the temperature of the store be approximately that of the stage itself. Backcloths and gauzes require long racks as they are usually stored rolled on their respective battens. One useful position for storing them is in a long trough at the rear of the stage which can also be used as a pit for lighting a cyclorama. Drapes require dustproof cupboards with plenty of slatted shelves to keep them aired.

Set pieces, such as trucks, rostra, etc, need plenty of room for manoeuvring. These pieces are often three-dimensional and are frequently tall, bulky and heavy and are, therefore, not easy to transport.

Construction and repair of scenery requires plenty of space within easy reach of the stage, good working conditions with supplies of gas, water and electricity, and the right conditions for storing timber. All storage should be easily accessible from backstage without going through the auditorium.

At the same time, the storage and working space should be separated from the stage by soundproof and fire-resisting construction.

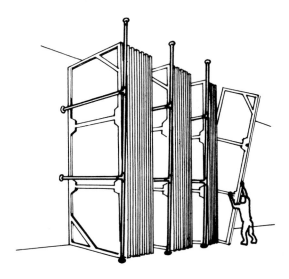

Method of storing flats.

11   Stage lighting

The first function of stage lighting is illumination of the actor and his setting. The earliest theatres were in the open air where the source was the sun itself. Dramatists exploited the situation and Euripides, for instance, made references to the sunrise in 'Iphigenia in Aulis', which coincided with the time of day when the play was actually performed.

But when the theatre came inside under cover, there had to be artificial light. People made do very well with oil lamps and candles until the nineteenth century when they changed briefly to gas lighting before electricity took over. Each change made possible a greater measure of control until at the present time stage lighting is capable of achieving much more than mere illumination of the action. It is used as a means of artistic expression and has become a vital component in the drama. As the action unfolds it can draw attention from one character to another or from one area to another and by changing the direction, intensity or colour of the light, a great variety of atmosphere and moods can be conveyed. This versatility is demanded in all sizes of theatre with all forms of actor-to-audience relationship. The pattern of lighting seldom remains static for long; it changes from production to production, scene to scene and often many times during a scene.

The lighting process   Before describing the technical provisions that should be made for an effective stage-lighting installation, it will help to have an understanding of the process of setting up the lighting for a production. The director of a play or opera or the choreographer of a ballet is concerned with the total effect, aural and visual, of the production and this includes the lighting. In recent years the great advances and consequent technical complications in multi-lantern stage lighting have made it very difficult for a director to devote to lighting the time it demands without taking that time from his main task – directing the performers. The work is now usually in the hands of an additional member of the production team: the lighting designer. His contribution is a creative one, but he is part of a team and the measure of his success is in the integration of his lighting with the total conception of a production.

The lighting designer should attend early conferences with the director and scene designer so that he is aware of the visual style decisions which are taken and he should see that the model or drawings of the set have made allowance for large enough openings through which lighting units can operate without obstruction before they are sent to the workshops for construction to start. The first opportunity the lighting designer will have to try out his scheme will be with the scenery in position on stage. All the other departments will have time to rehearse, improvise and alter before the production reaches the stage, but the lighting can only be set up at the end of the preparation period. Time is limited and the operation must be carefully planned to avoid, as far as possible, the delays which can be caused by having to rig lanterns more than once. The lighting designer will have prepared a layout plan of the stage showing the position of each lantern, its type, its colour filter and the dimmer circuit to which it is to be connected. Using this layout the lanterns are rigged in position, plugged into the right circuit and each one is angled and focused on to the area of the stage chosen for it. This process of 'setting' the lanterns is best done one by one with all the other lights out, a difficult ideal to achieve when all the other departments are pressing to complete their work. At this time the filaments of the lamps are hot and at their most vulnerable as they are moved. When they fail, they more often than not take the fuse in the dimmer room with them. An emergency like this shows how important it is for the lighting positions and the dimmer room to be easily accessible.

With all the lanterns set, the lighting designer will sit in the auditorium with the director and the scene designer and build up each picture by calling out on the intercom the circuit numbers to the operator of the stage-lighting control desk and deciding the intensity of the light on each one. Each picture must flow into the next with the right timing. The lighting plot is recorded so that it can be reproduced on cue at the right moment in the script. This recording usually has to be done in longhand and can be tedious especially when it is decided that alterations have to be made. The process has been greatly simplified by introducing computer memory devices which allow a particular selection of circuits at particular intensities to be instantly recorded and instantly recalled when desired.

The procedure just described is followed for a new production which is destined for a run after which it will be dismantled. The situation is different when the production is to slot into a repertoire of productions which may be changing every day. The time available both for rehearsal and for readjusting lighting between performances is even further curtailed and compromises have to be made.

It is possible to have an entirely different set of lanterns for another production, but for several shows this would become extravagant and there may not be room to hang so many units. Certain basic lanterns may have to remain in position for all the productions and alterations and redirection of the rest reduced to bare essentials. Where the policy is to play in repertoire accessibility of the lighting equipment is vital and sophisticated control systems show their value.

Light sources

All stage-lighting schemes, whatever the theatre, must begin on a basis of general illumination. In this role, lighting must be seen as the source of the sight line. The actor and his environment are illuminated and the light reflected from them to the eyes of the audience. However good the position of the audience in relation to the stage, the contact is lost if the actor is not properly illuminated.

Illumination of the acting area (as distinct from backcloths, etc) is rarely achieved by using sources throwing a wide angle beam of light.

The task is to build up a pattern of illumination from a number of localised lighting units each fed from its own electrical circuit. The pattern can then be altered by increasing or reducing the intensity of light from the appropriate units, and the principal instrument for this purpose is a centralized lighting control through which all circuits pass.

Once the general field of illumination has been established, attention can be turned to the provision of lighting to achieve specific dramatic or decorative effect, or a suggestion of the origin of the illumination – sunlight, moonlight, etc – known in the USA as 'motivating lighting'. These results may be achieved in a variety of ways using colour, direction and intensity in a manner characteristic of each individual designer. In theory, all means used for stage lighting must be versatile; lighting units should have widely adjustable beams capable of being expanded and contracted and in many cases of being shaped. Light must not stray outside these intended beams; it must fall only on the specific area of the stage desired at the time. Accurate delineation of beam edge is particularly important in open staging where the audience is often very close to the glare.

Stage lighting installation

While it should be flexible in use, the electrical wiring and control of the stage lighting installation must have a degree of permanence. The mobile part of the system is the lighting equipment which is fed and controlled from the fixed part. The permanent installation includes not only the electrical wiring but the mountings to which lighting equipment will be attached and the means of access to them. An electrical supply at a point where nothing can be fixed or reached for adjustment is useless. This applies particularly to the lighting positions in the auditorium.

Lighting positions   **Proscenium or end stage:** To meet the demands upon it, the stage-lighting installation must make provision for lighting any part of the stage from as wide a range of angles as possible. If these angles are restricted as in the case of a forestage which can be lit only from vertically above, the installation will be inadequate. There are basic lighting positions which are essential if the performance and setting are to be seen with clarity. But when these have been provided still other angles and directions of light may be required to build up an effective composition.

Some light must come from the general direction of the audience. The source need not always be in the auditorium itself; for instance, an actor standing upstage in a proscenium theatre could be lit from the audience direction by using lights downstage, but still inside the stage area. When the actor is downstage close to the audience, some lighting positions must be in the auditorium. This is even more important in theatres where there is an orchestra pit which can be raised to form a forestage. In such circumstances additional front-of-house lighting positions will be necessary. A large part of the lighting from the direction of the audience should be arranged so that it strikes the actor's face at about 45° above horizontal. If the angle is much steeper it will produce dark unflattering shadows under the brows and if it is at a shallow angle there is the danger of unwanted shadows on the set or on other actors. Spotlights are rarely directed straight at actors, but are usually crossed.

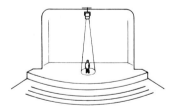   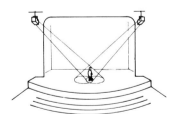

No. 11:1   *Spotlight directed straight at actor.*   *Spotlights crossing onto actor.*

The preferred angle of 45° cannot, therefore, be used to locate the lighting positions on a section drawn on the centre line of the auditorium, but if these positions are sited at an angle of elevation of about 55° to the actor's face, the light will strike him at approximately 45° after crossing diagonally. Obviously, the width of the stage and height of the lighting equipment will also affect the angle, but these principles should be sufficient to locate the lighting positions.

The principal overhead positions can be located in the same way.

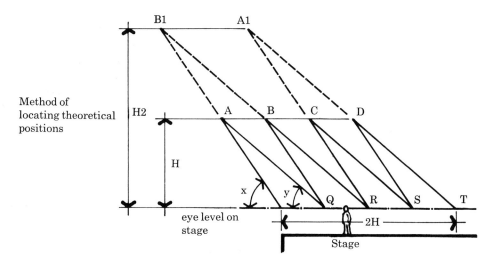

No. 11:2   *Method of locating theoretical positions.*

Spotlights at A will light an actor at the edge of the stage at 55° in section, about 45° to 50° after crossing, but as the actor moves in from the edge the angle will decrease. At Q it is only 40° in section, about 35° after crossing and this is the minimum. It is, therefore, necessary to provide another lighting position, B, which will cover the area Q to R within the same range of angles and then positions C and D, lighting areas R to S and S to T. Where, as with proscenium and end stages, the audience sit only on one side, A, B, C and D will be preferred positions for overhead lighting.

In proscenium theatres A and B correspond to the front-of-house lighting positions and C and D to numbers 1 and 2 spot bars. More bars may, in fact, be required if the theoretical angles of coverage shown in the diagram, are obstructed by the scenery. These overhead positions should be supplemented by vertical bars, both in the wings and on the side walls of the auditorium, close to the proscenium to give coverage from a much wider range of angles than can be shown on the diagram. The diagram also shows the effect of height on the layout of the lighting. Where the lighting grid is only half the stage depth above the eye level, four bars are required, but where the height is the same as the stage depth, only two, A1 and B1 will give the same coverage. The factors determining the height on proscenium stages will be the dimensions of the effective openings and the borders which may lead to several bars being required.

Arena and thrust stages: The same principles apply when locating the lighting equipment in arena and thrust stages. Here, with the audience surrounding the stage on three or all sides, to achieve the preferred angles of light with the actor facing in any direction, the number of lighting positions would have to be doubled at least.

But in practice the arrangement of the audience tends to restrict the number of lighting positions that can be used. Most of these will be disposed so as to follow the plan of the stage. Some will be over it and some will be over the audience. A typical arrangement has lighting bars running in two directions at right angles over the stage and audience areas forming a grid.

When lighting is set up great care has to be taken to avoid lighting units glaring directly into the eyes of the audience seated on the other side of the acting area from the source. The illumination of a front row of embarrassed knees can be distracting. Spectators are sometimes troubled by the reflecting of incident light from the stage surface. The remedy for this lies in choosing a non-specular floor finish.

When a theatre is designed to be adaptable, from one audience-to-stage relationship to another, including thrust stage and theatre-in-the-round the demands upon the lighting system are even greater. Changing the lighting equipment to accommodate a different form of staging may involve a great deal of time and labour costs, some of which can be saved by having an extra number of circuits and additional stocks of equipment. The situation is greatly eased where the acting area is planned to remain in the same position for whatever audience-to-stage form is in use.

Access to lighting positions over the stages

All lighting positions have to be reached so that individual units can be directed, focused, colour filters changed and the fittings maintained. It is most convenient if the electricians can reach the lanterns from permanent walkways or platforms with room to walk without stooping, but this is not always possible over the stage where hanging space is in great demand. Most smaller theatres will not be prepared to relinquish the vital space just inside the proscenium which would be neutralized by a heavy lighting bridge. In large opera houses and similar buildings where the productions in a repertoire are changed everyday, the saving in electricians' time and labour may justify a bridge. In buildings of this scale the proportion of space taken up is less crucial than in an average-to-small theatre. The question of whether to sacrifice some flying space for a bridge should be discussed with the users before a decision is made. It may be that most of the functions of the traditional bridge can be performed by a lighting bridge just on the auditorium side of the proscenium where there is no interruption of the flying system. There is one disadvantage in this position when a house curtain is used: the scene cannot be lit from sources in the auditorium until the tabs have opened far enough to clear them. This is a limitation which can be taken into account by directors and lighting designers.

Lighting over the stage is usually suspended from bars attached to counterweight sets or winches. It should be remembered that the ability to raise or lower these bars does not make it possible to adjust the angle or focus of a spotlight before hauling the bar into place. Such adjustments can only be made when it is in its final position. There is a limited range of lanterns which can be directed from below by means of a pole, but this is at best unwieldy and adjusting from a step ladder is usually a surer method. Step ladders, however, are dangerous and inconvenient and in recent years access towers of light aluminium tubing have almost become standard equipment in theatres. One such is the Tallescope, manufactured by Access Equipment Ltd, which has a platform on top of an extensible framework tower. It has outriggers at its base which are folded down to improve its stability. While it is much safer and more convenient and generally useful than a step ladder, it shares with it the inevitable disadvantage of obstructing the stage when it is in use.

Lighting bridges and wall slots

The objection to lighting bridges over the stage itself have been discussed, but elsewhere over the auditorium they are, without doubt, the best solution. Access to positions in the auditorium ceiling from step ladders or towers is even more perilous and tiresome than reaching the spot bars over the stage. Lighting equipment on bridges can be altered, adjusted and serviced if necessary during a performance without the electrician having to pass through the auditorium. Side positions in the walls of the auditorium are extremely useful and it should be possible to reach these too without bringing ladders into the auditorium. If the lighting equipment is put in wall slots provision can be made for access from outside the auditorium or from catwalks in the ceiling. The absence of slots will not prevent these valuable lighting positions from being used and bars will soon sprout from the walls if they are forgotten in the first place.

The diagrams show the recommended sizes for lighting bridges and for wall slots. The dimensions depend upon the size of lanterns. Within 18 m of the stage usually only the smaller units will be used, but at greater distances more powerful and, therefore, larger equipment may have to be accommodated. Even close to the stage a large 5 kW projector may sometimes be needed and there should be a platform, say 1100 mm wide, where one can be set up in a forward position.

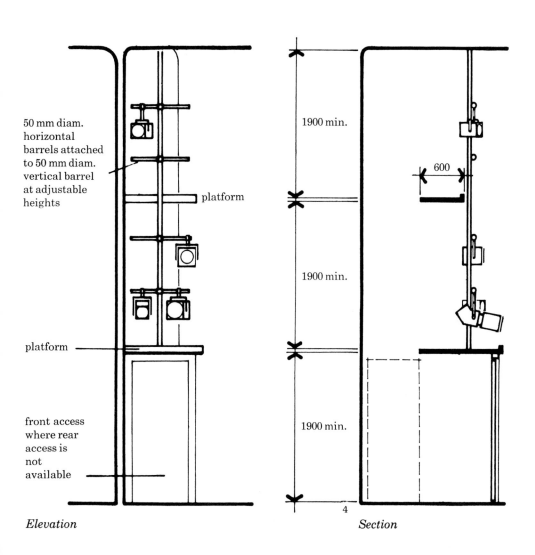

50 mm diam. horizontal barrels attached to 50 mm diam. vertical barrel at adjustable heights

platform

platform

front access where rear access is not available

1900 min.

600

1900 min.

1900 min.

4

Elevation

Section

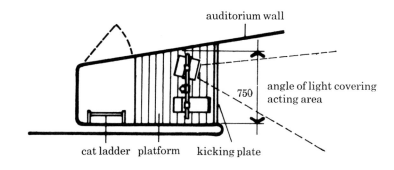

auditorium wall

angle of light covering acting area

750

cat ladder   platform   kicking plate

Plan

No. 11:3   *Auditorium wall slot.*

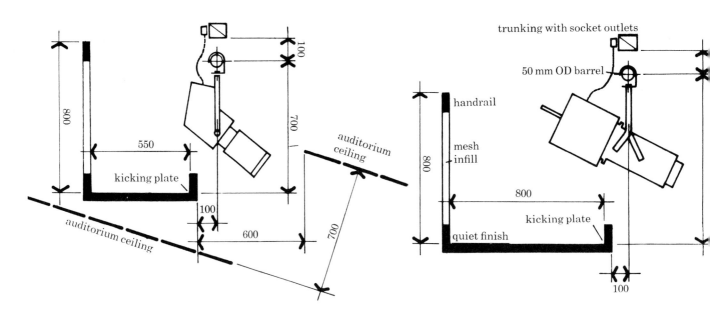

No. 11:4   *Auditorium lighting bridge.*   *Auditorium lighting bridge. (large lanterns).*

No. 11:5   *Lighting bridges over the thrust stage at the Crucible Theatre, Sheffield.*

Access to the lanterns from bridge and slots should be easy and safe. It may be necessary to kneel down to make some adjustments to the extremities of the lanterns, but this is no reason to expect technicians to reach lighting positions by crawling on all fours. There should be proper headroom of 2 m over all access routes so that people can walk naturally without having to crouch. Platforms and walkways should be finished in a material which is quiet to walk on and reasonably comfortable to kneel on. Wood or linoleum are suitable and have another advantage in their electrical insulation which reduces the risks if a technician touches a faulty lantern. Kicking plates must be provided at the edges of walkways to prevent small items being knocked off.

All the bars mentioned for suspending stage lighting equipment should be 50 mm outside diameter tube which has a recommended span of 1950 mm. A span of 2400 mm should not be exceeded. This is the usual scaffold tube and other sizes or square section tube will not take the standard hook clamp used for attaching lanterns and are therefore, unsuitable.

Storage   Storage space and racking for spare lamps, equipment, colours and cables should be available on or adjacent to bridges and slots. The

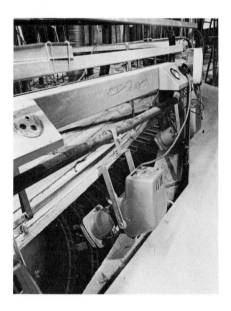

No. 11:6   An auditorium lighting bridge.

No. 11:7   A lighting control board in use (Rank Strand SP 80).

amount of space required is difficult to determine precisely, but it is reasonable to provide for 20% spare lanterns, coils of cable, spare colour frames, tools and accessories. The fitting-out of the space can be left to the users of the building.

Reflecting surfaces

There is inevitably some light spill from lanterns and to avoid distracting reflections, all those auditorium surfaces near bridges and slots should be of low reflectance. In particular, polished surfaces which give specular reflections should be avoided.

Lighting control

The lighting-control equipment is the nerve centre of the stage-lighting installation. Instead of the switch and distribution panels of a normal electrical system, the stage-lighting circuits are each controlled by a dimmer. The control equipment can be combined in one instrument, but above 20 channels it is usually split into two constituents: the control desk and the remotely controlled dimmers.

The electrical power handled by the dimmers is considerable. Though they are talked of as 'lighting' circuits, the lamps they feed often take 1 kW or 2 kW and sometimes 5 kW. They are the equivalent of large electric fires; in fact the ratio of light to heat output is so low that they give out almost as much heat as electric fires of a similar rating.

The thyristor dimmers regulating the current feeding these lanterns give out a certain amount of heat which must be dissipated by mechanical ventilation. As this is never completely silent and the thyristors themselves can emit a low hum or buzz, it is better to house the racks of dimmers in their own separate compartment.

The dimmers in their turn are controlled from the control desk or console, but here the signal currents are very small indeed when compared with the load on the stage-lighting circuits. The cables joining the desk with the dimmer room are, therefore, much lighter and consequently cheaper than those going from dimmers to lighting circuits. The lighting control room can be in the most convenient position for the operator, without its remoteness from the dimmers adding significantly to wiring expense. The siting of the dimmer room, on the other hand, can have a material effect on cable costs. A heavy main from the electrical intake goes to the dimmer room where it is split up to feed the various stage-lighting circuits. The shorter these routes the better for wiring economy and in this way, the voltage drop along all these cables can be reduced to a minimum.

The other factor in siting the dimmers is their accessibility, the importance of which has already been explained. It is, of course, possible to split up the dimmers, mount them individually or in large installations, to group them in different rooms sited to serve, for example, the stage floor, the flys and the front-of-house. In this way an electrician on a catwalk in the auditorium ceiling may be spared a trip to the basement to replace a fuse.

Types of dimmer

Over the years there has been a continuous process of development in dimmers and many different methods have been tried. Resistances, transformers, saturable reactors, thyratron valves and magnetic amplifiers. At the present time, the solid-state thyristor has replaced all the others. Considering it was introduced as a theatre dimmer as late as 1964, this is a remarkable testimony to its efficiency. However, technology is developing at such a rate that it may well be replaced by some other device in its turn. Thyristors are usually mounted on racks in multiples of twenty. They are normally wired in, but sometimes plug-in modules are used.

The lighting control desk

One of the main objectives of stage lighting is a smooth flow from one lighting picture to the next. The simplest control desk has a series of faders usually in the form of levers, each one controlling a channel of stage lighting. By adjusting the faders, the various intensities of light can be balanced until the desired lighting picture is obtained. Once the intensity of each individual channel has been set up the whole can be controlled by a master fader. The next problem is how to change from one set of dimmer intensities to the next; from one stage picture to the next. In its simplest form we have a duplicate set of faders known as a preset, controlling the same lighting channels where the next set of lighting intensities can be set up while the first one is still in operation. When the cue for the change to the new lighting pattern comes up the master fader controlling the preset with the new setting is brought up to full while the master controlling the first set of levers is brought to zero. Very often a third set of faders is added giving the opportunity to set up three preset lighting patterns.

Changes are made by cross-fading from one preset to another and individual channels can always be adjusted by hand. It is, of course, possible to have more than three presets, but the resulting system tends to become clumsy and expensive. The system can be made more versatile by providing grouping so that each preset has two or three masters instead of only one. By operating a switch on each channel, groups of circuits can be connected to one or other or both master faders.

Memory systems

So far we have considered control desks where one preset is controlling the lighting on stage and has its master at full while the other preset is being adjusted to set up the next lighting pattern. The operator reads the new levels from his lighting plot and when cues follow one another quickly, he is involved in some very intricate finger work with a large number of levers. With an automatic memory system added the whole process of recalling previously determined lighting patterns can be greatly simplified. An elementary form of group memory system can be added to a normal preset board enabling selected channels to be recalled at will as a pre-determined group. This is an extension of the switch selection of groups which has just been described and with controls of over eighty channels the plotting and manual dexterity required of the operator are much reduced.

Used in this way the memory system is an addition to an orthodox preset board, but with the introduction of dimmer memory systems, the operator is no longer tied to a limited number of presets and groups. When at a lighting rehearsal the stage lighting picture has been composed, the levels of all the various channels can be instantly recorded into a memory. Each succeeding lighting plot can be built up and stored away without any tedious plotting on paper. Each cue thus memorised can be played back in any order at any speed required by the production. The controls at the desk will still have a manual over-ride which enables immediate alterations of any individual lantern before, during or after a cue has been invoked in playback and such modification can be re-recorded if required. For repertoire work all the recorded information for a production can be taken out on magnetic or punched tape and kept in store until it is required again to re-programme the principal memory when the show comes back.

No. 11:8   *The console for a stage lighting system with memory control (Thorn 'Q'-File).*

Each recorded lighting state is recalled from the memory banks in readiness for the next change. Cross-fading from one to the other can be done manually by the operator, but automatic fade controls which can make a change at a pre-determined speed, can now be provided. All the operator has to do is initiate the change though he can modify it manually while it is in progress.

The control desk should give an indication of the state of lighting at any particular point in time. This can be done by a mimic panel containing one or two lamps per channel or by illumination of channel dimmer lever scales, rockers or push buttons. Mimics usually only indicate whether a channel is on or off and the actual intensity of the channel has to be checked on a scale or dial. A sophisticated dimmer memory system has the following advantages over other lighting controls.

(a)   A single operator can control a large number of circuits.

(b)   The lighting states achieved at rehearsal are recorded virtually instantaneously. The tedious plotting time is completely eliminated.

(c)   Each recorded lighting state can be reproduced precisely an unlimited number of times.

(d)   Any recorded cue state can be summoned up from the memories in any order. Sudden decisions to change the running order of a show present no problems.

(e)   It is possible to carry out rapid cue sequences completely unobtainable on non-memory controls.

The lighting control room

The best position for the operator of the lighting-control board is in a control room in the auditorium with an observation window allowing him an unrestricted and undistorted view of the stage, wing to wing and floor to borders.

In a tiered auditorium the rear of the stalls is preferable, but the floor level must be arranged so that the operator's view is not obstructed by any member of the audience standing or sitting in front or by the overhang of the balcony.

The control room houses the lighting console and the operator and needs space for writing the lighting plot, storage and maintenance activity. A space 3 m wide × 2·4 m deep should be allowed initially, but this may have to be revised depending upon the equipment to be installed. Some equipment may require extra height, but there is a tendency towards miniaturisation in the latest control systems and a smaller space may be sufficient. The normal access to the control room should be outside the auditorium and preferably separate from the public areas, but a door direct into the auditorium is desirable for rehearsal. There should be an easy connection from the control room to the stage and dimmer room and any associated data stores without having to go through the auditorium. The entrance door must be light trapped to avoid light spill into the auditorium through the observation window and also to avoid disturbing the operator's dark adaptation. Direct access to stage lighting positions in the ceiling of the auditorium is desirable.

The sound control room

The sound control room will usually be situated near to the lighting control room, but it has different requirements and is better separated and sound insulated from it. An interconnecting door has the advantage of rapid communication and in small theatres it may be acceptable to combine the two.

Projection box

Where a film projection box is included the question of its relation to the control rooms must be considered. In general it is better for it to be separate and fire precautions may make this essential. There are certain auditorium lighting controls which will have to be duplicated in this case. The projectionist should be able to dim the auditorium lights and operate the curtain without having to go into another room.

The observation window

The size of the window should be governed by the sight lines from the operator to the stage and lighting equipment which he should be able to see. A typical size would be 1200 mm × 600 mm high. During rehearsals the window often has to be open but during performances it must offer good sound insulation. This can be done with 12 mm plate glass or better with double glazing designed for sound insulation. Reflections of the illuminated part of the control board in the window may distract the operator and on the auditorium side reflections of stage lighting can be a nuisance to performers. This can be eliminated by angling the glass. Tinted or one-way glass which affects the true colour or intensity of the operator's stage-lighting picture is totally unacceptable.

Control room lighting

For lighting the control room itself two distinct situations have to be met. During performances, localised illumination of the operational area of the lighting control are needed. A method of adjusting the intensity and direction of this lighting locally in the control room must be selected, bearing in mind that unless they are to broadcast system standards, thyristor dimmers can cause interference in sound equipment. The placing of this lighting should be arranged to avoid reflections of the source in the observation window.

The other system of general lighting should be of normal intensity for plot writing, cleaning and maintenance.

Electric power supplies will be needed for permanent or semi-permanent equipment and for portable maintenance equipment. At least three socket outlets should be provided and the lighting control desk and auxiliary control panels may also need a separate power supply.

Ventilation   Since daylight must be excluded, silent dust-free ventilation, thermostatically controlled, is necessary. Ventilation must not conduct noise or smells from other rooms or public areas.

Finishes   The floors, walls and ceiling of the control room should be dark and non-reflective. A soft finish, such as carpet, on the floor both absorbs sound and muffles it at source. The walls should also be lined with sound-absorbing materials.

The manufacturers of the control board will give details of the positions of entry of control cables and access points required for maintenance. Flexible cables will need protection. A false floor may simplify the positioning of equipment and improve the accessibility for alterations and maintenance.

Additional controls   Good communications with stage management, other lighting staff and, during rehearsals with the production desk, are essential. The chapter on communications discusses the whole system, but a reminder is not out of place here that the lighting operator does not often have a hand to spare for a telephone when rehearsals or a show are in progress. For administrative purposes there should be extensions on the internal telephone system and sometimes on the external GPO system, but these should have lamp calling signals not bells. A two-way talk back system with the dimmer room is essential.

A considerable number of controls for ancillary services accumulate in the lighting control room and it is an advantage if these are housed in a purpose-designed unit mounted within convenient reach of the operator, for instance, on the side wall or above the window.

The following may have to be accommodated:

1   Colour changing controls.
2   Auditorium lighting controls.
3   Local lighting intensity control.
4   Clock, with sweep second hand.
5   Cue lights and/or buzzer.
6   Stage working light master controls and/or indication.
7   Cleaners' lighting master switch.
8   Controls for remotely positioning spotlights.
9   Indication of safe/unsafe ambient temperature of dimmer room.
10   Safety lighting indication.
11   Volt meter and selector switch to monitor stage lighting supply.
12   Communications and show relay speakers.

13   Orchestra pit lighting dimmer controls.
14   Curtain-dressing and call-lighting controls.

Provision may also have to be made for mounting a broadcast television monitor.

In theatres where it is intended to play a repertoire or a complicated programme of different activities a simple control desk should also be provided at stage level to allow lighting units to be reset without the necessity for an operator in the lighting control room. The same panel can be used for rehearsal lighting and to set lighting suitable for concerts.

Design of electrical installation

The design of the electrical installation in a theatre, and not only that of the wiring for the stage lighting itself, is a highly specialised matter and the proper advice should always be taken.

Wiring methods

All electrical wiring in a theatre should, of course, comply with the current edition of the *Regulations for the Electrical Equipment of Buildings* issued by the Institution of Electrical Engineers (the IEE Regulations). In addition, the fire insurance company insuring the building, the local supply authority, and sometimes the local licensing authority also impose their own regulations. In the opinion of the ABTT the IEE regulations should be sufficient.

The wiring between the dimmers and the socket outlets to feed the lanterns needs more careful consideration in an open-stage theatre. Behind a proscenium with a fire curtain quite liberal amounts of temporary cables can be used, especially if the production is short term. Nearly all the wiring for an open stage is out among the audience, probably hanging over their heads. This demands a good standard of finish and safety. In any case there is little point in paying for almost rewiring the place each time a show is put on, which virtually happens where temporary wiring is used. The layout of lanterns may differ from show to show in the way they are angled and focused, and in the number which hang over a particular area. Some forethought will, however, show that complete flexibility is unnecessary, since certain positions are a 'must' if the show is to be lit, and a very large number of positions are excluded owing to the risk of glare and sheer inutility.

It is convenient and does not greatly increase cost, to terminate circuits in pairs of socket outlets side by side at their stage end. It is essential to use the same size of socket outlet connector throughout for the lighting circuits. This should be 15 amp (BS 546 gauge) for all 2 kW outlets. A 5 kW channel needs a 30 amp socket outlet, but should have a changeover device to two 15 amp 3-pin sockets. The 13 amp fused plug and socket for ring mains is considered unsuitable as fusing local to the lighting units is not always practicable for stage work. Fuses or circuit breakers must be centralised and accessible during the show. To convey the wiring between the control and the various points, there are two methods which are particularly suitable: the first is a trunking of metal, with removable lids so that the wiring is protected, but can be added to or altered when necessary, and the second, which is coming into use, is the wiring tray. In this case MICC wiring is buckled with simple clips to an open mesh tray with shallow edges.

The technique of stage lighting is developing rapidly and the amount of equipment to which connection has to be made in any theatre, always increases with time. It is, therefore, most important to take all possible steps to ensure that expansion of the number of circuits can be made easily. As an example, electric trunking and cable trays should always be significantly larger than is required to accommodate the amount of wiring envisaged when the theatre is first brought into use, while apertures through concrete walls and beams, etc, should either be much larger than is required for the trunking and conduit which will be installed initially or be capable of easy enlargement.

Notes on phase balancing

While responsibility for the phase balancing rests with the engineer designing the installation, the following remarks may be helpful.

The use of a stage-lighting installation varies so widely and so rapidly that it is impossible to ensure a good balance under all conditions. Under 'full-up' conditions with modern techniques, no diversity may be assumed and it is likely that the heaviest load will be found front-of-house and the next heaviest from hanging equipment on stage. This applies particularly when a forestage is used.

The most convenient division is likely to be:

front of house	phase 1
flys	phase 2
stage floor	phase 3

As equipment hanging from bars may be connected from either end, the outlets at each side of the stage, either in the flys or at low level, should be on the same phase. Small installations up to 30 ways can be conveniently connected to single phase supplies.

In small theatres, there is the possibility of looping cables from the flys to the dips or vice versa.

It is sometimes worth considering splitting the stage lighting installation across two phases only, one front-of-house and the second backstage, with the dressing rooms or other ancillary spaces connected to the third phase. This is safer and unlikely to lead to a greater out-of-balance under average conditions than any method of splitting the stage lighting across three phases. This method is unlikely to be practicable in medium-sized and large theatres.

Working lights

In stage areas such as the fly gallery, the grid and lighting galleries, a high level of illumination is needed for maintenance and setting up. This is provided by a system of working lights, but during performances unwanted light must not stray into the auditorium or stage and another system of low-level lighting offstage for working the show is needed. The switching of all these working lights should be centralised near the performance control point (prompt corner).

Auditorium decorative lighting

The brightness of the auditorium affects the scale of intensity required on the stage, and if the audience have become accustomed to too high a degree of brightness before the play begins, it becomes very difficult to establish the effect, for instance, of strong sunlight.

The Illuminating Engineering Society Code: *Recommendations for Lighting Building Interiors* 1968, gives a level of 100 lux for theatre auditoria and this should be regarded as the upper limit for the light which the audience will need to read their programmes. However, the appearance of the auditorium and the adaptation level of the audience's eyes are determined not so much by the light falling on the programme, or other special objects of regard, as by the brightness of the seating, carpets, walls and ceiling. These should have finishes of low reflectance (which does not exclude the use of strong colours) and little light should be directed at them.

Large polished surfaces should be avoided in the auditorium, as they will pick up reflections from the stage which move as the actors move and can be most distracting. This applies not only to glass and similar materials, but even to polished wooden panelling and marble, etc. Further, there should be no bright glaring sources of light in the auditorium and where chandeliers are used to add sparkle they should be fitted with low power lamps and shades. Fluorescent lighting is at present very difficult to dim effectively without flickering. It cannot match the smooth response to control of incandescent lamps to say nothing of their warmth and sparkle.

All lighting in the auditorium, should, of course, be controlled through a dimmer operated from the same position as the stage lighting itself. In large auditoria several dimmers may be used so that the lighting can be faded sequentially. The foyers are likely to be strongly lit, either by daylight or artificial light and it is necessary to ensure that the passages leading from them into the auditorium offer a gentle gradation of brightness from one level to the other. All daylight should be excluded from the auditorium at all times, and it is especially important that there should be means of preventing daylight or artificial light leaking in through the exit doors. Curtains, which should never for safety reasons come right to floor level, are unlikely to be satisfactory and the fittings and windows immediately outside the exit doors must be placed in such a way as to prevent shafts of light distracting the audience as latecomers or ushers move in and out. In buildings designed for more than one use it may be necessary to have a higher level of lighting available. In this case the supplementary lighting should be separately controlled. It may be unnecessary to arrange for dimming of the supplementary lighting and switches are often sufficient. In any auditorium separate lighting is required for rehearsal and cleaning purposes. The switches should be located outside the auditorium, readily accessible from it, but where they cannot be operated accidentally by members of the public. In some areas a 'panic switch' is required under the control of the manager, which will enable him to bring lighting on in the auditorium in the event of an emergency.

Safety lighting and management lighting

All parts of a theatre or similar building to which the public have access, and all main escape routes for staff from backstage and elsewhere, must be adequately lit at all times, from two independent sources of supply when the building is open to the public.

The licensing authority is responsible for determining the requirements, and in fact most authorities follow BS CP 1007:1955, *Maintained Lighting for Cinemas*, compliance with which will normally be deemed to fulfil the statutory and other requirements. This code of practice deals with the maintained lighting which in the absence of daylight is intended for use during the whole time the public is on the premises: it includes the management lighting fed from the mains and the safety lighting fed from some source independent of the mains. Two electric service cables from the supply are not normally accepted as 'independent'. Generally speaking the safety lighting must be fed from a battery normally charged from the mains except for very large premises where it might be worth considering a diesel set. Even then, a battery is likely to be required to cover the interval while the diesel starts.

Inside the auditorium the management lighting will be the minimum required to enable the staff to see their way about and perform their essential task of controlling and assisting the audience. The amount of light required will vary with circumstances, but it will be greater in cinemas with continuous performances, where people are coming in and going out all the time, than in buildings with fixed times of performances. Outside the auditorium the management lighting will normally be the whole of the lighting although in some buildings, part of the foyer lighting is switched off as an economy measure once the show has started. The safety lighting must be sufficient to enable the public and staff to leave in safety even after total failure of the mains supply.

The standard of safety lighting in the auditorium required by the code of practice is between 0·01 and 0·025 lux depending on circumstances, and provided that the light is adequately distributed. Measures must be taken to ensure that nosings of treads, the perimeter of blocks of seats, changes in the direction of gangways, etc, are treated in such a way that they stand out from their surroundings. Certain critical areas may require a higher illumination, but sharp changes of intensity should be avoided. Outside the auditorium a higher standard of safety lighting, not less than about 1 lux is required.

Internally illuminated exit notices must be provided to mark the escape routes from both auditorium and back stage, etc, fed from both sources of supply. There is a British Standard (BS 2560:1954) for exit signs for cinemas, theatres and places of public entertainment which goes into a great many unnecessary details of construction and lays down even the style of the lettering. Those provisions which are relevant are that the lettering should be not less than 125 mm high and so designed that there is sufficient contrast between the lettering and surround to make the word EXIT clearly legible even when the internal lighting is not on. The exit notices have to be illuminated continuously whenever the public is admitted to the building.

The rest of the maintained lighting in the auditorium may be turned off for short periods when required by the action of the play provided that some responsible person in, or in immediate contact with the auditorium has control of the switches whenever this lighting is turned off.

The wiring for safety lighting must be completely separated from all other wiring, except that, as in exit notices, one lighting fitting may contain lamps fed from both mains and safety systems, provided that the fitting is properly constructed and is of fire-resisting materials.

In recent years self-luminous exit signs have begun to be more widely used. They depend on the substances (phospors) which are excited to luminescence by the radiation from radio-active materials. Radiation from the sign is negligible and there is no danger to health. They require no wiring and once screwed in position need no further attention. In time there will be a slight diminution in brightness, but this will not be appreciable for many years. Though they are initially more expensive than the orthodox box signs the savings on wiring two systems may redress the balance and the complete elimination of maintenance cost in replacing bulbs and the cost of electric current is a further advantage.

Battery rooms for safety lighting

The battery room should be located where it will be easily accessible and yet not so close to the intake position that it is liable to be affected by fire or explosion in the mains voltage apparatus. The plan area of the battery room should be approximately 0.15 m² for every 100 W of safety lighting provided, with a minimum of 2 m². No single dimension should be less than 1 m. The minimum height is 2.2 m.

The battery room should have good natural ventilation to the open air independent of any other ventilated spaces. Batteries give off gases which can, in certain conditions be explosive, or in others can be poisonous. If forced ventilation is unavoidable the fan motor should be outside the air stream.

The battery room should be of substantial non-combustible construction, having a fire resistance of one hour; the doors should be of half-hour fire resistance and kept locked. Except in the case of small buildings with a small self-contained metal cabinet housing both 'sealed' type batteries and charging plant, the battery room should not be used for any other purpose.

The walls and floor should be of acid-resistant materials and easily washable. A gulley for hosing down is an advantage. Inside the room or nearby, there should be a porcelain or earthenware (not steel) sink and a cold water supply.

The battery room should contain space for racking for carboys of distilled water in addition to that for the batteries themselves. Battery racks are normally provided by the manufacturers, but if made up by a contractor they should be of substantial timber construction and the shelves covered with lead sheet, ceramic plates or other acid-resisting material.

Except in the case of self-contained units described above, the charging plant should not be accommodated in the battery room, but in an adjacent room.

Television requirements

At the time of writing, colour television outside broadcasts are in an early stage of development. They require an intensity of light which will, with development of new techniques, be unnecessary in the future.

The engineering department of one of the television companies should be consulted before provisions are made in new buildings. At present a mobile control room vehicle will be essential for colour television outside broadcasts from theatres. It will require 14 m × 4 m parking space during rehearsals and performances and other essential vehicles will need additional space three times this area. There should be 4 m of headroom, the turning circles are approximately 25 m diameter and weights are up to 14 000 kg. The parking area should be close to the side of the building with easy routes for personnel both to the auditorium and the stage. As the broadcast is likely to take place while the public is present, cables and equipment must not interfere with the normal audience flow and means of escape, nor must they interfere with the light and weather insulation of the building. There is some preference for access to the front-of-house areas, if a choice is necessary, but proximity to the stage door is also valuable.

Cable access

Good cable routes both to the auditorium and the stage space are essential. The main entry point near where the control vehicle will be parked needs an aperture in the wall of 0·2 m², about 300 mm above ground level leading into a corridor or an easily accessible duct. In corridors the cables may be supported in trays or on hooks. They must reach stage-floor level, the stalls, and the first tier if there is one. Where they pass through fire-compartment walls, holes of 300 mm diameter should be provided, which, when not in use, should be sealed with fireproof caps or shutters. When the cables are in position the broadcasting organisation will plug the gap with fireproof packing. All the cable ducts should be as short and straight as possible.

Power supply

A colour mobile control van may require up to 100 amp 240 V single-phase ac from the theatre mains. Present practice is to take this supply direct from the busbars in the main intake switch room using temporary connectors supplied by the broadcasting organisation. Again, a cable route to the parking area will be needed and this must be as short as possible. A normal theatre lighting installation, must, at present, be supplemented for colour television. The power required will vary according to the size of the set from about 100 kW for a small house to 300 kW for a large opera house. This power too will be taken from the intake switch room and distributed to switch or dimmer trucks on the stage and in the auditorium usually in the circle.

Cable routes of approximately 150 cm² cross section should be provided between each area.

House dimmer control

Television technicians would prefer to make use of the house control board and operator, but there are certain conditions which few theatres can meet. A large number of 5 kW dimmers must be available with sockets in suitable parts of the house. 10 kW dimmers may also be needed but can be provided on a temporary basis if necessary.

The house lighting control board must have room for a television adviser in addition to the normal house operator. The control room will have to accommodate a colour picture monitor 600 mm × 600 mm × 900 mm weighing 70 kg, and a sound communication panel. Cable routes to the mobile control room are essential and these should have a cross-section area of 25 cm². If the control room is designed in accordance with the recommendations given elsewhere in this chapter, it should answer the requirements of television.

If the house board is unsuitable or unavailable for some reason, portable dimmers and a portable control panel will be brought in by the television company. The dimmers will be placed close to the lamp loads at the sides of the stage, the ends of the circle, in the boxes or on the fly floor.

The control panels will usually be at the front-of-house and preferably at circle level. So long as the cable routes, including a 25 cm² hole through the proscenium wall, are provided, there is seldom any difficulty in setting up this equipment.

When working on a stage with theatrical lighting already rigged the television equipment is usually supported underneath on spare lines or auxiliary bars hung below the normal lighting bars. The extra load on the suspension gear can be up to twice the weight of the standard equipment and this should be taken into account at the design stage.

When a forestage is in use, a temporary scaffold grid may have to be hung over and in front of the playing area. Provision should be made for loadbearing connections in or through the ceiling at design stage.

A feature of television lighting is the emphasis on back lighting from upstage bars and this should be taken into account when considering grid loading.

Camera position   It is not possible to predict exactly how the television cameras will be used. Platforms and tracking rails will be built to suit each production and it is helpful if seating can be easily removed in the stalls and front circle areas.

Stage sound   Television lighting will probably use thyristor dimmers and the temporary lighting wiring may run close to house microphone circuits. A special microphone cable can be obtained which virtually eliminates the risk of interference, but wiring enclosed in ferrous conduit or trunking is equally satisfactory. Balanced cables and careful earthing are, however, essential.

Types of stage lighting equipment   The following list is intended to be a series of definitions only. The symbols are internationally agreed.

Floodlight: A lantern with a beam angle of 100° or more and with a cut-off not less than 180°.

Special floodlight: Unit with a specified beam angle (less than 100°) and a specified cut-off angle.

Reflector spotlight: Lantern with simple reflector and adjustment of beam angle by relative movement of lamp and mirror.

Sealed beam lamp: Lamp with integral reflector giving an even beam.

Lens spotlight: Lantern with simple lens and with or without reflector and capable of adjustment of beam angle by relative movement of lamp and lens.

Fresnel spotlight: As a lens spotlight, but with stepped lens providing a soft edge to the beam.

No. 11:9   *The demountable stage at the Piccadilly Theatre, London, was removed to accommodate the Prospect Company's set for Edward II. The production first appeared on the open stage of the Assembly Hall, Edinburgh, and toured several other theatres with widely differing forms of audience-to-stage relation. While it was at the Piccadilly a television recording of the play was made by the* BBC.

Profile spotlight: Lantern giving hard-edged beam which can be varied in outline by diaphragms, shutters or silhouette cut-out masks.

Effects spotlight: Lantern with optics designed to give an even field of illumination of slides and well-defined projection of detail using suitable objective lenses. The slide can be of the moving effects type or stationary.

Softlight: A lantern of sufficient area to produce a diffuse light causing indefinite shadow boundaries. For stage lighting purpose this is taken to cover batten flooding equipment, two such symbols being joined by a line.

Bifocal spotlight: As profile spotlight above, but fitted with two sets of shutters or other such means at the gate so that the profile may be composed of either hard or soft edges or a combination of both.

Proposed list of definitions of dimmer and control systems expected to be adopted by the C.I.E. Committee

Dimmer: A regulating device in the electrical circuit controlling the intensity of the light.
Fader: The operational control element associated with the dimmer (or dimmers).
Dimmer curve: Relationship of control element to light output.
Linear Law: Assuming that the control handle travel is divided into ten equal sections with 100% light represented by 10 and zero light by 0, then the percentage of light corresponding to each position is 0, 10, 20, 30, 40, 50, 60, 70, 80, 90, 100%.
'S' Law: A dimmer curve that does not follow a simple mathematical relationship, but is 'S' shaped, thus light output changes slowly at the beginning and end of the control handle travel.
Square Law: Assuming the control handle travel is divided into ten equal sections with 100% light represented by 10 and zero light by 0, then the percentage of light corresponding to each position is 0, 1, 4, 9, 16, 25, 36, 49, 64, 81, 100%.
Cube Law: Assuming the control handle travel is divided into ten equal sections with 100% light represented by 10 and zero light by 0, then the percentage of light corresponding to each position is 0, 0·1, 0·8, 2·7, 6·4, 12·5, 21·6, 34·3, 51·2, 72·9, 100%.
Non-dim: A channel without a dimmer (switched only).
Circuit: An independent route from power source to load.
Patch panel: A device for connecting a number of channels to a

larger number of circuits (this normally refers to a power patch). See also 'control patch'.

Control patch: A device for connecting a number of controlling elements to a larger number of dimmers.

Channel: The control element (fader) complete with intensity control unit (dimmer).

Master: A means to control more than one channel at the same time. (The channels to be so controlled, preferably being selected at the will of the operator.)

Master Fader: A fader which controls a number of dimmers simultaneously.

Group selectors: Controls to enable channels to be formed into groups (which can be common to all presets or, alternatively, unique to each preset).

Group master: A fader giving an overriding effect to those channels grouped therein.

Preset: A means of setting up dimmer channels in advance while other levels are held on the same channels.

Preset master: A fader giving absolute master dimmer effect in respect of a preset.

Cross Fader: A single fader which effects the transfer from one preset to another (common channels at the same settings will not change).

Platten control: A system in which hand-set miniature channel controls are carried in sets on removable plattens or trays which are then inserted to be read off as a preset.

Memory: A process for recording information automatically (requiring neither hand nor any kind of mechanical sorting).

Group memory: A means of collecting a number of channels on to a group master automatically.

Intensity memory: A dimmer system which memorises and re-produces dimmer levels (this assumes instant and random access – for others see 'intensity recording').

Intensity recording: A dimmer system which records and re-produces dimmer levels (e.g. punch cards).

Lighting plan: A plan view of the lighting equipment.

Lighting plot: A statement of the time sequence in proceeding from one lighting state to another.

12   Sound installation and communications

This chapter is based upon the ABTT *Recommendations and proposed standards for wiring requirements for a sound system in a new theatre*. The subject is a complex one, technology is continually advancing and specialist advice should be taken at an early stage in a project.

Some degree of standardisation of sound equipment would be of mutual benefit to theatre owners and organisations that will use the theatre for broadcasting and recording. The aim should be to make the best possible use of common equipment such as microphones and loudspeaker circuits and to avoid the wholesale use of temporary cabling for special functions. The installation should conform to the conditions given in British Standard Code of Practice No. CP 327.300(1952) *Sound Distribution Systems*.

Sound control point
Many of the factors influencing the location of the lighting control room apply equally to the sound control room and they are often placed side by side. They should have a sound insulated division between them but it is an advantage if this has a window or door in it which can be opened for direct communication between the two operators. The sound control room should have an observation window giving an unrestricted view of the stage and the orchestra pit and if possible, of some of the audience. There are occasions when it is better for the operator (sound mixer) to monitor the sound direct from the stage as the audience hears it, rather than rely on sound relayed by a loudspeaker. This can be done by operating either the observation window itself or a panel opening to the auditorium. The room will have to be adequately and quietly ventilated and the internal acoustics should, as far as possible, be similar to those of the auditorium.

All the permanent wiring of the sound system will terminate in the control room. It is recommended that all lines are brought to a GPO type jackfield panel with standard Post Office type jacks

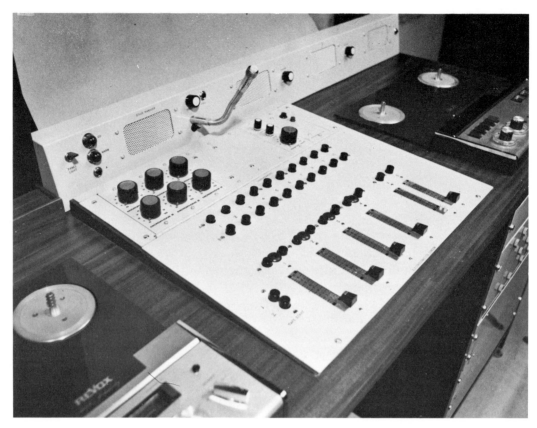

No. 12:1   Sound control console with 4 inputs, 2 groups and 10 loudspeaker circuits.

of the 'tip, ring and sleeve variety'. With equipment of this type it is an easy matter for a broadcasting or recording organisation to use any particular circuit by withdrawing the usual link and replacing it with special equipment that will split the microphone signal. One output may then be connected to the broadcasting equipment and the other to the sound system and by this means the common microphone circuit is shared between the two parties.

The sound equipment can be powered from standard 13 amp sockets and after all the permanent equipment has been served at least three extra sockets should be allowed for additional equipment which from time to time may be required. It is an advantage if all the mains points around the building, solely for the sound equipment, are controlled from a main isolating switch, fitted with a pilot light, situated in the sound control room. To avoid possible interference, this supply should come from as near the main intake as possible rather than from a local distribution board. A good earth is essential.

Microphone points

The following is a typical list of microphone points which might be required in a proscenium theatre:

Location	Number of points
Orchestra pit	4
Floats	6
Stage – prompt side	3
OP side	3
working side flies	4
grid	1
understage (centre)	1 (for possible rising microphone).
Auditorium roof	2 (in the dome or other convenient position)
Stalls level prompt side	1
OP	1
back	1
Circle prompt side	1
OP	1
back	1
Upper circle prompt side	1
OP	1
back	1
Front of house	1 (in the main foyer)
OB *point* (*outside broadcasting*)	6 pairs of cables

It is important that the screen of the cable is earthed at the equipment rack or other central apparatus position and not at or near the termination of the cable.*

Power points

The need for socket outlets in the sound equipment room has already been mentioned but other power points will be needed elsewhere. The following is a typical list:

Location	Number of points
Orchestra pit	1 near to microphone
Stage	3 each side of proscenium arch
	1 on working side of flies near to microphone points.
	1 on grid near to microphone points

---

*   It is recommended that the screened microphone cables are connected to a cannon plug type XLR–3–14. Pin No. 1 is connected to the screen of the cable and care should be taken to see that the other two pins are connected in correct polarity throughout the system. The number of the socket for these plugs is type XLR–3–11C.

Auditorium	1 in roof area near to microphone point.

Loudspeaker points

The typical sound system we are describing would have loudspeaker points distributed as follows:

Loudspeaker	Number of points
Orchestra pit	3 equally spaced on the back wall.
Stage	3 either side of the stage which could be conveniently placed in small traps.
	1 on either side of the flys
	1 in the grid
Auditorium	2 in the main roof area
	2 prompt side
	2 OP
	2 back. These to be at each level and should be sited adjacent to microphone points to act as control lines when required.
OB (*outside broadcasting*) point	6 pairs of cables
Front of house	1 in foyer and crush area
	1 in each bar and restaurant area.
	1 on the front canopy
	1 in the car park area, if any

In some of these positions loudspeakers will be installed permanently in which case the wiring should terminate in a screwed terminal block.*

Cables

All permanent cables should be run in solid drawn, heavy-gauge screwed conduit or metal trunking. The specification and placing of microphone cables is particularly important because interference from outside sources is possible. The screened cables must be spaced at least 150 mm from any ac mains cables and kept well clear of switch gear, transformers and dimmers. Where, as is usual today, thyristor dimmer lighting circuits are involved this space should be increased to at least 2 m. The Code of Practice Clause 802(III) gives information about suitable cables and there are many

---

*   Where loudspeakers are plugged in on a temporary basis, the socket type recommended is Cannon XLR–4–13C and the loudspeaker cable plug to suit this socket is type XLR–4–12C.

different makes on the market. The insulation of the conductors should be in pvc or rubber and the outer sheath should be in a similar material if the cable is encased in conduit or duct.

Loudspeaker cables are usually heavier than microphone cables but do not have to be screened. Individual conductors are insulated and the whole will be sheathed in pvc or tough rubber. When either of these cables emerge from the protection of conduits or trunking they should have a heavier sheath of pvc or tough rubber and they should be kept at least 150 mm apart.

Outside broadcast point

This subject has been discussed in detail in the chapter on stage lighting. In the recommended list of microphone points and loud-speaker points it has already been mentioned that six screened pairs should be allowed for each of these linking the sound control room with the outside broadcasting unit. If the cables themselves are not provided a route should be available in the form of conduits or divided trunking. In either case arrangements should be made for the cables to be divided into two groups of six.

Loudspeakers

Loudspeakers for speech reinforcement, public address and repro-duction of music have to be placed so that sound comes from the direction of the stage. In a proscenium theatre this usually implies that provision has to be made in the design at either side of the proscenium opening. Because of their directional qualities and compact design, line source speakers are widely used in theatres. They have the advantage of limiting upwards and downward radia-tion and their directional properties help to reduce the danger of acoustic feed-back from microphones.

Line source speakers were originally intended for sound rein-forcement where clear speech is required, but for more flexibility in use, compromises are made in the design to make them suitable for both music and speech. It is in some cases desirable to install specially designed wide frequency range loudspeakers comprising base bins coupled with multi-cellular horn units to handle the higher frequencies. These speakers, similar to those used in most cinemas, produce a high quality of reproduction with very great power output efficiency. The main drawback is their size and weight. However, base bins have not the same directional quality as line source speakers and therefore can fairly easily be built into the fabric of the building. On the other hand the multi-cellular unit is highly directional and has to be critically adjusted by a specialist. Many of the loudspeaker points in our typical list will have speakers permanently installed, but the theatre should have several portable loudspeakers for the reproduction of music and effects within the stage area, and some of the points in the audi-torium area itself could have portable units plugged in when the occasion arises. Certain specially designed loudspeakers may be used such as the highly directional type mentioned in another chapter which has been used for prompting on open stages. In a sound-system it is important to keep a consistency of quality and power handling capacity in all sound equipment.

Foyer loudspeakers

It used to be considered sufficient to ring bells to signify that the performance was about to begin and to summon the audience back from the bars after the interval, but now it is common practice to install a loudspeaker system in the foyers, bars and other front-of-house areas. This can relay emergency announcements, curtain-up announcements, electronic warning tones, recorded announcements or recorded music. Normally announcements will be made from the stage manager's control point, but it is a good idea to have an alternative access to the system in the sound control room. The layout of loudspeakers has to be carefully devised to avoid the system being too loud in some areas while being inaudible in others.

There are many suitable types of loudspeaker which can be built into walls or ceilings. Speaker units with cone sizes of 200 to 250 mm would be typical. The enclosures for these speakers would be approximately 300 mm square × 150 mm deep for the 200 mm cone and about 400 mm square × 200 mm deep for the larger cone. When a loudspeaker can be rigidly mounted on a suitable wall or ceiling the enclosure may not be necessary, the wall or ceiling forming an infinite speaker baffle. Wherever it is placed it should be accessible because it might need to be replaced at some time. There are acoustic hazards to be reckoned with in resonant cavities behind false or suspended ceilings and in resonances from ventilation trunking systems. A rough guide to the effective spread of an ordinary cone loudspeaker unit is 45° all round the centre line of the unit. If the speakers are in the ceiling, this gives a clue to the spacing which will give a complete coverage. If the ceiling is low the units have to be spaced rather closely together, and if the ceiling is too high, say, 6 m or more, this type of mounting is not really suitable. In very spacious areas clusters of small column loudspeakers might be a good technical answer. The number and bulk of necessary speakers is by no means negligible and if they are to be integrated into the design of the building provision must be made for them at an early stage.

Microphones

Microphones of a cardioid, that is uni-directional type, should be provided for outlets positioned in the float position along the front edge of the stage; the number depending on the width of the stage. They should be provided with shock absorbent fixings so that vibrations from the stage itself do not affect the microphones. An alternative to float microphones is the use of long-range gun microphones facing across stage from front-of-house positions. These have proved effective in musicals and have the advantage of picking up less noise from feet, on the stage. Theatres need at least one general purpose microphone on the list of permanent equipment. This would be used for off-stage announcements, special effects, speeches, singers etc. An omni-directional microphone is most useful and it should have a pedestal stand and enough cable to allow movement over the stage. Risers are usually only required for the variety or music hall form of entertainment. They can be operated in four ways:

(1) by hand with the microphone mounted on a rod which in turn is mounted on some form of guide and pushed up through the stage by a stage-hand, a cheap but not very elegant method;

(2) the microphone riser mechanism can be winched to the required height by the stage manager;

(3) the operation can be by electric motor operated by push buttons which control the rise and fall to predetermined positions, or,

(4) the operation can be electric but with continuously variable limits.

Microphones employed in this position should be physically as small as possible and the type will depend upon the use to which they are to be put and the acoustic conditions of the auditorium. It is important to mute the microphone while the riser mechanism is in operation. A small trap is provided centrally near the front of the stage, the flap or lid of which is connected with the riser mechanism so that it opens and closes as the microphone rises and falls without damaging or coming into contact with the microphone itself.

Radio microphones have many applications in the theatre. The absence of a cable gives great freedom of movement and they can easily be concealed on an actor's person. A Post Office licence will probably be required before a broadcasting device can be used and in any case expert advice should be sought.

Control room equipment

The location and layout of the control room for the sound operator have already been discussed and the following is an outline of the equipment which has to be installed in it.

There should be two gramophone turntables of transcription quality with pick-up arms of matching quality, although in certain circumstances it is possible to make do with one turntable.

A groove-locating device is not strictly necessary if the pick-up arm dropping device is sufficiently accurate. At least two tape decks will be needed, one of which should have recording facilities. One should be portable so that it can be used outside the control room for recording rehearsals, etc. Ideally both should be fixed and a third portable unit used for outside work. The others should be removable for cleaning and maintenance. The decks should take larger spools, they should be fitted with safety devices to prevent accidental tape erasure and their running speed should include 7·5 IPS. The sound operator should have a remote control on the desk

No. 12:2   The sound mixing desk and auxiliary sound desk for the Wyvern Theatre and Arts Centre, Swindon. (Stagesound)

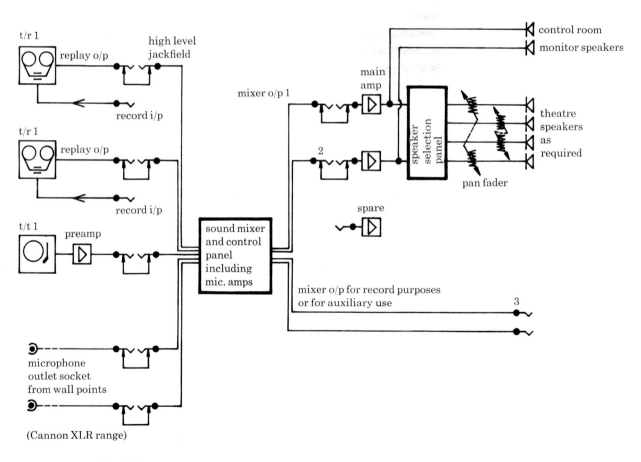

No. 12:3

enabling him to start and stop the decks. At the mixing desk each signal input from tape, gramophone or microphone can be routed to various amplifiers and loudspeakers which go to make up the sound system. At the mixing desk the level of the input signals and the amplifiers can be adjusted. It should be possible to switch the input from one amplifier to another in case of failure. All loudspeakers should be switchable to any of the amplifier channels. If there are only two it should be possible to fade the sound from one speaker to another when only one amplifier is being used. This is referred to as a pan fader. There should be tone controls and oral and visual means of monitoring individual signals. An echo device is a worthwhile extra if it is intended to use the desk for the preparation of recorded effects. The quantity and power output of the amplifiers depends upon the design of the particular installation. Usually, the stage effects are fed from a separate amplifier from that used in the auditorium.

Impedances

It is now standard practice in broadcasting organisations for individual items of equipment, tape decks, gram units, mixers, amplifiers, etc, to be low-impedance output and high-impedance input. It is recommended that all inter-connected sound circuits associated with the mixing desk and other equipment, be from low-impedance balanced sources of less than 100 ohms resistance and that inputs be high impedance bridging greater than 2k ohms balanced.

Stage management control equipment

A variety of means of communication are brought in to assist in the control of the performance organisation. Telephone links, loudspeaker intercom systems, radio loops, lights, bells and buzzers all have their part to play. Stage management control of the performance is the most vital function which these mechanical aids can assist. This control is operated from the prompt corner which is probably a misleading term to the uninitiated. Prompting, let us hope, is the least frequent of its uses and the proper position for it is certainly not tucked into a corner. It is, in fact, the point from where the stage manager controls and co-ordinates the various operations which combine to make up a theatrical performance. 'Performance control point' would be a more accurately descriptive term, but the traditional name will surely continue to be used at least in proscenium theatres. It is to theatres of this type that most of the recommendations in this chapter apply. Performance control is operated from the stage and as close to the acting area as possible, but in open stage theatres where no part of the stage is masked from the audience, performance control is usually operated from a control box in the auditorium. The physical separation of the stage manager from the stage has many disadvantages and some compensating advantages which we will discuss later.

No. 12:4 *A prompt corner showing both the portable control desk and the fixed control panel.*

No. 12:5 *A combined cue board and intercom panel. This panel is combined with a desk, not shown in the photograph. The desk and cue board unit is portable and has a flexible multicore cable connection to allow movement. The controls in this panel are limited to cueing and intercom.*

The ideal position has a direct view of as much of the acting area as possible while remaining masked from the audience. A position downstage of the curtain line recessed into the proscenium wall will give the best line of sight if it is structurally possible. A mirror can be used to extend the field of view to a certain extent.

Closed-circuit TV is becoming more important and can be a great aid to the stage manager where his view of the acting area is restricted. However, definition on the monitor screen must be detailed enough for such visual cues as the actor's hand on the light switch. The stage manager also needs to be able to see off-stage into the wings as well as the acting area. In an open stage theatre his view from the control box is the same as the audience's so that off-stage control has to be delegated to one or more assistant stage managers stationed as near as possible to the acting area. They must be in immediate two-way communication with the stage manager in the control box. The best position for the prompt corner may vary from one production to another. The stage manager's control desk, cue board, etc, should therefore be made movable by being mounted on castors and connected by armoured multi-core cable. The traditional position for the prompt corner is on the actors left side of the proscenium opening and this side of the stage is always called the prompt side. It may be more convenient at times to have the prompt corner on the OP or opposite prompt side or even in the orchestra pit. It should be possible to plug the multi-core cable into either of these positions. It is important to keep the movable part of the equipment as compact as possible otherwise an unwieldy structure will result which gets in everyone's way wherever it is put.

Working the show from the prompt corner requires concentration and accurate timing. All equipment should be kept as simple as possible to operate and different switches and controls should be readily identifiable even in a dim light.

The desk   If full-size musical scores are likely to be used, the desk will need to be 430 mm $\times$ 760 mm. It may have a gentle slope but enough flat space should also be provided for a notebook, pencils, rubber torch and various sound effects such as a door or phone bell pushes. A clip board and stop watch should also be provided for. There must be sufficient lighting to illuminate the page without spilling into the audience's field of vision. It should be possible to dim this light and change from white to blue so as to reduce the effect of spill during blackouts.

The cue board   The cue board is a panel of switches and pushes controlling cue light, bell and buzzer outstations. It is often combined with the intercom control panel. Standard cue light systems provide two coloured lights, red for 'stand by' and green for 'go' at all outstations where actors or technicians will need cues. Each outstation will be controlled by its own 'on/off' switches on the cue board. One 'two-way and off' switch for both lights is not satisfactory. Red and green master switches for group control may be useful. Indicator lights on the cue board in series with the outstation provide a check that the system is in order. Two or three 'pear' switches on long leads which can be plugged into the 'go' light or buzzer circuits to the main technical outstations, should be provided. These will enable the stage manager to move away from the cue board in order to see a visual cue that will be out of sight from the cue board. The outstations most likely to require sockets for the purpose are switchboard, sound control, projection room, follow spots, flys and house tabs. The use of expanding coil cable will prevent the long leads from trailing on the stage. The pear switches should be of different shapes and colours for easy identification and should remain on only while pressed and have a positive action so that the moment of switching from 'off' to 'on' and back, can be felt.

Some systems provide a cancel switch in the 'standby' at the outstation cue light to indicate that the operator is ready for the cue. This is not always satisfactory as the operator must either switch the standby off and leave it off, which leaves it indistinguishable from a failure in the system, or he must flash the

light in which case the stage manager will have to stare at the
indicator light on his cue board waiting for it to flash. A better
method for some positions such as flys and house tabs is to provide a
third circuit in which a switch at the outstation operates a third
light (amber) on the cue board. An alternative system is to provide a flashing standby light which can be switched at the outstation to a maintained or steady circuit. Though costing a little
more this method not only acknowledges the signal but is more
likely to attract attention at the outstation.

The stage outstations should not be in fixed positions but should
be equipped with extension leads so that they can be placed in
whatever position is required for the current production and this
could be on the scenery itself.

It would simplify the stage manager's job, especially when on
tour, if the layout of cue boards in all theatres were as standardised
as a typewriter keyboard. On the other hand, a stage manager who
is resident at a particular theatre, will wish to design the layout to
his own specifications which are unlikely to coincide in all respects
with the personal preferences of other stage managers. However,
the following suggested layout of a combined cue board and intercom panel is given as a basis suitable for most theatres and most
types of productions. The controls for each outstation should be
arranged vertically above one another with the intercom control at
the top of the panel and the call lights from an outstation adjacent
to the control for that outstation. The individual outstation controls, when lined up on the panel, would have all similar switches
laid out in horizontal lines. Below the intercom switches and call
lights there should be two rows of switches and indicators controlling 'warning' and 'go' cue lights, the 'warning' controls being
above the 'go' controls. At the end of each row there should be a
master control contrasting in appearance with the individual
switches. A typical order colour of the switches from left to right
would be:

Outstation	Colour of switch
Switchboard	White
Sound control	White
Projection box	White
Follow spots	White
Flys	Green
Stage left down stage	Green
Stage left up stage	Green
Under stage left	Green
Under stage right	Green
Stage right down stage	Green
Stage right up stage	Green
Orchestra pit	Blue
House tabs	Green

Below the row of 'go' switches the main technical outstations will have a buzzer push, which can be used in cases of a light failing or when circumstances make an audible cue more convenient than a visual one. Audible cues may be better for the switchboard operator. Some outstations will not need audible cues and a blank should be left in the row of pushes where this would have gone. Sockets for plugging leads are also provided for these buzzer circuits. They should have a locking device to prevent the jack being pulled out. In an attempt to get some standardisation of colour coding, the ABTT recommends that colours should be used as follows:-

Lighting & sound outstations	White
Stage working areas	Green
Orchestra dressing rooms, etc	Blue
Public areas, foyer bars, etc	Red

In addition to the cue and intercom controls the cue board will also have to carry such accessory controls as the talk-back volume control and possibly the loudspeaker. All these should be incorporated in the design of the panel.

Intercom system

The performance control by sound intercom is in some ways more vulnerable to mechanical failure than cue lights because the cue light system has the indicator lighting in series to warn the stage manager of failure. There should be alternative methods of communication which can be used if the main system fails, but the first indication of a failure may still be the non-appearance of some vital scenic or lighting effect which can ruin the performance. Everything possible should be done to guard against failures in the first place and to give adequate warning if they do occur. Good maintenance of the system is the first safeguard but precautions against some kinds of performance failure should be part of the design. Relays should 'fail safe', jacks and plugs should lock into sockets. The outstation speaker in the lighting control box should have a direct feed from the performance relay which is not cut out when the stage manager's selector key is on. Apart from this being essential in a soundproof box, it also means that the switch board operator is immediately aware of a failure and can report to the stage manager before the next cue has to be given.

Outstation speakers

The volume of speakers in the stage and flys areas should be adjusted to a level which cannot be heard by audience or actors. Several speakers may have to be spaced along the length of the fly rail so the fly men are always close enough to hear one of them. Another way to get round this difficulty is to use head sets instead of speakers. The connecting flex may restrict movement too much to make them practicable, but where an induction loop or radio system is in use, this problem does not, of course, arise.

The stage manager's microphone should be on a flexible stem and there should be an alternative plug-in hand microphone on a wandering lead. This should be a noise-cancelling microphone incorporating an on/off switch.

Selector key

The selector keys for the intercom system are best grouped with the cue light system on the prompt corner control panel. They must be clearly marked for easy identification and even if they are separate from the other switches they should have the same colour code as that used for the cue light system. The selector key for public areas, bars or foyers should be placed apart from the others and be spring-loaded so that it has to be held in the 'on' position. All other keys should stay in the 'on' position without being held. It is sometimes necessary for the stage manager to leave several outstations switched on for a series of cues so that all his instructions are heard at all technical outstations. A simple and reliable system for performance control would be one where all outstations were on a single circuit and no selection was possible. The stage manager usually gives verbal identification of the outstation to which the cue is addressed, for example 'stand by for electrics cue 15', or 'flys cue 9 go', so that selection of individual outstation keys during a rapid sequence of cues is not necessary. A separate selection of calling (paging) circuits to dressing rooms, staff room, band room, green room, etc, would still be necessary.

Certain outstations should have a talk-back system to allow for two-way conversation with the stage manager. The key technical positions use the talk-back outstations during rehearsal and in case of emergency during a performance. It may also be used for verbal cueing during a performance, but care should be taken that neither the stage manager nor the outstations can be heard by the audience.

During rehearsals, particularly of musicals, there should be a direct talk-back intercom between the director in the auditorium and the stage manager in the prompt corner.

Reply indicators are sometimes provided in the prompt corner so that artists can acknowledge calls from their dressing rooms, but they are not considered necessary in all theatres.

Other equipment

So far we have discussed the stage manager's cueing and intercom controls, but there are a number of other pieces of equipment which should be within his control somewhere in the prompt corner area. Strong lighting is needed by the stage staff to 'set up' on the stage, in the flys, the grid, and the lighting galleries, and this must be under the control of the stage manager. He will also control from the prompt corner, rehearsal lighting for which there should be a few lighting circuits available without having to use the main switchboard. The stage manager has to make sure that no rehearsal or working lights are left on during a performance and for this a change-over switch should be provided. When in the 'performance' position it carries out several safety functions such as making inoperative all bright working light circuits, switching telephones from audible to light signals switching on 'performance in progress' signs in dressing rooms, corridors, etc. The prompt corner will have a connection to the internal telephone system. It is doubtful whether this should have a bell or buzzer at all. During a performance it would have a flashing light with a slightly audible click. The conductor's desk should have a telephone link with the prompt corner either on the house phone system or by a specially provided link.

Very often when the house curtains are down, the stage manager cannot see whether the house lights are full on or off. There should be an indicator light to tell him in the prompt corner. He should have a clock which must be silent and have a centre sweep seconds hand. It must be illuminated but not too brightly.

Safety curtain and drencher controls must be in the vicinity of the prompt corner, placed so that the operator can see the full line of descent of the safety curtain. They must be well guarded against accidental release and clearly marked so that the drencher can never be released instead of the safety curtain.

If the house curtain is power-operated the controls will be in the prompt corner. There may be occasions when remote control on a wandering lead is necessary. In any case the emergency manual operation must be within easy reach of the prompt corner. The stage manager may have other special controls in his care such as pyrotechnic effects. Flash boxes, bomb tanks and the like should be connected through switches which can only be operated by inserting a special key.

Other controls in the prompt corner would be those of the rise and fall microphones, which have already been discussed on page 143. If a production calls for a lot of rising microphone cues they will probably be controlled by a special operator who must have a good level view of the microphones. Alternative plugging arrangements to enable the rising microphone controls to be moved to the OP side of the stage will keep the mike operator and stage manager out of each other's elbow room. When there is an orchestra pit lift one set of controls will be in the prompt corner. Setting the lift in motion at the wrong time could be very dangerous and this is another control which should have a key switch.

Some sound control systems

In the description of the stage manager's control equipment in the prompt corner, the essentials of the intercom system have been outlined. Microphones pick up the sound of the performance and

No. 12:6   *A stage manager's control panel. This panel is fixed and is*
complementary to the movable cue board. It carries controls of stage
equipment other than cueing and intercom. When the house lights are
on, the panel to the right of the clock is illuminated and reads
'HOUSE LIGHTS'.

relay it to all dressing rooms and other selected outstations which
need to be in touch with the performance and are unable to hear it
direct. The stage manager also uses the system to pass messages to
the dressing rooms and other outstations. The loudspeakers at these
outstations may be fitted with volume controls, but these should
affect the show relay only; messages from the stage manager would
be reproduced at full volume. It can be arranged that only the
outstation called has the show relay interrupted and announcements are made to an individual outstation. Some outstations
where the performance can be heard need only to receive calls from
the stage manager and will not require show relay. Sometimes the
stage door keeper has a control unit which enables him to make
calls to certain of the outstations served by the system, but the
stage manager must have priority over the stage-door keeper at
all times. The diagrams which follow show some possible systems
starting with the most simple and growing in complexity.

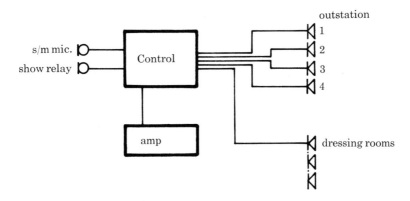

No. 12:7   *This system with one amplifier has a loudspeaker in each dressing room and any other areas needing to receive calls. Separate keys would be provided for each outstation with one key for the dressing rooms. An additional facility with this system would be to have volume controls fitted to each of the loudspeakers, adjusting the show relay but not, of course, interfering with the stage manager's call.*

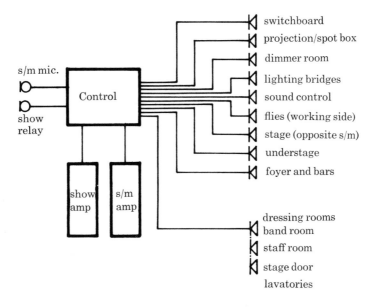

No. 12:8   *This system has one control with two amplifiers providing uninterrupted show relay to areas where required plus selected switching of stage manager's calls to the outstations.*

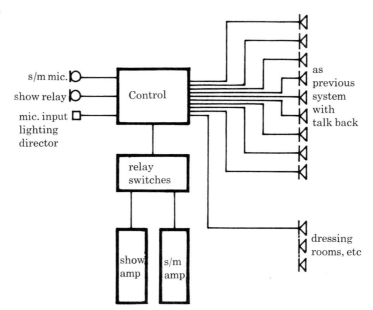

No. 12:9   *This adds to the previous system, talk-back facilities from selected outstations, and a unit which can be plugged into one or more sockets in the auditorium so that the lighting director may talk to and receive replies from various outstations. Again, the stage manager's microphone must have priority at all times.*

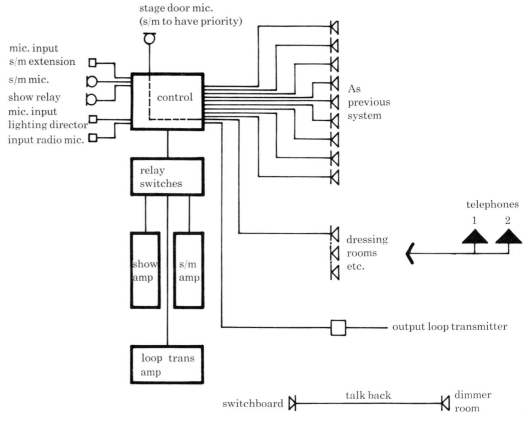

No. 12:10   *In this system with three amplifiers the director of lighting may talk back to selective outstations at the same time as the stage manager is conversing with other outstations. The stage manager still has priority at all times so that when he actuates a call by selecting an outstation already being used by the lighting director, the latter's microphone drops out of circuit. The third amplifier also acts as a standby switchable from the stage manager's control position. Another system would be to have a completely separate intercom system for the use of the lighting director.*

13   Film projection

This is not intended to be a comprehensive treatise on the design of cinemas, but films are so often shown in places intended primarily for live performances that an outline of the subject is necessary.

An auditorium which has evolved from balancing the acoustics and sight lines required for films will not be the same as one based on the requirements of the live theatre. Even the pre-war cinemas where live shows were a regular feature of the programme were very limited in the sort of performance that could be staged. Sometimes in the more important movie palaces quite elaborate music and dancing acts were put on and even in the relatively small suburban houses the cinema organist would contribute a live element. In the design there was a balance between the needs of film projection and the live theatre though it was heavily weighted in favour of the movies. Most new cinemas no longer make provision for anything else but film shows. On the other hand there have been cases in recent years of buildings designed for tactical reasons as theatres which for commercial reasons very soon turned over to the movies. Film shows can be viewed quite comfortably in a theatre, but the demands of live productions are more extensive and exacting and if the architect's brief calls for both it is the requirements of the live performance which must take precedence.

Projection systems   The four standard types of film are described by their width: 8 mm, 16 mm, 35 mm, 70 mm and each has its appropriate type of projection equipment.

8 mm film is for home movies and at the other end of the scale 70 mm film is at present used for very large screen spectacles and needs special equipment that is most unlikely to find its way into a theatre regularly used for live performances.

Projectors for 16 mm film   16 mm projectors are generally used for educational, scientific, advertising and entertainment purposes where audiences are rather small.

When the light source is an incandescent lamp the equipment is comparatively simple, compact and portable. The sound reproduction systems are combined with the projectors. The largest size of incandescent lamp available is 1200 W and if the screen has a matt white surface its size should be limited to 2 m × 2·7 m. It may be possible to project a larger picture successfully if the stray light from all other sources falling upon the screen does not exceed 1% of the luminance at the centre of the screen.

If it is desired to show 16 mm film on a small scale within an auditorium licensed for cinematograph exhibitions, projectors with incandescent lamps may be set up in the auditorium provided that no flammable film is used, no repairs are made to the film in the auditorium with a flammable substance and a clear space of a metre round the projector is roped off to keep people away. This sort of temporary arrangement is not at all satisfactory and should be avoided if possible. The projectors make a noise and spill light and the projectionist causes more distraction as he handles the film cases. 16 mm films can be exhibited on screens up to about 3·5 m × 5 m using projectors with carbon arc, xenon arc or pulsed discharge light sources, but in this case they must be treated just like regular 35 mm projectors and have to go in a projection room. Attachments are available to enable 16 mm films to be shown on 35 mm projectors.

35 mm projectors

Portable or semi-portable 35 mm projectors fitted with incandescent lamps are often used in lecture theatres and similar places where better picture quality is required than can be obtained with 16 mm film. Because of the larger image, bigger screens can be used. On premises licensed for cinematographic exhibitions 35 mm projectors must be in a projection room.

35 mm projectors with carbon arc, xenon arc or pulsed discharge light sources are standard equipment for commercial cinemas throughout the world, and are widely used for high-quality, non-commercial work. Present day standard spools contain 600 m of film which passes through a projector in about twenty minutes. Thus in most cinemas and wherever films lasting longer than this are shown it is necessary to install two projectors if the programme is to be seen without a break.

Light sources

The various different types of light source have different requirements for power supply, ventilation and water cooling. The choice must be known in advance so that the right provision can be made.

Carbon arc lamps

At present the light source which gives the best quality of projection is the carbon arc lamp. The light output is constant, its distribution is almost uniform and it gives very good results when projecting colour films. The carbons burn during the process and the products of combustion must be carried away in ventilating ducts to the open air. In many of the high power carbon arc systems water cooling is essential. The attention of a skilled projectionist is needed all the time to adjust the carbons if necessary. This is not a process which lends itself easily to automatic control.

Xenon arc lamps

Xenon lamps are less adaptable than carbon arcs. They are manufactured in only five sizes ranging from 450 W to 5,000 W and cannot be inter-changed in any one lamp housing. Their principal advantage is that they require no attention other than replacement and are easily controlled automatically. Light output diminishes with age and as the lamps operate under high negative pressure, they are likely to implode if cooled suddenly. Operators must wear goggles and protective gloves when handling them. There are no combustion products, but the arcs ionize the surrounding atmosphere and produce ozone to which some operators may be allergic. This can be avoided by providing ducts from the lamp housings to connect with the open air.

Pulsed discharge lamps

Pulsed discharge lamps can be used only in specially designed projectors made by Philips of Eindhoven. They are manufactured in two sizes – 800 W and 1000 W. The larger of these being bright enough to illuminate screens up to 9 m wide. Double lamp projectors are available which can be used on screens up to 12 m wide. They give a satisfactory distribution of light and do not deteriorate in the way of xenon arc lamps. They are not good for colour films unless colour filters are used to correct the quality of light, which they do at some sacrifice of light output.

Pulsed discharge lamps have the advantage that they do not require skilled attention or special ventilation. When a lamp fails it is instantaneously and automatically replaced. They do require a continuous water supply and drainage at a rate of 5–7 litres per minute. But similar supply and drainage is also required for other high-powered light sources.

Projection systems

At present three methods may be used for film projection: direct, indirect and back projection. The first is by far the most commonly used. Indirect projection requires mirrors and is used as an expedient where direct projection is impracticable. Rear projection has limited uses, but some advantages in special circumstances.

Direct projection

The ratio of width to height (w:h) is known as the aspect ratio. The standard aspect ratio is 1·375 to 1. It is derived from the standard size of frame on cinematograph film, the screen representing a direct enlargement of it.

In the diagram 13:1 the simplest case is shown with the projector axis horizontal and centred upon a vertical screen. In

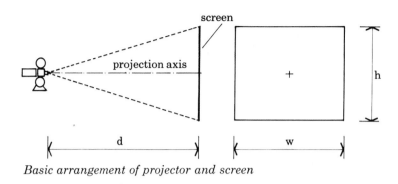

Basic arrangement of projector and screen

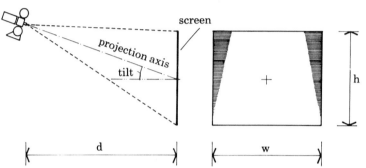

No. 13:1   Distortion of projected image caused by tilt of projection axis

practice this is not always convenient to arrange and so the projector axis is put at an angle to the horizontal. This angle is known as the projector rake. If the screen is vertical the projected image is then distorted as seen in diagram 13:1. Similar distortions occur if the projector axis is tilted up or is set sideways to the screen. Within certain limits these distortions are not important if the outline of the picture is kept rectangular by placing black masking along its edges. For the standard aspect ratio limits for deviation of the projector axis from the horizontal are 18° for 16 mm film and 15° for 35 mm. Distortion of the image can be corrected or reduced by tilting the screen from the vertical so that it is at right-angles, or nearly so, to the projector axis. It is usual to tilt the screen to an angle equal to one half of the projector rake.

Wide screen   The human field of vision normally extends to a wider arc sideways than vertically. Increasing the magnification to the standard aspect ratio gives less value than enlarging the width of the picture. Thus aspect ratios of between 1·65 to 1 and 1·85 to 1 have been adopted since 1950. British Standard 2784: 1956 *Aspect ratios for 35 mm motion picture films*, lays down 1·75 to 1 as an optimum for wide screens. The proportions chosen will depend upon the structural shape of the particular auditorium and the type of film which it is proposed to exhibit. For example, foreign language films usually call for 1·65 to 1 so that subtitles can be shown below the picture.

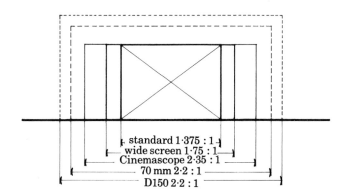

standard 1·375 : 1
wide screen 1·75 : 1
Cinemascope 2·35 : 1
70 mm 2·2 : 1
D150 2·2 : 1

No. 13:2   Screen aspect ratios

Mirror projection

If provision for film projection is included in the initial brief, it should be possible to include direct projection even if the primary use of the building is for live performances, but when converting an existing building, structural considerations may make ideal cinema conditions impossible. These difficulties have been overcome by using either rear projection or mirror systems or a combination of both. Mirror projection can only work if the light source is powerful enough and if the screen does not exceed 9 m in width. The advice of a specialist consultant should be sought.

Rear projection

Rear projection is not practicable for a large curved screen but the system has certain advantages in small auditoria and in lecture halls. Direct rear projection involves a lateral reversal of the screen picture unless specially adapted projectors and sound heads are used. Mirrors also reverse the picture and where rear projection is to be used it is often convenient and an economy to introduce mirrors.

Projection suites

Projection suites may include a projection room, a re-winding room, a dimmer and switch room, a work room and store, remote control room, a projection staff rest room and a lavatory. Unless automatic control equipment is installed, a projectionist must be on duty in the projection room whenever the projectors are in use.

A convenient size for a projection room containing a minimum of equipment is 2·9 m × 4 m. If an effects lantern and spotlight are included, the minimum size should be 5·5 m × 3·9 m. The essential items of equipment are two projectors, sound amplifiers and controls. Ancillary equipment may include an effects lantern, a

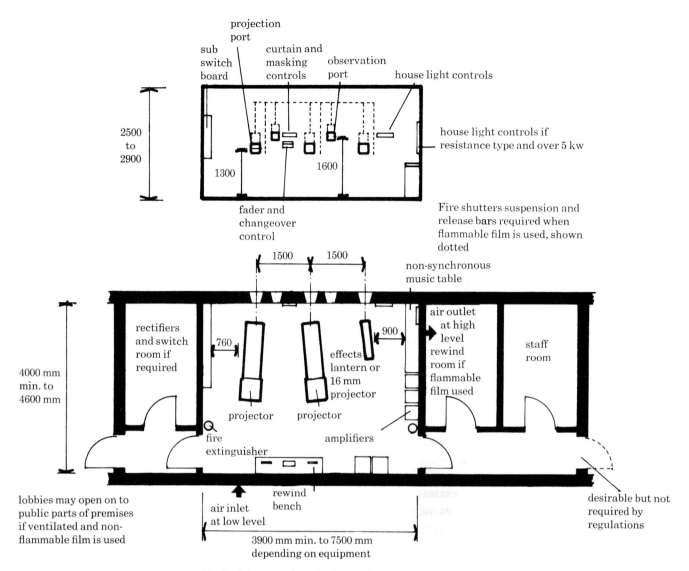

No. 13:3   *Typical layout of projection suite*

non-synchronous music desk, a rewind bench, rectifiers and screen masking controls. Some of these may be in separate rooms.

Projectors are usually placed 1·5 m apart centre to centre which leaves the projectionist about a metre clear in which to work. Statutory regulations demand that there is enough space round the projector and other equipment for the projectionist to work freely. The minimum clear space is 750 mm. A typical layout for the projection room is shown in the diagram. The effects lantern which may double as a follow spot, is normally to the right of the projector and adjacent to non-synchronous music equipment and dimmer controls for the auditorium lighting. There should be an observation port close by.

Ports   The wall separating the projection room from the auditorium will have a projection port for each projector, an observation port for each projectionist and a port for an effects lantern. The projection and lantern ports are glazed with optical-quality glass while the observation ports are fitted with plate glass. Cleaning is simplified if the glass is fitted into hinged metal frames. Where flammable films are used all ports must be provided with fire shutters made from heavy-gauge sheet (3 mm steel) in steel guides and designed so that the shutters fall to cover the ports when released. The regulations require that fire shutters can be released both from within the projection room and from a position in the auditorium, usually at the back. Where non-flammable film is used these fire shutters are not required by regulations, but shutters of some kind should be provided to prevent stray light reaching the screen through the ports.

Amplifier racks

The position of the amplifier racks themselves is not critical, but the controls and change-over switches must be fitted between the projection ports unless a remote-control system is in use. The racks may be placed against side or rear walls of the projection rooms. Some types have to be pulled forward half a metre to gain access to wiring for maintenance or repairs. The diagram shows three amplifiers which would be necessary for stereophonic sound reproduction; monophonic sound only requires one amplifier and a power pack.

Projector power supply

16 mm portable equipment needs a 13 amp or 15 amp socket outlet. For 35 mm equipment with arcs requiring up to 45 amps a single-phase supply is sufficient, but above this three-phase supply is necessary.

Lighting

Lighting in projection rooms has to be arranged with care so that no light is accidentally spilled through the ports. Bracket fittings on the front wall of the projection room to the right of each projector or narrow beam spotlights on adjustable arms suspended from the ceiling are usually considered suitable.

Water supply

Pulsed discharge lamps and all 35 mm projectors with carbon arcs operating at more than 55 amps have to be water cooled. A 15 mm diameter supply pipe and 20–25 mm drainage pipe are enough. Some authorities will not permit direct connection to the water mains and in such cases a closed-circuit system can be used. This requires a tank of up to 700 litres capacity and a circulating pump working at about 2 kg/cm². As a precaution a standby pump should be fitted. In either case water is used at a rate of between 5 to 10 litres a minute.

Heating

Where non-flammable film is used the temperature should not be allowed to fall below 10°C especially when film is stored overnight. Electric heaters controlled by a thermostat are often used. A suitable temperature for working is 18°C and heating must be provided to maintain it. Incandescent lamps or pulsed discharge lamps give off enough heat themselves, except in very cold weather or in large projection rooms.

Ventilation

Projection rooms, rewinding rooms and lobbies connecting them must have a ventilation system entirely separate from the auditorium. Ventilation can be natural or mechanical according to circumstances. Where carbon arcs are used draughts can cause uneven burning and hence changes in light intensity during film projection. Care must be taken to ensure that the ventilation provides a non-fluctuating volume of air at low velocity. Grilles both for input and extract of air must be provided separate from any skylights or windows. Regulations require that there shall be not less than 174 cm² effective clear area per projector installed. The need for additional outlet ventilation for projectors and effects lanterns equipped with carbon or xenon arc light sources have already been mentioned. It may connect directly with the open air by ductwork. If the route to the outside air is at all complicated an extract fan will be needed at the end of the ducting.

Access panels will be needed in the ductwork so that it can be cleaned along its full length. Typical connections to lamp housings are shown in the diagram.

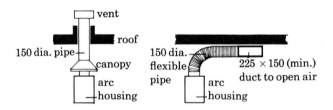

No. 13:4   *Alternative methods of venting projection arc lamps.*

Fire-fighting equipment

No special structural precautions other than those required under the building regulations are necessary where non-flammable film is used. In such cases the Home Office merely recommends that two 2 gallon (10 litre) soda acid or water gas expelled extinguishers shall be provided. Where inflammable film is used an asbestos blanket is required.

Rewinding room

When a reel of film has been shown it has to be rewound and stored for the next showing. Most 16 mm film projectors incorporate a mechanical rewinding device but it is nevertheless better to rewind on a bench so that films can be inspected. Only when flammable films are used is a separate rewinding room required otherwise it may take the form of rewinding space fitted with a bench within the projection room.

Rewinding benches

These are bench tops 600 mm wide at least 1200 mm long and 600 mm high, with a small frosted glass panel set centrally and illuminated from below. This enables the film to be inspected as it passes between rewind heads fitted at each end of the bench. These are made to accommodate various sizes of spool and have to be suitable for the type of projection system in use. There are seven sizes of standard spools for 16 mm film of which the largest is 600 m representing 55 minutes showing time. Larger non-standard spools are sometimes used. 35 mm film is kept in standard spools of 600 m (22 minutes showing time), but some projectors are made to accommodate 1800 m spools, three standard lengths joined together.

Rewind benches are used for splicing together a film which has been broken or torn. Close to the bench or underneath it there should be metal lockers fitted with divisions and spring-loaded, self-closing flaps.

Cinema screens   In the early days of the cinema a small picture was projected on to a flat, matt white screen with an aspect ratio of 1·375 to 1. This is still the usual practice for 8 mm and 16 mm films, but when large and wide screens are used as with 35 mm and 70 mm some important factors must be considered. With a large picture on a flat screen the

No. 13:5   View of a film projection room.

distance from the optical centre of the lens to the edge of the screen is appreciably greater than the distance from the lens to the screen centre. Either the outer parts of the projected pictures are out of focus when the middle is in focus or vice versa. To keep the whole of the picture in focus it becomes necessary to curve a large screen to keep its surface reasonably equidistant from the centre of the lens. The surface of the screen should really be part of a sphere which would be difficult and expensive to make. This is another reason why the standard aspect ratio of 1 to 1·375 has not been used for very large screens. A broader aspect ratio permits screens to be curved in one plane only. Another important consideration is the amount of light available from projection light sources. Twofold to fourfold increases in areas of cinema screens have not been accompanied by equivalent increases in light output from these light sources. If the original type of matt white surface were used in such circumstances, picture luminance would be insufficient. Instead screens have a surface with partial specular reflection characteristics which give an increased luminance within a limited forward sector. It becomes necessary to curve the screen to provide a uniform distribution of the increased luminance but the required curvature depends upon the reflection characteristics. The actual curvature adopted is a compromise between the needs for picture focus and uniform distribution of luminance in the auditorium seating area. This requires the advice of a specialist consultant.

Screen position   Screens are usually spaced on the centre lines of auditoria and normal to them. In the case of curved screens centre lines are normal to the chord of the screen arc. Screens may be tilted from the vertical plane according to the location of the projector, the type of auditorium and the system of projection. Masking is normally adjustable at the sides and sometimes at the top. This black serge masking contains the picture and obtains the maximum apparent brightness.

In auditoria designed for both stage performances and cinema exhibitions many compromises are necessary. A flat picture screen up to 6 m long can be fitted in the proscenium opening in front of the safety curtain or main curtain. It can be housed on a roller in a wooden box set into the forestage and can be raised electrically or by hand. In such cases retractable davits are used to support the top of the screen. Another position for housing the box is under the proscenium arch and hidden from view by a pelmet or valance. The screen is then lowered into position when required.

Variable masking is not practicable for these types of rolled screen. Curved screens or those more than 6 m wide, have to be fitted on the stage behind the proscenium opening. Probably the best solution is to hang them on counterweights from the grid. They tend to take up valuable flying space especially if they are curved. There must be enough flying height under the grid to get the screen well clear of the proscenium. It is possible to hang a lighting spot bar underneath them thus making use of hanging space which might otherwise be lost. Another method is to move them away on castors which is possible if there is plenty of room on the stage to store the screen and if there is plenty of room to manoeuvre it without getting in the way of sets for live performances.

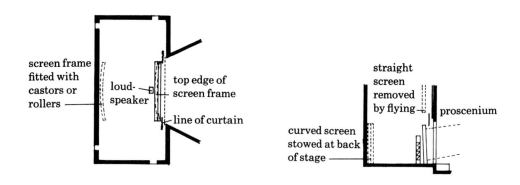

No. 13:6   *Removal of screen by rolling or flying.*

Removal of screen by rolling or flying

Another method is using a screen frame traveller as shown in the diagram. This has the advantage that the screen is protected from damage when it is stored away but it does require the whole of the stage to be cleared before the screen can be brought out.

Screen construction

Screens are generally made from a flame-resistant material such as pvc or metallised fabric, stretched into position by cord lacing to hooks on a special frame, usually made of steel or aluminium lattice construction. Such a screen can be free-standing but lighter construction is possible when the frame is supported by brackets fixed to the rear wall, ceiling and floor. The size is determined by the largest type of picture that will be shown. To this size 80–230 mm is generally added all round to allow for fitting eyelets and localised rucking of fabric when stretched. A further 160–230 mm has to be allowed for lacing. Screen frames are thus 460–920 mm larger overall than the maximum size of picture.

Screen surfaces deteriorate and have to be replaced from time to time. New rolled screens will be delivered in a roll which measures

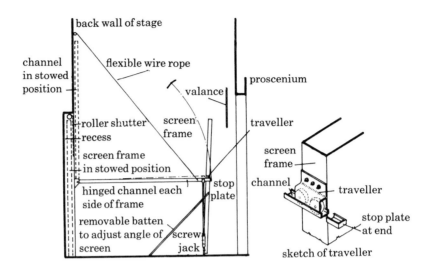

No. 13:7   *Removal of screen by screen frame traveller*

about 1 m in diameter and has a length of about 600 mm more than the height of the screen. These have to be manoeuvred into position without being bent. Masking is usually done with black wool serge fixed along the bottom edge of the screen, but carried on rails attached to the top and sides of the screen and adjusted by cables over pulleys connected to hand or electric controllers.

Screens mounted on stages

Stage screens should have the whole of the back, including the back and sides of loudspeakers, covered with heavy felt or asbestos cloth. Forestages should be carpeted with black carpet or heavy black felt to prevent reflection of sound or light. The stage must have some background heat to prevent condensation on screen and speakers. This also serves to prevent movement of warm air from the auditorium through the screen which can cause deterioration.

Cinema auditoria

Satisfactory viewing conditions in a cinema depend upon each spectator having an unobstructed view of the whole of the screen without picture distortion. The size and position of a cinema screen must be related to the shape and rake of the auditorium floor.

Viewing conditions

The diagrams show what are considered satisfactory viewing angles for 16 mm films and 35 mm films. One geometrical limit which has already been mentioned is the angle between the centre line of the projector lens and the centre line normal to the screen. Other limitations depend upon the dimensions of the screen itself. The angle between the top of the screen and the eye level of the

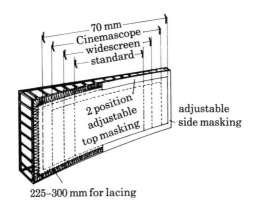

70 mm
Cinemascope
widescreen
standard

2 position adjustable top masking

adjustable side masking

225–300 mm for lacing

No. 13:8   Construction of screen.

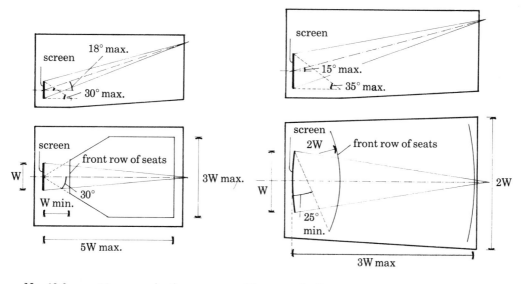

No. 13:9   16 mm projection   35 mm projection

first spectator should not exceed 30° for 16 mm films. A committee set up by the Illuminating Engineering Society to consider 'Eyestrain in Cinemas' recommended that the angle should not exceed 35° for 35 mm film and this has been adopted by the GLC and many other authorities as a condition for the grant of a cinematograph licence.

The position of the closest and furthest seats from the screen are fixed in terms of the width of the screen and the width of the seating area on plan is also limited by the width of the screen. Where 70 mm film and various special wide-screen forms of projection are used there are other dimensional limitations, but these are matters for a specialist.

Acoustics for films   The sound track of a film is complete in itself and the ideal conditions for listening to it would be by direct sound untrammelled by any acoustic characteristics of the space in which it is played. It is common for cinemas to be equipped with quite elaborate stereophonic sound systems and these do not profit from any extra reverberation in the auditorium itself. The ideal cinema auditorium is acoustically dead. This is not possible to achieve in practice, but the low levels of reverberation that can be achieved give poor conditions for live performances. A theatre auditorium is not, therefore, ideal for showing films though it probably has the advantage of a lower level of extraneous background noise than is usual in a cinema. The musical sound track of a film is there not only to underline the dramatic mood but also to drown the level of unwanted noise filtering in from outside and caused by the audience coming and going, eating popcorn and crushing plastic cartons.

Loudspeakers   In cinemas loudspeakers are usually housed behind the screen. For monophonic sound only one speaker unit is required but for multichannel and stereophonic sound reproduction from 35 mm film, three units are used with one on the centre line and the other two spaced equally on either side. Special wide screen processes can have more elaborate speaker systems with five units behind the screen and others placed round the auditorium.

The typical cinema loudspeaker unit is usually much more powerful than any single unit in a theatre sound system. It comprises one horn or cone with a bass response and one or more responding to higher frequencies. Being both bulky and heavy it presents problems of storage and mobility in theatres where films alternate with stage performances. A space of 1400 mm clear between the back surface of the screen and the back wall or any other obstacle on the stage is required. Best results are obtained when the speaker has a solid base such as a brick pier but this is seldom possible in a movable system. The more massive the base the less likely are sympathetic vibrations at harmonic frequencies. Probably the best place to store the speaker is in the wings, but it is possible to have a trap in the stage through which the unit can be lowered to a storage place in the stage basement. This imposes a limitation on the use of the stage floor which may not be acceptable to the stage management. It is inconvenient to have to keep a central area of the stage clear of a stage cloth or any other covering.

14 Administration

The extent of the office accommodation is determined by the administrative structure of the company which is to occupy the building. The needs will vary widely according to the kind of operation anticipated.

If productions are not to originate in the building the administration will be mainly concerned with the box office, the front of house and maintaining the building in general. Touring theatres and most West End theatres come into this category but companies running repertory or repertoire resident in a particular building, will need space for all their staff including those concerned with initiating and mounting a production. Before listing the offices that may be needed we shall outline the staff structure which is likely to be encountered. This cannot be done definitively as each organisation will be different and the responsibilities within it may be distributed amongst the staff in a variety of ways. In small companies one person may have to look after several jobs which in a larger organisation are split into separate departments. The tasks that have to be performed are, however, similar though they will vary in complexity according to the size of the operation.

The ultimate responsibility for the conduct of a theatre will probably lie with a Board of Management or Trust whose Chairman will act as a spokesman. Depending on the ownership of the theatre the members of the Board will be unpaid and elected or appointed to represent local interests. The artistic policy will be in the hands of the artistic director who, once the Board has appointed him, will ideally, take full responsibility for that policy. Looking after the legal and financial side and the running of the box office and front of house, becomes the responsibility of the administrator. These two must work closely together and it should not be thought that their departments are hermetically sealed off from one another. There is a range of tasks that must be attended to and the division of responsibility is broadly as follows.

The artistic director will have under his leadership the acting company, musicians, singers, etc, designer and the production manager. He may also have associate directors, conductors, playwrights and composers working with him. The production manager in turn co-ordinates the work of the stage manager and his staff, the electricians, the workshop staff, the scene painters and the wardrobe. The administrator will be in control of the house manager and his box office staff, usherettes, cleaners, caretaker and boiler man and building maintenance staff, the catering manager and his bar, kitchen and serving staff and the publicity and press department.

There is some confusion in the use of the terms 'director' and 'producer'. In the theatre, the person who gives the actors their moves and conducts rehearsals used to be called the producer. In film making, on the other hand, these functions and the choice of camera positions and shots are always carried out by the director of the film. The producer is the business manager for a particular film production. This anomalous use of titles is one reason for the change in terminology which has now been generally accepted in the theatre. The term producer has been dropped and the person who directs the action and controls the production is now called the director. He may be called in for a particular show or he may be a permanent member of the company. Very often plays will be directed by the company's 'artistic director', but this title implies a wider range of responsibility extending to the whole policy of the company.

Function

Theatre Board meetings will probably take place every two or three weeks but a smaller management committee may meet more frequently.

Artistic Director:
Responsible for choice of plays, artists, etc.

Assistant Director:
Assists artistic director.

Associate Directors:
Conductors:
A company may have directors whose responsibility is for particular productions. Their appointment may be on a permanent basis or just for a specific task.

Accommodation

A board room big enough for the whole board to meet in comfort. Between meetings this room should be available for other compatible uses such as production conferences and committee meetings.

An office large enough to hold meetings and conferences of heads of departments.

Office space close to the artistic director.

Where the establishment is known, the office space can be included in the schedule of accommodation. It is useful to provide space that can be allocated to visiting directors and conductors. For the latter, this would be in addition to the changing room for a performance.

Instructors:
Repetiteur, Ballet Master:
The size and programme policy of the
company may require specialised personnel
– fencing masters – mime instructors, etc.

If these posts are known to exist they will
need office space which may be in the
administration area or close to the
departments with which they are most
concerned.

'Dramaturg', Playwright:
Some companies may have a resident
playwright or a writer whose job is to adapt
new material for the stage.

As above.

Musical Director, Composer:
Where new musical productions are staged
or incidental music is composed or arranged.

The musical director should have space
for a piano in his room.

Library:

This may vary from a few shelves or a
bookcase to a separate room and a librarian.

Music Library:

This is necessary where operas, ballets and
concerts are produced.

Interview Room:

A room is needed where interviews can be
held without interruption from other
members of staff. Auditions would probably
be held on stage or in the rehearsal rooms.

Production Manager:

His office can be associated with either the
general administration or with his workshop
or stage staff.

Designer:

The designer will need drawing boards
and a place to make models. It is probably
better for his department to be close to the
workshops and paintshop.

Lighting Designer:

Where there is a separate lighting designer
he should be closely associated with the
designer.

Costume Designer:

Costume design cannot be separated from
the actual making of clothes and the
costume designer should, therefore, be
placed next to the wardrobe.

Stage Manager:

In larger organisations the stage manager
may have an office located with the general
administration but usually his work is
concerned with the running of the stage
during rehearsals and shows and his office,
therefore, should be closely related to the
performance organisation.

Deputy Stage Manager:

The stage manager's second-in-command
will only have a separate room in larger
establishments.

Assistant Stage Managers:	The stage manager will allocate various tasks which are part of the running of the production, to assistant stage managers, e.g. looking after props and dressing the sets. Their work will largely be on stage and in the property store, but they should have a room near the stage with changing facilities.
Master Carpenter: *Property Master:* *Wardrobe Mistress:*	Except in very big organisations these people will not require separate offices but will have places within their workshops.
Chief Electrician:	The electrician will require a workshop for the repair and maintenance of stage lighting equipment, lanterns, etc. This should be situated where it has easy access to the stage or the lighting galleries.
Electricians: *Flymen:* *Stagehands:*	All the backstage and workshop staff will require changing rooms, cloakrooms, lavatories and access to showers.
The Administrator: Works closely with the artistic director.	An office with easy access to the general office and secretaries.
Administrator's Assistants:	The administrator may have an assistant in larger organisations. He will have book-keeping and secretarial assistance but these will probably be housed in the general office.
House Manager: Supervises the box office and the front-of-house staff.	His office should be preferably close to the box office. He is the liaison between the public and the management and acts as host during the performance. The traditional practice is for him to wear evening dress as a kind of uniform to identify his function to the public. He should have a wash basin and somewhere to change, in or next to his office.
Catering Manager:	Where the provision of refreshments is on any kind of scale the person in charge will need an office and probably secretarial assistance. A location close to the restaurant is better than with the other administration offices. Larger restaurants may need an office for the chef.
Press and Publicity:	Places of entertainment must advertise their performances through the press, posters and mailing lists. Publicity and public relations are increasingly important and space will be needed for a press and public relations officer in the area of the general administration.

Assistants and Secretaries:

The administration bridges the division between stage and front-of-house and most of the secretarial and paper work can be grouped together to serve both the artistic director and the administrator.

Storage:

Space is required for duplicating and dealing with post, a store for stationery and office supplies, a store for archives and a store for publicity material, programmes, etc.

Lavatories and Cloakrooms:

The office staff should be provided with lavatories and a cloakroom for both men and women.

Whether all these administrative activities are accommodated in one office or are divided depends on the client's policy and the scale of the scheme. There are offices which are better related to the departments which they control and however neat it may seem, it is not often practicable to centralise all the administrative functions in one part of the building.

The detailed design requirements of the offices for theatre type buildings do not differ from those of other types and it is not proposed to discuss them here. The subject has been dealt with at length in other publications.

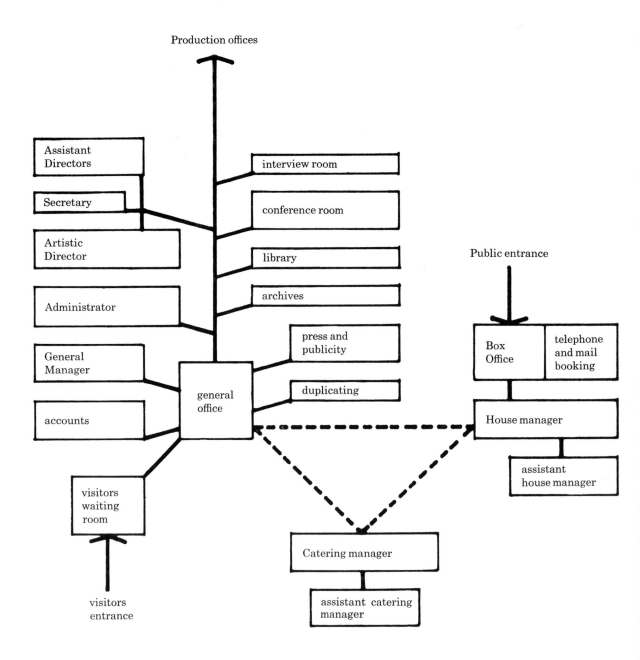

No. 14:1   Administration

15 Performers' accommodation and rehearsal space

Many of the older theatres are so poorly provided with accommodation for the cast that actors have had to put up with near slum conditions which would hardly be tolerated in other industries. Actors may have to spend long hours in their dressing rooms, not only during and between performances but also during rehearsals.

A distinction should be made between dressing rooms used by actors and other performers for changing into costume and applying stage make-up, and changing rooms for musicians and others who change from outdoor clothes into evening dress, for instance. The scale of provision of dressing and changing room accommodation depends on the type of production and will range from one shared room each for men and women, to a complex including special rooms for stars, shared rooms for other performers, chorus rooms, musicians' rooms and rooms for conductors and soloists. It will be seen that the status of the performer tends to produce a hierarchical order in the arrangement of dressing rooms. This can be in conflict with flexibility which is essential to meet the varying demands of different types of production. It is not economical to provide for the largest possible cast. In a theatre where most plays have an average of about ten actors, occasional large-scale production will entail temporary dressing room arrangements in, for example, a rehearsal room or a committee room.

The tables which follow give dressing-room and changing-room requirements for various types of production.

Opera house This schedule is for a resident company producing a full repertoire of large-scale operas. Smaller scale works can do with less and if it is understood from the start that the productions cannot comfortably include the more extravagant works of Wagner, Richard Strauss, etc, then accommodation can be reduced.

If an opera house only takes touring companies the demands on space are less. The economics of touring large productions force such companies to limit their repertoires and the scale of presentation.

Opera dressing rooms

Type of performer	Number	Occupancy of room	Remarks
Male principals	3	single	Should be at stage level. At least one room for each sex should have a piano or there should be a performance practice room. These star dressing rooms should be planned to allow for visitors and dressers.
Female principals	3	single	
Male minor principals	20	up to 4	These rooms should, if possible, be at stage level. They would be allocated according to the size of cast and though 4 could be accommodated they would more usually have two or three occupants.
Female minor principals	20	up to 4	
Male chorus	35		
Female chorus	35		
Extra chorus	30	up to 20	It is an advantage if these large shared dressing rooms can be sub-divided into smaller spaces if required.
Male ballet dancers	10		
Female ballet dancers	10		
Male supernumeraries	40		Make-up in these cases may be done by specialists in a separate room.
Female supernumeraries	12		
Children	20		The employment of children is governed by regulations. They will have to be separated from other performers and will have to be accompanied by responsible adults. A separate w.c. must be set aside for their sole use.

Ballet dressing rooms

Type of performer	Number	Occupancy of room	Remarks
Male principals	3	single	Should be at stage level and it is desirable for them to have their own showers and lavatories. These star dressing rooms should be planned to allow for visitors and dressers.
Female principals	4	single	
Soloists (male and female)	24	up to 4	These rooms should if possible be at stage level. They would be allocated according to the size of the cast and would more usually have 2 or 3 occupants.
Male corps de ballet	25	shared	The numbers will depend on the kind of company and the size of the stage.
Female corps de ballet	25	shared	
Children	20		Children must be chaperoned, accommodated separately from the rest of the cast and must have their own lavatory accommodation.

Changing rooms for opera and ballet

Type of performer	Number	Occupancy of room	Remarks
Conductors (visiting)	2	single	The room should be large enough to accommodate an ensemble of 6 musicians for rehearsal. These rooms are for use during performances and rehearsals. A resident conductor would have separate accommodation.
Orchestra leader	1	single	
Section leaders	6	shared 2 – 4	
Musicians	120		The sexes should be segregated but as the proportions vary large rooms should be capable of sub-division.

Variety, musicals, spectacles: dressing rooms

Type of performer	Number	Occupancy of room	Remarks
Principals	4	single	Should be adaptable for 2 occupants.
Minor principals	30	up to 6 per room	Capacities of rooms can be varied to take a maximum of 3, 4, 5 or 6 performers. As many as possible of the principals' and minor principals' rooms should be at stage level.
Chorus, etc.	60	shared up to 20	The size of cast will vary with the size of the production but this should be sufficient for the average maximum.
Children	variable	they may be accommodated in one of the chorus rooms.	Regulations for child performers require that they be separately accommodated and properly supervised.

Variety, musicals, spectacles: changing rooms

Type of performer	Number	Occupancy of room	Remarks
Conductor	1	single	The room should be large enough to hold auditions.
Musicians	30	shared	Divisible for male and female musicians, e.g. 5 rooms to take a maximum of 6 each.

Drama dressing rooms

Type of performer	Number	Occupancy of room	Remarks
Principals	2 – 6	single or occasionally two.	The principals and as many minor principals as possible should be at stage level. The allocation of dressing rooms will vary continually according to the scale of the production and they will only be fully occupied for large shows.
Minor principals	16 – 20	shared 2, 3, 4, 5 or 6.	
Supporting cast	20 – 40	shared in rooms holding up to 15.	

The scale of operation of a theatre for drama depends very much upon the policy of the company using it. The figures above would be adequate for most repertory theatres but a specialised company like the National Theatre or the Royal Shakespeare Company, running several productions at the same time, would require more accommodation. Theatres mainly for amateurs do not need as much.

Changing rooms are not often needed when a theatre is used mainly for drama, but, the programme for most theatres is bound to include the occasional musical production. For instance, most repertory theatres have an annual pantomime. Though this seldom calls for more than three or four musicians, a larger orchestra is occasionally desired and a reasonable allowance would be a shared changing room for about 15 musicians. It is preferable to have two rooms so that the sexes can be segregated, but if musical performances are rare it may be necessary to make temporary arrangements in one of the dressing rooms. Where they are regularly performed, the accommodation should be similar to that recommended in the previous table for variety, musicals and spectacle.

Concerts: changing rooms

Type of performer	Number	Occupancy of room	Remarks
Conductors	2	single	
Soloists (instrumental)	4	single	There should be a piano in at least one room.
Leader of orchestra	1	single	
Musicians	120	shared	As the proportion of male to female musicians varies there should be flexibility in the changing room provision, say, 6 holding 20 each.
Soloists (singers)	4	single	There should be provision for making-up.
Choristers	250	shared	The sexes should be segregated and a flexible system adopted to allow for varied proportions.

Recitals: changing rooms

Type of performer	Number	Occupancy of room	Remarks
Conductors	2	single	
Soloists (instrumental)	2	single	There should be a piano in at least one room.
Soloists (singers)	2	single	
Musicians	40	shared and segregated	For flexibility it should be possible to sub-divide larger rooms or provide several smaller ones which can be suitably allocated.
Choristers	40	shared	

Dressing room equipment and layout

The most specialised function of a dressing room is putting on stage make-up which has to be done in artificial light of similar quality to that used on stage. It does not follow, however, that all daylight must, therefore, be excluded at all times. Actors often have to spend long hours in their dressing rooms during and between performances or rehearsals and in addition to natural light and ventilation it is of great benefit psychologically for them, to have contact with the outside world through a window. Blinds and/or curtains cut out the daylight when they are making up. For applying stage make-up each performer must be able to see in the dressing room mirror head, shoulders and head-dress while in a sitting position.

Hinged side mirrors are sometimes provided, but these lead to difficulties with the lighting and most performers will have a hand mirror as part of their make-up kit. The make-up top itself should not project further than 450 mm from the face of the mirror or the actor will be pushed too far away to see properly.

Dressing room lighting

Traditional dressing room lighting is bare tungsten bulbs ranged round the mirror and this is still the most usual method. The bulbs themselves should not be more than 40 watt to avoid dazzle, but most actors insist on at least 60 watts to make up by. It is important that some light should come from above so that hairdo's and wigs can be adjusted. Some special effects may depend on a particular colour of light on a particular colour of make-up in which case a colour filter can be rigged up. Fluorescent lighting must not be used.

As an alternative to bare bulbs or in addition to them, lights on flexible arms can be fitted to either side of the mirror. This has

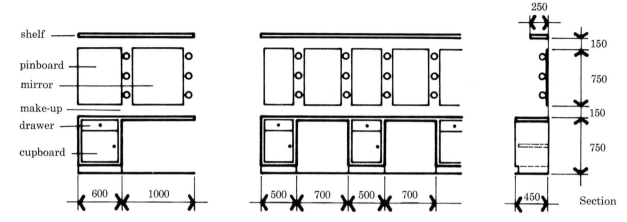

No. 15:1   Single dressing place.   Two or more dressing places.

advantages of greater adjustability and helps to avoid glare. In
chorus rooms and where space is very limited a continuous run of
mirrors with the bulbs above it may be used. Performers can be more
closely spaced, but illumination from above alone is less effective
than from all sides.

These dressing-table lights should not be the sole illumination
in dressing rooms and each position should be individually
switched. When make-up is complete and actors want to relax it is
a great advantage to be able to switch off the more dazzling lights.

Each dressing room should be provided with one long mirror so
that performers can check their costume before leaving to make an
entrance on the stage. Lighting should be arranged so that they are
illuminated when standing in front of the mirror.

Power sockets   Shaving sockets should be provided between each pair of dressing-
room positions.

The authorities have often frowned on ordinary power sockets in
dressing rooms largely because there has been a tendency to misuse
them for plugging in electric fires and cooking equipment likely to
cause a fire hazard. However, if the dressing rooms are properly
heated and there is a green room where brewing up can be done,
these abuses are less likely. Power sockets are useful for hair driers
and curlers and similar gadgets. They are also useful for vacuum
cleaners for cleaning carpets and costumes.

Storage in dressing rooms

A small cupboard underneath the make-up top between each position is useful for personal possessions and a drawer should also be included.

Management policy may be for locks to be provided on these cupboards, but in many theatres there is a continual change round of cast and keys are easily lost or taken away by mistake. The stage-door keeper or someone on the stage management staff should have the responsibility for issuing and looking after keys. Performers have to store their day clothes and any changes of costume for the production they are engaged in at the time. When they are performing in repertoire, they may have to keep costumes for more than one production, but it will be the policy of most wardrobes to store all costumes not currently being used in the wardrobe department. A minimum length of hanging rail of 600 mm should be provided for each performer, but double this where there are likely to be numerous changes and a repertoire of productions.

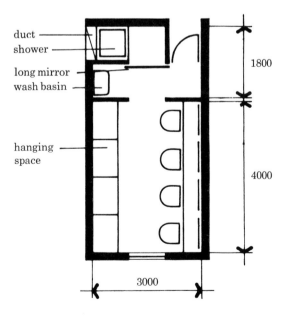

No. 15:2   *Dressing room for 4 performers   Area 17·4 m².*

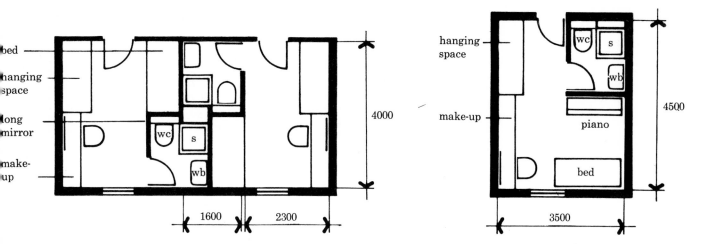

No. 15:3   Single dressing rooms. Area 14·4 m². Single dressing room with provision for piano. Area 15·7 m².

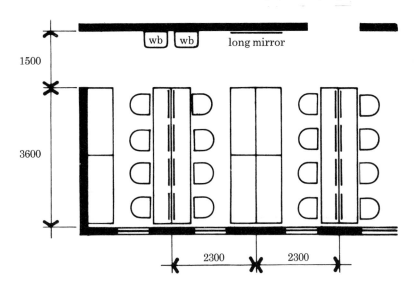

No. 15:4   Communal dressing room. Area 8·3 m² each bay.

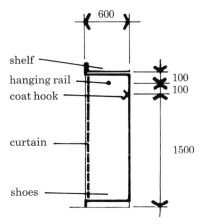

No. 15:5   Section through hanging space.

In chorus dressing rooms the amount of fixed hanging rail can be reduced to 300 mm each.

A convenient method of temporary storage of costume is on wheeled racks which can easily be moved to and from the wardrobe. It is best to hang all clothes and costumes on hangers, but for changing rooms, coat hooks could be used instead.

Hats and wigs need a shelf which can be over the dressing-table mirror or over the hanging rails, and boots and shoes should have a rack under the hanging space. Hooks at 1 m height are useful for hanging swords and similar costume accessories.

Pin boards are an essential provision in dressing rooms, for greetings telegrams and notices and these are very often put alongside make-up mirrors.

No. 15:6   *A dressing room at the Wyvern Theatre, Swindon.*

Furniture

Most dressing room furniture is built-in, but loose chairs will be needed. The most useful chair is an armless, upholstered, swivelling and adjustable type. It is desirable to make room for a day bed or sofa in every dressing room or at least in the star dressing rooms. If there is no room for a bed, there should be some easy chairs in the other dressing rooms. The floor finish should be soft for the comfort of bare feet and for quietness. Carpet is best, but soft-backed vinyl or similar materials might be used for economy. Waste-paper baskets are essential in every room, at least one to every two performers.

Washing and bathing

A wash basin with hot and cold water should be provided in every dressing room holding up to four performers. In larger rooms there should be at least one per four positions. Each basin should have a splash back and mirror over it and a towel rail within easy reach.

Showers should be provided on a similar scale to wash basins and the best arrangement is for these to open off the dressing rooms. However, for reasons of economy it may be preferred to group the showers together at least for the larger dressing rooms. In this case the access from the dressing rooms must be easy.

Lavatories

Lavatories for the cast will normally be grouped together but it is desirable to provide some dressing rooms with a private lavatory opening off a lobby. A star dressing room becomes something like an hotel room with its own small bathroom containing shower, wash basin and wc. The scale of provision of lavatories for performers may be laid down by the local authority, but this minimum is seldom sufficient. As a guide, one wc should be provided for every five females, one wc for every eight males and one urinal between every five males. Each wc compartment should have a coat hook in it. Wash basins should equal the number of wc's and urinals. There should be lavatories close to the entrance to the stage and for each sex on each level of dressing rooms.

Circulation

The most important circulation link for the dressing rooms is with the entrances to the stage. The best position is at stage level close to the main entrance to the stage and at least the principal rooms should be located there. Site limitations and the complications of fitting in many other essential parts of the building close to the stage make it unlikely that all the dressing rooms can be at stage level. Ideally, they should not be more than two floors up or down and the vertical circulation should be close to the stage entrance. Passenger lifts are not usually acceptable to connect performers with the stage. This attitude is due to a fear of missing an entrance through being trapped in a lift which has broken down. There are situations, particularly on restricted city sites, where valuable space could be saved at ground level and better conditions could be created for performers if the dressing rooms were to be located higher up, even over the fly tower. Passenger lifts would in this case be essential, but they would have to be exclusive to the dressing rooms and their use would have to be carefully disciplined to ensure that they were never out of action during a performance. The performer may often have to go quickly from dressing room to stage wearing an elaborate costume. The doors through which he passes should not be less the 850 mm wide and the corridor should not be less than 1500 mm to avoid encounters with another performer, similarly attired going in the opposite direction. Corridors should not be less than 2400 mm high to allow for head-dresses. The designer must take care when choosing the ironmongery to avoid door handles which tend to catch in clothing and with hazards like the unprotected end of a handrail or a hose reel projecting from the wall. It is very likely that the corridors will have various pieces of equipment in them such as asbestos blankets, fire extinguishers and telephones. These must be recessed or situated where they do not encroach on the clear width of the circulation.

Entrances to stage

There should be a lobby between the route from the dressing rooms and the stage to prevent light straying from one to the other. It should also be remembered that the human eye takes an appreciable time to accommodate from a brightly lit to a dimly lit area. A sudden transition from one to the other may result in a few moments of temporary blindness. The lighting in the backstage area should, therefore, be contrived to reduce in intensity before the lobby to the stage is reached.

The lobby also acts as a sound lock preventing noises from the dressing rooms filtering through to the stage. There are occasions when an actor listens for a cue before making an entrance through the door to the stage. This is more likely to occur in open stages where the doors may be in full view of the audience.

There should be at least two entrances to the stage, one on either side and in large theatres and opera houses there may be three or four. Sometimes a separate entrance for the chorus is necessary in opera houses so that there is no danger of the principals getting tangled in the crowd. In the proscenium type of theatre a way round from one side of the stage to the other is essential. A corridor running round the back of the stage possibly serving the dressing rooms at the same time is the straightforward answer. Where space is limited the cross over may have to be on the stage itself behind the set and in this situation the more depth of stage the better. The disadvantage of the cross over on stage is that performers have to creep round as silently as possible in dim light, avoiding the obstacles such as stage braces and cables which are likely to be lying about. If they are close behind a backcloth or a cyclorama they may set this moving merely by the draught they cause.

In addition to entrances for performers at stage level, there are often others from under the stage through traps and at high level to a Juliet balcony. In open stages and particularly in theatre-in-the-round, the actors come through the auditorium. They should have entrances segregated from the members of the audience to avoid clashes with latecomers or other straying spectators. These entrances must be on the same level as the stage or with an easy ramp in case props have to be rolled or wheeled on to the set. In any case it is very difficult to make a rapid entrance or exit which entails running up and down steps and in the dim light often necessary for dramatic purposes, steps are a physical danger.

Specialist make-up room

Professional performers and most experienced amateurs will put on their own stage make-up, but children and novices have to be made up by specialists who require a room in which to do their work. If this is a rare occurrence, probably one of the dressing rooms will be used, but when it is a regular procedure a room will be needed especially for this purpose. It is basically a dressing room with mirrors and lighting but with plenty of room for the make-up expert to move round the subject rather like a barber round a barber's chair.

Children's dressing rooms

When there are children in the cast there are strict regulations about how they are treated. In the dressing rooms they have to be segregated from the adult members of the cast in separate rooms where they are looked after by chaperons, and they must have lavatories for their exclusive use. Some managements may include a child supervisor on their staff who will need a small office with a desk, chairs and a filing cabinet.

Changing rooms

Many of the recommendations for dressing rooms apply equally to changing rooms without the emphasis on the arrangements for stage make-up. Single rooms for conductors, soloists and singers need a minimum area of about 10 m², but if an upright piano is to be accommodated this should be increased to 14 m². For communal changing rooms a minimum of 1·5 m² should be allowed for each person.

Single rooms need a hanging cupboard for street clothes and top coats, a cupboard and drawer for personal possessions, a wash basin with mirror over, a long mirror, a wide shelf (600 mm) covered with something resilient like linoleum for resting musical instruments, a table and chair (armless), a sofa and/or an easy chair. At least one single room in a concert hall or opera house should have a piano. Sometimes a conductor's room has to be big enough for him to hold auditions there or ensemble practice in which case space is needed for a baby grand piano. These activities may, of course, be carried out elsewhere, in a practice room for example.

In shared rooms, each user needs a chair, hanging space and some table space. It may be worth considering lockers for clothes and personal possessions particularly for resident companies. There should be a long mirror in each room and some other mirrors on a scale of one between two or three persons.

It is preferable for single rooms each to have their own wc and shower, but they may have to be grouped for economy. The shared rooms will have access to lavatories and if possible to showers though this is not essential.

Orchestra assembly area

The members of an orchestra should have an assembly area next to their entrance to the orchestra pit or concert platform connected to it by a sound lobby which will also act as a fire check between the auditorium and backstage areas. It should have benches and a broad shelf for musical instruments. In opera houses and theatres the conductor will probably use the same route, but in a concert hall there should be a separate entrance to the platform for the conductor and soloists.

The circulation of the orchestral musicians and choral singers should be segregated from that of the conductors and soloists. In an opera house, the conductor's changing room will be grouped with the dressing rooms of the principal singers.

Instrument store

The storage arrangements for musical instruments depend upon their size. The smaller ones will be looked after by individual musicians who will need the broad shelves which have already been mentioned in their changing rooms. The larger instruments and their cases should be stored near to the musicians entry to the orchestra pit or concert platform. The route from the loading bay to this store should be direct and without steps if possible. Openings and corridors should be wide enough for a grand piano. If the piano does have to be taken to a different level it must have a lift to move it. In theatres with a forestage convertible to an orchestra pit, the lift for this can be used.

Green room

The green room is the performers' common room, rest room and canteen where snacks and drinks can be served. For a small theatre one room of about 20 m² might have to serve all these purposes while in an opera house playing in repertoire with a resident ballet company and orchestra a separate dining room with a canteen kitchen, a bar, a lounge and a writing room might have to be provided. The scale of green room facilities depends on the policy of the management. In a repertory theatre the whole company including performers, stage technicians and workshop staff might use the same room. In another situation the stage staff might have their own common room and the musicians theirs. If the principals have well-equipped and spacious dressing rooms where they can entertain visitors, they are less likely to use the green room.

As it is for the use of the actors during performances and rehearsals the green room should be near the dressing rooms, the stage and the stage door. It must have daylight and, if it can be arranged, a pleasant outlook helps to improve the atmosphere of relaxation which it is the main purpose of the green room to provide. The room should be furnished with easy chairs, coffee tables, sofas, some writing tables and chairs, a television set and the floor should be carpeted. Refreshments should be available served from a counter on a self-service basis. A small kitchen with sink, cooker, refrigerator, and crockery and cutlery storage should be included. If the budget allows for the employment of someone responsible, alcoholic drinks can also be served and there will have to be a lockable bar and store. In smaller organisations a vending machine for various kinds of hot drinks has the great advantage of saving staff time. In any case there must be some provision for serving hot drinks to the green room, dressing rooms and changing rooms.

The stage-door keeper

The entrance for artists and technicians to the backstage areas is normally supervised by the stage-door keeper who has a small office strategically placed so that he can check and if necessary stop anyone coming through the stage door. For the artists he will receive mail and post it in a rack of pigeon holes, take messages and look after valuables. He probably keeps the keys on a keyboard including those of the dressing rooms rather in the manner of the chief porter at an hotel. He will take care of visitors, both wanted and unwanted. The usual planning arrangement is to have the door-keeper's office with a counter open to a lobby just inside the stage door. The lobby acts as a sound lock between the outside and the corridor leading to dressing rooms and the stage. It also acts as a reception area with seats and a table where visitors can wait. A notice board will be required in a prominent position just inside the stage door.

The stage doorman will usually receive outside telephone calls for the artists with whom he is connected by extensions in the dressing rooms and green room.

Not all small theatres can justify the expense of a full-time stage-door keeper in which case his duties have to be divided amongst the stage management. Outside telephone calls have to be made and received through a coin-operated call box situated in the dressing-room area preferably somewhere near the green room.

Rehearsal spaces

All types of production need space where they can be developed in rehearsal. The stage or platform will at times be used for this purpose and final dress rehearsals must take place on the stage so that scenery and lighting technicians can practise their contribution to the show. In a busy theatre or opera house there will be great demands on the stage area and it will not be available long enough or at the right times for a continuous programme of rehearsals. Very often companies have to find space away from the theatre, a situation which can be expensive and is certainly inconvenient.

A rehearsal room is what we shall call a place where the whole company can prepare a drama or opera. A rehearsal studio is the term given to a space for the preparation of dance and ballet productions and, like the rehearsal room, its dimensions must be related to the size of the stage upon which the production will eventually appear.

Other spaces for the practice and tuition of speech and movement, music and singing, need not be related to the size of the acting area. These we call practice studios.

Rehearsal rooms

For opera and drama the rehearsal room should be as big as the acting area of the stage plus a margin of about a metre at the back and sides and space of two or three metres at the front for the director to have a broad view and for the performers to have some space into which they can project their performances. The height of the room should be related to the height above the stage floor which can be used by performers.

The rehearsal room should be close to the dressing rooms and it is an advantage if it is also close to the stage and workshop. If, for example, a production involves rostra built on the stage it is very useful if these can be moved into the rehearsal room so that the actors can practise their moves in conditions closer to those which will apply on the stage.

For some, nothing short of a replica of the stage and all its equipment will suffice, but it is most unlikely that this can be economically justified.

Flexibility of use

More often than not a rehearsal room will have to serve other purposes. For instance, if it is to be used as a chorus dressing room it should have provision for make-up tops and mirrors in some portable or dual-purpose form. There should be wash basins within easy reach and portable hanging rails for clothes and costumes. If it serves as a ballet practice room it should have a barre and some wall mirrors as long as there is some means of covering these or hiding them away when they are not wanted.

A room of the size of a rehearsal room has obvious potential for other activities and it is most likely that it will be used for experimental productions to which the public will be admitted. If this is the case, a separate entrance accessible from outside will be needed and the circulation of the public should be planned so as to avoid routes used by the actors.

If there is no easy connection with lavatories for the public in the main foyers, provision should be made for both sexes near the entrance to the rehearsal room.

A small stage-lighting system will be needed consisting of some lanterns hung from a grid of 50 mm diameter tubes hung from the ceiling. The control can be of the simplest kind with slider dimmers, for instance. A small sound system with speakers, amplifier with inputs for microphone, tape deck and turntable pick-up will normally be sufficient. It is best to house these controls in a cubicle off the main rehearsal room floor, preferably with a view over the heads of an audience.

The rehearsal room will be equipped with a piano, probably an upright. Chairs and one or two tables will be needed for the director and other technicians and if the room is used for performances to the public an appropriate number of chairs will be required. The stacking variety is probably best with means of linking chairs together. Rostra may also be needed for the audience to sit upon and it is clear that a good deal of storage space is necessary to house all the equipment which may otherwise clutter the floor while rehearsals are in progress. The room should, in any case be properly heated and ventilated, but if public performances are given and there are say between 100 and 150 people present the quantity of fresh air required is quite considerable and a system must be designed specially to cope with it. As with any auditorium, the noise of the ventilation must be kept to a minimum and this cannot be achieved with the cheaper and cruder methods.

When the only use is for rehearsals it may be possible to get sufficient natural ventilation through windows, but for a performance these have to be blacked out and artificial ventilation becomes essential.

Orchestra and choir rehearsal

Whereas rehearsal rooms for drama or opera should have a flat floor, one for an orchestra, choir or opera house chorus should have rostra similar to a concert platform so that all musicians and singers have a clear view of the conductor or coach's instructions.

The size of an orchestral or choir rehearsal room depends upon the number of members who will be using it. Choir members need about 0·6 m² each and orchestral players 1·1 m². A grand piano is essential and chairs and music stands should be provided.

Rehearsal studios

Rehearsal studios for dance and ballet productions have many requirements similar to those of rehearsal rooms for drama and opera. They need, if anything, more space round the acting area of the stage and they need height of about 4·5 m. A sprung floor is essential. The walls require large areas of mirror up to a height of 2·4 m which can be curtained off on occasions and a practice barre at a height of 1·2 m and 300 mm from the wall. The studio will be furnished with a grand piano, a table and a few chairs.

Practice studios

Individuals or small groups may wish to practise or rehearse without the necessity for the full dimensions of the acting area or the orchestral rostrum. For this purpose, practice studios or practice rooms, sized according to the number likely to use them, should be provided. They would be used for speech and movement practice, singing practice and by musicians. They often act as classrooms.

Finishes and lighting

All rehearsal spaces need good sound insulation to avoid disturbance both of and by rehearsals taking place in them. They should have a floor finish similar to that of the stage but wall and ceiling finishes may need some sound absorbents to improve the acoustics.

Artificial lighting must give a high evenly distributed illumination, but daylight should not be excluded. Some windows with a view outside have a psychological advantage, but wall space and a background which does not distract are essential. Most windows should, therefore, be at high level. Where a rehearsal room is used for performances before an audience, it must be possible to exclude all external light with lightproof blinds.

16 The performance organisation

In other chapters, various aspects of the technical working of a stage have been discussed and many of these come within the 'performance organisation', a title which indicates the group of activities which are involved in a live performance as distinct from those which are essentially part of the preparation for a performance.

In general these activities are under the control of the stage manager and his task can be made easier by careful planning of the areas concerned. During a show, a rehearsed sequence of events is taking place depending on split-second timing not only by the performers themselves, but also by the technicians controlling lights, sound, stage machinery, curtains and scenery. Their duties often have to be performed in near darkness and as silently as possible. All entrances to the stage or technical spaces open to the auditorium must have adequate sound insulation. Doors should have solid cores and be provided with acoustic sealing strips all round. Where there is likely to be much coming and going during a performance a lobby should be formed with doors at each end. There must be a very thorough sound insulation between any workshop and the stage and, for this purpose, a metal roller shutter is inadequate.

The performance organisation should function independently without being interrupted by or interrupting the work of general preparation for other presentations. It is unwise, for instance, to put a paint frame on the stage where the scene painters can only work when there is no performance and only under difficulties when there is a rehearsal. For that matter there should be a rehearsal room for most of the early work on a future production so that the current set need not be disturbed by rehearsals on the stage.

Compromises may be forced by economic restrictions and may be quite acceptable in small scale schemes and where the main use is for amateurs. But a busy theatre working in repertory or repertoire needs to have its performance organisation independent of all activities not directly concerned with the actual performance.

Scene dock

There are also storage and maintenance spaces which should come within the performance organisation. The scene dock is the place for storage of scenery for the current production or repertoire of productions. The desirable size depends on the scale of productions and on the number of sets likely to be used in repertoire. Its clear height should allow for the highest pieces of scenery plus $\frac{1}{2}$ m or the same as the height under the fly gallery in theatres where this occurs. Storage space is always in demand, but the scene dock close to the stage is probably in a position where space is at a premium and it is not sensible to use it for long-term storage. The most economical use of the scene dock is for the current production or repertoire of productions and the management should either be ruthless with old sets or if they must be stored they should find somewhere less important to put them.

The connection between the stage and scene dock should be generously sized, going to the full, clear height and wide enough for rostra, built pieces and boat trucks to be trundled through. Three m wide would usually be sufficient, but circumstances may vary this. The fire authority will probably require a fire separation of the scene dock from the stage area and may also require an automatic smoke vent at high level similar in detail to that over the stage tower.

The dock door

This is the place to mention the 'get-in', which is the term used for the process of bringing scenery, lighting equipment, props and costumes onto the stage. There should be a route for a large pantechnicon to approach the stage end of the building where it can back up to a loading bay, preferably at tailboard height, and have its cargo discharged under cover. In very large schemes it may be possible for lorries to drive right into the building, but it is more likely that loading and unloading will be through the dock door either directly onto the stage or into the scene dock from whence it will be moved again to the stage. The dock door should be as high as the tallest item that will go into a pantechnicon plus 500 mm and the width 2–3 m. A door such as this, opening straight onto the stage from outside, presents a noise hazard and it must be carefully detailed to reduce sound penetration. Again, a roller shutter is not satisfactory. It is better to have a solid wood door with acoustic sealing strips all round and, if the area at the rear is near a road or is likely to be noisy for any reason, some form of lobby or two sets of doors with a substantial gap between them should be considered.

Repair workshops

Minor repairs to the set during the run of a show can be carried out in a small workshop opening off the stage or the scene dock. Here the stage carpenter should have a bench and vice and storage space for tools, nails, screws, etc. In a touring theatre or a long-run theatre in the West End, where scenery is not made on the premises, this workshop has a greater importance and should be large enough to handle the biggest flats or built pieces that may be used. A repair and maintenance bench near the stage is useful in all theatres, but if the main workshops are in a close and convenient relation to the stage it is probably better for large pieces of scenery to be taken there for repairs.

Wardrobe repairs

A similar situation arises with the wardrobe. There should be provision for running repairs and minor alterations to be made to costumes in the current production. This activity comes within the performance organisation; it will be linked closely to the laundry and dressing rooms and it is essential in all theatre, opera and ballet operations. Where productions are initiated and there is a costume-making workshop, it may at first appear that a separate wardrobe unit for the current show is not needed, but on further examination it may be found that the main workshops are not geared to cope with the sort of emergencies which occur during a performance. They may even be well enough organised for their staff to work from 9 till 5 rather than uncivilised theatrical hours. The wardrobe mistress should, therefore, have a small workshop with a sewing table, hanging space for costumes in the current production, racks for footwear, hats and accessories and an ironing board. The laundry should be alongside.

Property store

Properties are of two kinds, those which are part of the set such as furniture, chairs, lamps, etc, and hand properties which are used by the actors as a part of the action of the play, such as a letter or a tray of food or drink. These are all the responsibility of the stage manager and his team. A property store, either opening directly off the stage near the control point (prompt corner), or close to the main actors' entrance to the stage, will be needed to lay out those hand properties which are essential to the action of the drama. Often food has to be eaten on stage and this will usually be prepared by an ASM who needs a sink and small cooker either in or close to the property store. Larger pieces of furniture and set dressings will probably be stored in the wings if there is more than one setting in the production. For longer-term storage there should be a furniture and drapery store, but this is not really part of the performance organisation any more than the property-making workshop and storage would be.

Electrician's workshop

The electrician's workshop has been mentioned briefly in the chapter on administration. Its place is with the performance organisation because it will be used directly in connection with the current production. It is unlikely that there will be any other workshop on the premises dealing with electrical work and it must, therefore, cope with all the general maintenance and repair of lanterns and electrical equipment. It needs a workbench with metalwork vice and storage for tools. The electrician's duties as part of the performance organisation influence the location of his workshop. It should open directly to the stage area, but not necessarily at floor level where there is always a great demand for space. The majority of lanterns will be suspended above the floor, many of them on lighting galleries in the auditorium ceiling or in lighting slots reached from above and it can be an advantage for the electrician's base to be near these. He should also be within easy reach of the dimmer room where he may urgently need to replace a fuse at short notice. While quick access to these parts of the stage and auditorium complex is essential, the workshop itself ought to have daylight, if possible, and its connection with the quiet area should be well insulated against noise.

Theatres can collect a great many lanterns which begin to clutter up floor space if they are not put away in a store. The best way of keeping them is hanging them on lighting bars, i.e., 50 mm barrels. Another vital commodity which must be stored away, preferably under lock and key, is the stock of lamps or bulbs for all the stage lighting equipment. The electrician will probably also be responsible for re-lamping the auditorium lights and the light fittings throughout the rest of the building. This store should have adjustable shelves to deal with all the various sizes of lamps and tubes which may be used. He also needs hooks on which to hang the coils of flexible cable used for extensions to lanterns, space for stands, clamps and other accessories and there are smaller items such as his stock of colour filters which should be found a place. These should be stored flat, they need an area 1300 mm × 650 mm of shelf or drawer and a bench space of a similar area where they can be cut to shape.

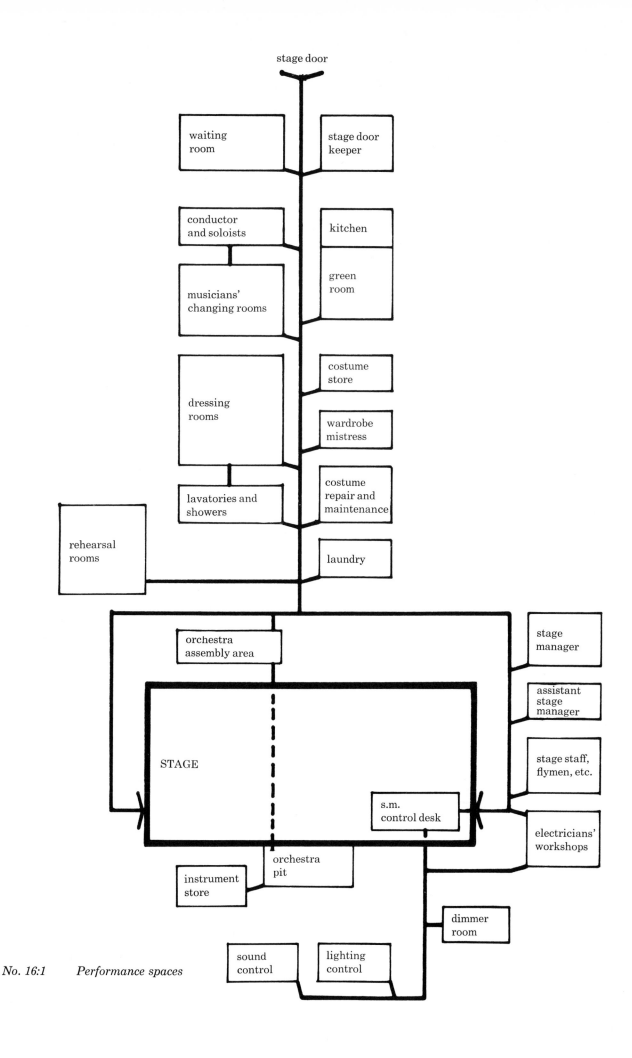

No. 16:1　　*Performance spaces*

17　Production spaces

Areas for the activities described under the section on performance organisation will be needed in all places where live performances involving scenery and costumes are to be presented. Production spaces, on the other hand, are only needed where productions actually originate.

They do not have to be part of the building complex or even on the same site as the rest of the building though there are obvious advantages when they are. Site conditions or the high cost of land within a city centre may bring economic pressures to bear on the location of what is, in effect, a light industrial activity. The production spaces are workshops manufacturing a range of specialised products. Their industrial nature should be understood and they should be planned to make the process of manufacture as simple and and efficient as possible. This objective is easiest to achieve outside urban areas where there is plenty of space, rather than on a congested site in the centre of town. However, all the advantages of moving out may be outweighed by the cost of transport, the labour of loading and unloading and the time wasted in traffic delays.

There are some specialised items which will be made elsewhere or sub-contracted out for even the best endowed companies. Only the biggest organisations will, for instance, make all their own wigs. The more that can be done under the control of the company's own designers, the more complete is the opportunity of artistic expression. It is very desirable to have the resources of elaborately equipped workshops at command but it may be difficult to justify on economic grounds. Where an organisation has extensive production workshops it will, from time to time, have capacity to spare and it may be able to take on work for other companies. Very often it is worthwhile setting up a hire department, a useful and lucrative sideline, particularly for the wardrobe whose stock of costumes will be in demand for amateur productions. The first priority in the provision of production spaces must go to the workshop for building and painting scenery. Stage sets are often bulky and they are expensive to move about and to store. Professional companies, and many amateurs, will expect to have a set tailored to their own conception of the show they are presenting and to the stage upon which they will present it. The opportunities of hiring sets which will be really suitable for a particular application are very limited. No serious theatrical enterprise can get along without its own scenery being specially made. There are excellent commercial firms who make scenery for new productions in the West End, for instance, but not many undertakings will be able to afford to employ them. The situation with costumes is less restricting; they are easier to store and there are theatrical costumiers who both make up to special design and hire out their stock. It is, of course, desirable if a company can both design and make costumes to measure to suit its own actors, but for a short run this may be uneconomical. The demands of a particular production influence the resources needed to fulfil them, for instance, some classic plays not only have a large cast, but need several changes of costume for the principals. A series of such shows in repertoire will need a large wardrobe organisation to cope with the output required. Less ambitious enterterprises will develop a pattern where some things are made and some hired.

When the brief for a new project is being drawn up, these are some of the arguments which must be thought out before company policy on the extent of the accommodation for production spaces can be decided. It may be necessary for management and architects to carry out feasibility studies to arrive at a reasonable conclusion.

Carpenters' workshop   The process of manufacture of a set begins when the designer presents his sketches, working drawings and model to the head of the carpenters' shop. The most common materials used will be timber framing and scenic canvas and these are still the cheapest for stage scenery. The amount required will be taken from stores along with plywood for rostra. All kinds of other materials may be used provided they are sufficiently flame-proof and if they are not in stock they will have to be ordered.

Chapter 10 on scenery describes this in more detail. The frames will be made up on long carpenter's benches, canvas stretched over them and tacked down in the case of flats and plywood fixed to them for rostra. All kinds of special pieces such as steps, doors and windows, fireplaces, etc, may have to be made in the carpenters' shop.

Assembly area   The various components of the set as they are made will pass, together with any suitable stock items, to an area where a trial assembly can be made. The dimensions of this depend upon the

No. 17:1   *View of workshop.*

area a large set will occupy on the stage and there must be sufficient
height to clear the tallest flat.

It is useful to be able to fix blocks to the roof structure so that
parts of the set which will be suspended can be dealt with in a
similar manner for the trial assembly. The floor should be carefully levelled to make it easier to align the parts of the set which
must fit accurately together.

There must always be an assembly area but in smaller scale
schemes it may just be one end of the workshop or a clear space in
the middle with the work benches round the walls.

Workshop equipment   Carpenters' benches against the wall have easy access to power
sockets for hand tools and wall racks, but for handling larger
assemblies, a bench with space all round it is more useful. Some of
the larger woodworking machines must have a clear area in which
to manoeuvre the pieces of timber which are being shaped. The
diagrams give an indication of these requirements.

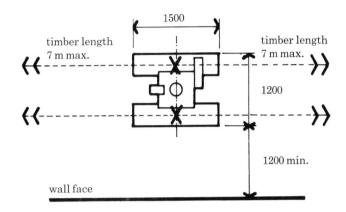

No. 17:2   *Space requirements for woodworking machine.*

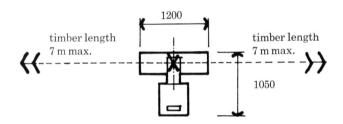

No. 17:3   *Space requirements for mortiser.*

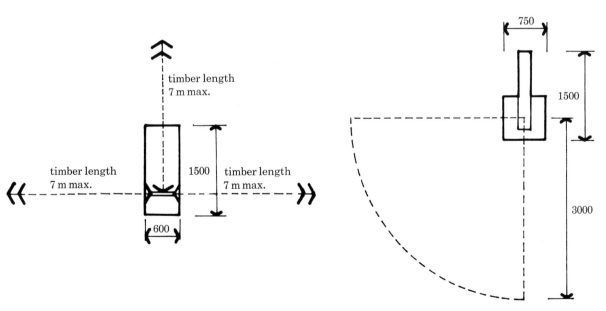

No. 17:4   *Space requirements for circular saw.*   No. 17:5   *Space requirements for band saw.*

The workshop should be planned to accommodate the following machines though the list is not exhaustive and special purposes may call for a different selection.

Circular Saw, Planer, Band Saw, Mortiser, Grindstone.

To work efficiently, the machines must be firmly bolted down on non-vibration mountings and it would be unwise to plan a carpenters' shop on the assumption that they are easily portable.

Electric power must be brought to the woodworking machines which may need three-phase supplies. For most smaller workshops it is probably cheaper to power the machinery with electricity, but there is much to be said for pneumatic equipment. A mortiser, for instance, working on compressed air, is much more efficient because it is not necessary to keep removing the cutting head from the work in order to clear away wood shavings. Pneumatic nailers and staplers are very much quicker and more accurate than a man with a hammer. The canvassing of flats can be done far more rapidly than by traditional hand methods. Another important use for a compressor is paint spraying in the paint shop.

Dust extraction

Sawdust and shavings have to be cleared away and for a busy workshop a dust-extraction plant should be installed. The system consists of extract points located close to the cutting blades of machines, from which sawdust will be carried away in metal trunking under the power of an extract fan to a discharge point where it will be collected in bags.

Heating

There is bound to be a certain amount of dust and sawdust in the atmosphere and for this reason it is not advisable to use a warmed-air system of heating. Probably the most comfortable environment for working in is provided by radiant panels overhead. The workshop has to be high and when the source is far enough away the unpleasant feeling of heat at head level, which is sometimes felt with low ceilings employing this form of heating, is avoided.

Ordinary hot water radiators are often used, but they take up valuable wall space. Piping and radiators should be sufficiently robust in positions where they could get knocked about. These remarks apply to cooler and temperate climates; the problems in hot countries will produce quite different answers.

Lighting

The walls of the workshop will sometimes be used to stack timber or pieces of scenery. Windows in them would be vulnerable and their existence restricting to workshop operation. There should, of course, be daylight but it is better for this to come from rooflights or clerestory windows high up out of harm's way. The best light is north light and if too much direct sunlight is allowed to penetrate there may be overheating problems in summer-time. Artificial light should produce the intensity of illumination recommended for woodworking shops by the Illuminating Engineering Society which is from 200 to 250 lux. Fluorescent fittings will produce this intensity most economically.

Finishes

Finishes in the workshop should be appropriate for industrial use: robust, easily cleaned and cheap. The surface which needs most thought is the floor. The importance of accurate levelling has already been stressed and this can be achieved in various finishes. Scenery is made for a timber stage floor and timber is for that reason alone a good choice. It can be made level, is fairly easily cleaned, fixings can be made into it and it is not particularly tiring to work on. On the other hand it is fairly expensive compared to some industrial finishes such as asphalt and its life in a workshop is limited.

The workshop should have a large sink with hot and cold water and a bench with a gas ring for heating glue and size. Timber storage may be in the workshop itself or preferably separate with easy access for long pieces of timber to the main workshop area.

Timber store

The maximum length of timber is not likely to exceed 7 m and a convenient method of storage is along a wall of this length on 50 mm galvanized tube cantilevered 900 mm from a wall at about 1200 mm centres. Rolls of canvas and other materials need shelves about a metre deep. Sheet materials keep their shape better if they are laid flat, but they are easier to select if they are stacked upright. The latter method is more convenient if the turnover of material is fairly rapid. Nails, screws, ironmongery and various odds and ends can go on shelves or in cupboards and drawers.

Staff room

The workshop staff should have a rest room with space for coat hangers or preferably lockers. There should be lavatories and showers for both sexes. These staff rooms can be shared with other departments if they are not too far away but should not be mixed up with the performance organisation.

Paintshop

The process of preparation now takes the scenery to the paintshop for the scene painters to get to work on it. Other scenic elements such as backcloths and gauzes will be taken direct from a cloth store to the paintshop. The dimensions of the paintshop should be such that the built-up pieces of setting can easily be reached, but the item most critical to its size will be the largest backcloth that is likely to be used on the stage. Painted backcloths are quite common in the proscenium theatre and are an essential element in operas and ballet. Their size is related to the proscenium and to the depth of the stage and this size in turn, determines the dimensions of the paint frame. In Britain, the common practice is to paint backcloths in a vertical position suspended on a paint frame,

No. 17:6   Paint frame with movable bridge.

but this is not the case in the rest of Europe where it is more usual for painting to be carried out with the cloth laid out on the floor. Designers there, who often do the painting themselves, prefer this method and it is one that should be considered if there is any likelihood of continental designers being invited to design sets in this country. Paint can be built up more thickly on a horizontal surface and there is no fear of drips running down. However, this method demands a great deal of floor space and where both budget and site area are restricted, economic factors favour a vertical method.

Paint frame   In a vertical position the problem of letting the painter get to all parts of the canvas from top to bottom, can be solved in two ways. Either the painter remains on floor level and the frame is moved up and down to suit him or the frame remains stationary and the painter is carried up and down on a bridge. There are advantages and disadvantages in both methods. Where the frame moves, the painter can at any time step back from his work to see the effect he has obtained, which is not recommended on a bridge. There has

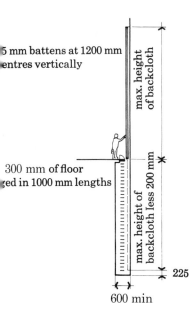

5 mm battens at 1200 mm
entres vertically

max. height
of backcloth

300 mm of floor
ged in 1000 mm lengths

max. height of
backcloth less 200 mm

225

600 min

No. 17:7
Section through paint frame.

No. 17:8   *Movable paint frame in slot.*

to be a slot in the floor so that the frame can sink far enough for a painter to reach the top of the backcloth, say 2 m from the floor. The vertical dimension of the wall against which the paint frame moves must, therefore be almost twice the height of the maximum size of the backcloth. If this is an outside wall without the rest of the building to brace and buttress it, construction could be expensive.

The pit into which the frame sinks should be accessible for cleaning and should have a drain so that cloths can be washed down.

The paint bridge travelling against a fixed frame is less convenient for painters, but does not involve the structural problems of a pit in the floor. It does have the advantage that high, bulky pieces of scenery that cannot be put on the frame can be painted from the other side of the bridge. One paint frame large enough to take the largest backcloth is sufficient for most operations, but where there is a heavy repertoire, and in particular in opera houses, it may be necessary to have several paint frames though they would not all have to be full size. Very often the painter is only concerned with painting flats; these can be done on a much smaller frame.

Paintshop equipment   The paintshop should be equipped with a large sink with hot and cold water for general use and a bench for preparing colours and cleaning tools. Gas rings will be needed, mounted on the bench or possibly in the form of a small cooker hot plate. Some of the paint will be applied with spray guns. If the workshop is already equipped with pneumatic tools, flexible airlines can be taken from the compressor plant to feed the spray guns, if not, small compressors will have to be connected to power sockets. When paint is brush applied a useful accessory is a mobile palette which consists of a trolley on castors holding colours, brushes, buckets and cloths which can be trundled around the paintshop. Scenery will eventually be seen on the stage under artificial stage lighting and there should be a few lanterns in the paintshop which can be rigged up to give similar lighting conditions. Most painters, however, prefer to work by daylight when they can. An even north light from above is best and direct sunlight should be avoided. The staff of the paintshop will share the facilities provided for the workshop. From the paintshop the set goes to the scene dock and from there it goes on to the stage.

The backcloth will be rolled and taken to the position on stage where it will be attached to suspension lines. A rolled cloth can easily be 15 m long and it is important that the relation between the paintshop and the stage should be carefully planned to enable an object of this length to be moved on to the stage without it causing too much havoc by being swung about. Paint frames have been put at the back of the stage itself. This can sometimes be justified when there is a very deep stage, but the more usual reason in smaller projects is to economise. A busy stage used for shows, rehearsals and perhaps cinema shows and recitals in between, will not leave the scene painters very much undisturbed time to do their work. In these situations the poor scenic artist usually has to work in the small hours of the morning.

It is far better to separate all workshop activities from the performance organisation. The fire authorities will probably insist on a two-hour fire barrier between workshops and stage, and in any case, acoustic separation is essential. The workshop staff should be able to work normal hours without fear of interfering with anything happening on the stage.

Property workshop   Properties are defined in chapter 10 on stage scenery. They may be made in a wide variety of materials such as wood, metal, plaster, fabrics, papier mâché, rubber and plastics particularly polystyrene and grp.

Properties made of wood can be made in the main workshop especially where it is equipped with a lathe, band saw, etc. Smaller items do not, however, need the height of the main carpenters' workshop. A room with 3 m head height would be sufficient.

Equipment

Equipment should consist of a sink with hot and cold water, a gas ring and working benches along the walls. These should be 800 mm wide and each working position should take up 1400 mm run of bench. There should be socket outlets for hand tools and storage space on shelves and in drawers. Daylight and artificial light should be as recommended for the carpenters' shop. If there is going to be a great deal of metal work, it is probably better to have a separate workshop. In recent years plastics have become more and more important, particularly expanded polystyrene which can be carved into all kinds of shapes very easily. Glass reinforced plastic (grp) particularly in the form of polyester reinforced with fibre glass, is a material which has largely replaced metal for such things as helmets and armour. During manufacture this material gives off a vapour with a very unpleasant smell and it should be given a well-ventilated room to itself.

Other techniques such as blow moulding of polystyrene sheet are also gradually being introduced. The painting of properties will probably be carried out in the property workshop rather than the main paintshop and it may be worth considering installing spray booths.

Storage of properties

The actual props being used in the current production will be in the property store which is part of the performance organisation, but there is also a need for a longer-term storage of properties, particularly if the company is performing in repertoire. Space must be provided for the following items: Furniture, which will include tables, chairs, sofas, desks, etc, carpets and stage cloths which can be rolled and stored on long shelves cantilevered from the wall, crockery, glass, cutlery, etc, which are better put away in a cupboard, and spears, swords and other weapons which are best hung in racks or from hooks.

A separate store is required for cloths, draperies, curtains, etc, some of which may be quite bulky and long shelves cantilevered from the wall are probably the best way of dealing with them.

Wardrobe

A distinction has already been drawn between a costume maintenance workshop which would be part of the performance organisation and the main manufacturing wardrobe which will now be described in this chapter.

Costume making is a manufacturing process which must be carried out in a proper sequence if it is to be efficient. In addition to cutting, sewing and fitting costumes, facilities should be provided for dyeing and painting cloth, for millinery, for making accessories and even for making boots and shoes.

The designer's sketches are discussed in the supervisor's office and a programme of work is decided. The actor's measurements are taken or checked with records and paper patterns are cut out on a drafting table. This would be about 900 mm × 1800 mm and should have space all round it. The next stage is cutting the cloth which is done at cutting tables 1200 mm × 1800–2400 mm. These must have access all round and there should be an allowance of 12–14 m² per table. During the rest of the process tailors' dummies are used. These will be mobile, but a person working at one will need about 3–4 m² of floor space. Each sewing machine on its table with a chair and a space round it, takes up about 1100 mm × 1100 mm. It is unlikely that hand- or foot-operated sewing machines will be used now and 13 amp socket outlets should be allowed in a convenient position for each electric machine.

The general lighting should be reasonably bright, but it is a good idea to have adjustable lamps near each sewing machine to give the operator extra light where it is needed. Other tables for sewing and general use should be 750 mm × 1200 mm. Each of these with a chair needs about 5 or 6 m² of floor space. Ironing tables can be built-in but it is more common to find the portable domestic type. There should be a bench nearby for standing irons and equipment. Each ironing board needs 6 or 7 m². Another useful portable piece of equipment is a wheeled cabinet or trolley with shallow drawers for boxes of pins and needles, cotton reels, etc. The costume shop should have a sink and draining board with both hot and cold water laid on.

Storage   It is probably best to store raw materials for costume-making in a separate room. Rolls of dress fabric are usually about 1 m wide, but curtain fabrics are more likely to be 1300 mm wide. A system of deep pigeon holes or shelves can be used for bolts of cloth and drawers or boxes on adjustable shelves for small supplies and haberdashery. Made-up costumes, while they are in the workshop, will be stored on hanging rails which can be fixed or, more conveniently, mobile. Tubular hanging racks on castors can be used for storing costumes temporarily in the costume shop itself and for taking the completed clothes along to the dressing rooms. If there is a lift nearby, the hanging rails should be designed to go into it. It has been assumed that men's and women's costumes will be made up in the same area, but it may be necessary to have separate fitting rooms. Each of these should have an area of about 10 m² and be provided with a wall mirror in which a full-length view can be obtained.

Dye shop   A separate area is needed for dyeing and painting cloth for the costume shop. There will be a heated dyeing vat alongside a large sink, plumbed with both hot and cold water. The dyestuffs and acids will be stored on shelves or in cupboards and will be weighed out at a bench traditionally topped with marble. Colours for painting cloth will be mixed at another bench faced with laminated plastic. The colours should be stored nearby on shelves or in cupboards. Painting would be done on a plastic-topped bench or table with working space all round.

Drying room

A drying room should adjoin the dyeshop. The wet cloth will here be draped over a drying rack which can be made of steel tube galvanised or plastic covered. The tubes of the rack should be fitted at about head height at $\frac{1}{2}$ m intervals and each tube should be about $1\frac{1}{2}$ m long. Moisture will drip on to the floor which should be laid to fall to a floor gulley. A suitable floor finish such as asphalt should be chosen. The speed of drying will depend on a good circulation of warm dry air.

Millinery and accessories

Millinery work will need its own area for making and storage. Though related to the work in the costume shop it should have its own separate accommodation.

Making hats and accessories involves sewing by hand and machine, but other techniques such as grp, more appropriate to the property workshop, are also employed. The work will usually be done seated at worktops about 750 mm wide with about 1 m run for each person. Each position should have a drawer for tools and shelves for materials, hatblocks and wig-blocks. The room should have a sink with hot and cold water and a bench with a gas ring. Each position should have access to a 13 amp socket outlet and, in addition to a good overall illumination from both daylight and artificial light, individual adjustable lamps should be provided for each position. Floor space should be allowed for a sewing machine and ironing board. Cupboards or a small storeroom with adjustable shelves will be needed for fabrics, paints, glue, wire and the accumulation of raw materials which come into use for this work.

Wig maker

Wig making would require similar accommodation. Even if wigs are not made on the premises, there should be a well-ventilated store room fitted with 300 mm deep shelves for storing them in boxes or on wig-blocks.

Shoemaker

Boots and shoes are an important element in stage costumes and some production organisations may include a separate shoemaker's workshop. Like the other work rooms it requires a bench, a sink with hot and cold water, good light both natural and artificial, power sockets, storage drawers and cupboards for tools and materials and racks for the products.

Jeweller

Jewellery for the stage is most often hired from specialist firms, but if it is made by the company it will probably be in a corner of the property workshop. The proper jeweller's bench is fixed at a height of about 1050 mm and has a semi-circular cut-out of about 450 mm diameter at each work position. Gas is needed for soldering and there should be a sink and drainer with resistance to the acid which is used.

Storage of costumes

When describing the dressing rooms, the necessity for a place to store costumes for the current production was stressed. When they stay within the building, costumes are best hung on rails either fixed or of the mobile rack type which has been mentioned already. When they are taken out of the building, to go on tour for instance, they are traditionally packed in skeps which are strong baskets, easily lifted and stacked by two people. Average dimensions are 900 mm × 650 mm × 650 mm and doors and corridors along the route they will take should be wide enough to let them pass. Skeps are usually moved about on trolleys and if they have to travel between floors there should be a hoist big enough to take them. It is convenient to be able to load them on to lorries from a loading bay at tailboard height.

Dark room

Photography can be used extensively in stage settings both in its own right and as an aid to scenery production. There is an increasing use of projected scenery as light sources become more efficient and more intense. Slide making will often involve photographic processes.

Publicity too relies to a great extent on photography and it may be worthwhile setting up a photographic department with a proper dark room to cope with all the various demands that can arise. The extent of the accommodation depends on the scale of the enterprise and on the kind of equipment it is proposed to install. The most important provisions are ventilation, drainage and a plentiful supply of water.

Recording studio

From time to time a theatre company will want to record sound effects or music for use in a production. It may be possible to do this in the auditorium itself which is equipped with microphones and has a sound-control booth, but the acoustic conditions will not be suitable for many types of recording. A company can employ the services of a professional recording studio if the need is occasional, but where sound recording is going to be a regular activity it is worthwhile for it to have its own studio. The first essential is for this to have extremely good sound insulation separating it acoustically from the rest of the building. Approach to it should be through sound lobbies with acoustic seals round doors and sound absorbents on the walls.

The ventilation system must be as near silent as possible. The recording equipment should be in a control room separated from the studio by a double-glazed sound-insulating window. There is little point in attempting to give sizes of recording studios as these will depend entirely upon the scale of use which a company proposes. If the proposals are ambitious and likely to be elaborate, expert advice is essential.

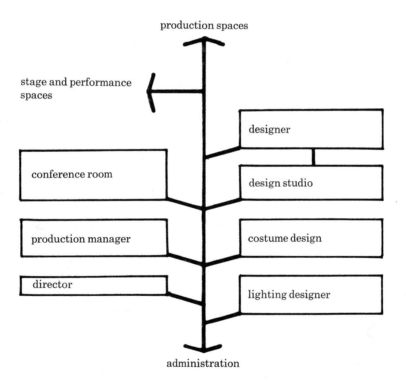

No. 17:9   *Production offices*

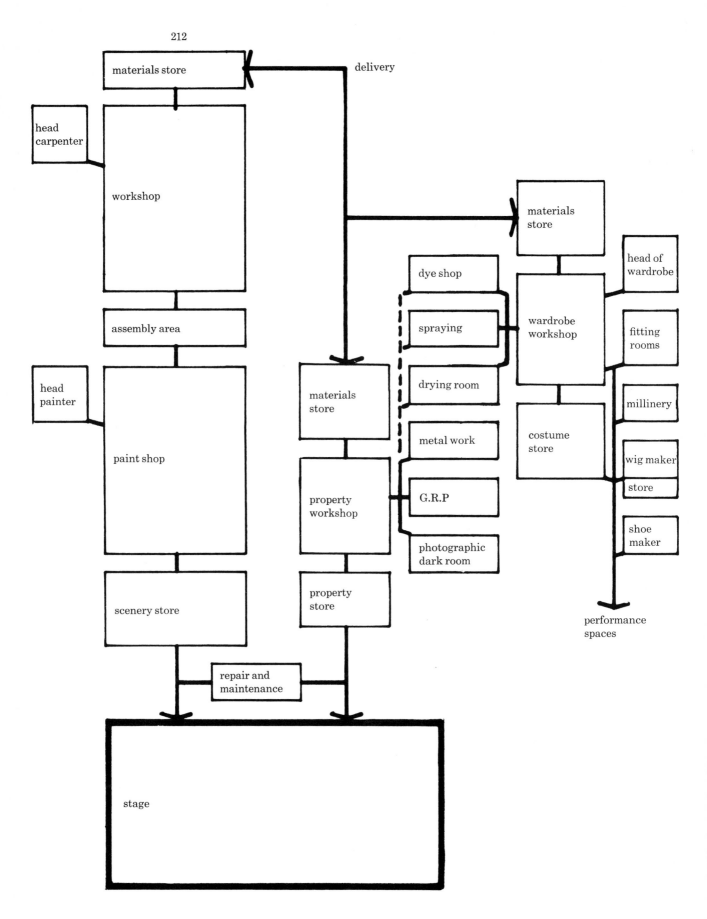

No. 17:10   Production spaces.

18 Public areas

Each age dictates the form of building it needs and one would not expect theatres built for a world subsisting without films, television, motor cars and aeroplanes to be ideal in the 1970's. A very different society with increasing leisure time and a range of staple entertainment on tap in almost every home, needs something of special interest to attract it away from its fireside or rather teleside armchairs. Fortunately electronic gadgets are still no substitute for the immediacy of being physically present at the moment of creation nor can they provide social contacts with other people.

There are times when people go to the opera, theatre or concert hall as much to be seen as to see. In the cinema it is usually only the film première which attracts this kind of audience, but for theatre and opera house patrons the social occasion is often as attractive as the performance itself. This motivation is considered unworthy by some serious-minded persons and it is true that there was a time when the social activity was clearly more important than the quality of the performance. Artistic standards were low and the intellectual content was trivial. A visit to a place of entertainment emphasised the stratified structure of society. The building itself stressed the segregation of society into classes. Patrons would dress according to the variously privileged parts of the auditorium for which they had bought seats, and the entrances and foyers serving the different tiers of the auditorium would often not connect one with another. The second world war finally ended the dress conventions and informality became the rule. The average audience made a rather drab and colourless, if not shabby, impression. We are unlikely to return to the conventional evening dress of the past but with the great interest taken in clothes, particularly by men in the last few years, we can expect people to dress up for the theatre once again though not in the uniform of conformity.

There is no shortage of 'canned' entertainment in the home and one of the distinctive characteristics of a visit to a place of live

No. 18:1   *Foyer of the Thorndike Theatre.*

entertainment is a sense of occasion. The public spaces where an
audience assembles before a performance must provide a suitable
setting for this occasion. Foyers have to meet functional requirements, circulation must be easy and uncongested but they should
also convey an atmosphere of anticipation and excitement. In the
past this was achieved by buildings being dressed in formal architectural motifs with gilt and crystal decoration, an exact parallel to
the evening dress and jewels worn by the audience. As society has
changed so has the attitude to both architecture and dress. There
has been some over-compensation and the reaction to decorative

No. 18:2   Foyer of the Nottingham Playhouse.

No. 18:3   Foyer of the Crucible Theatre, Sheffield.

excesses has produced some dull buildings which fail to provide a stimulating setting for the social aspects of attending a live performance. Success in this respect, depends upon the quality of the architecture, for which it is not possible to give a recipe here. However, the functional purposes of the public areas can be described.

The foyer provides circulation routes for the audience to the various entry points into the auditorium and access to the cloakrooms and lavatories. In it the audience assembles and takes refreshment before the show and during intervals. The minimum space which should be allowed is 0·5 m² for each seat in the auditorium and this excludes the areas required for lavatories, cloakrooms and vertical circulation. Where theatres have been built on restricted sites in the centre of cities with high land values, there has been pressure to reduce foyer sizes in a way which the public find less and less acceptable in new buildings. In busy towns where there is a profusion of restaurants, pubs and bars, it may not be essential to provide these amenities within the theatre building itself, but in smaller places there may be nowhere to get a meal after the show or before it for that matter. Theatregoers expect to find refreshment facilities at the theatre and even cinemas are beginning to provide licensed bars for their patrons. Probably the strongest argument for providing food and drink is that these departments make a profit whereas the live performance itself almost invariably requires a subsidy.

If the use of the public spaces is to extend beyond the circulation of an audience for particular performances, then the space allowance may have to be increased. Foyers will have places designed for the display of posters, photographs and details of current productions and it is an easy step to extend this to provide an area where exhibitions can be mounted. This can be open to the rest of the foyer for most exhibitions, but if it is intended to display precious or rare objects, it may be necessary to provide a separate gallery where there is some check on the security of the exhibits.

Wherever the exhibition space is situated it will need a flexible system of display lighting which can easily be adapted for a new layout without trailing wires across the floor. Once all the information required by a gallery to prepare for hanging a painting would be its dimensions. Now with the coming of kinetics it is often as important to specify its power consumption and whether it is AC or DC. The moral to be drawn is that exhibition areas must be liberally provided with electrical points both for lighting and power.

The foyer can provide an attractive setting for dancing but this is one activity which it is difficult to provide for while performances are being given in the auditorium. When such functions are held there will again be a demand for power sockets and it is always good policy to provide plenty in foyer areas if they are to be truly flexible in use.

No. 18:4   *Theatre bar and Exhibition area.*

**Access for
the disabled**   In Britain the Central Council for the Disabled has for years campaigned for provision to be made for disabled people in public buildings, but it is only recently that there have been any tangible results in places of entertainment. Licensing authorities and fire officers are less than enthusiastic about wheelchairs in escape routes and even when the physical provisions in the building have been designed in by the architect there may be reluctance on the part of the local authority to permit their full use. The essentials are that a person in a wheelchair should be able to enter any of the public parts of the building without having to negotiate any steps. Changes in level can be joined by ramps providing these do not exceed a 1 in 12 slope and providing there is a flat section at the top of the ramp. If the vertical circulation is greater than can be accommodated by a ramp there must be a lift large enough to take a wheelchair and attendant. In a place of entertainment, corridors and door openings will, in any case, be wide enough if they conform to the normal regulations. For the ambulant disabled not confined to wheelchairs, staircases will be sufficiently easy going and the necessary handrails will, in any case, have to be provided.

In the auditorium itself it is much more satisfactory to have a special area set aside for wheelchairs and their attendants than to expect the disabled to be transferred to ordinary auditorium seats. The degree of disability varies and for some, this may not be too difficult but many problems arise with storing the chair, retrieving it after the performance and obstructing the movement of the more fortunate fit. It is much better for the disabled to remain in their wheelchairs in a special position with a level floor. Given their own entrance to the auditorium they are not in danger of blocking the circulation of other members of the audience, but this cannot always be done and if they do share the exits with the rest, the rules of management will probably insist that they must stay put with their attendants until the last of the audience has left the auditorium. The management's emergency routine will have to include action to be taken when wheelchairs are present. If a lift is to be used as a means of escape it will be necessary to provide it with a method of operation independent of the electrical system, probably by hand.

The disabled must have a lavatory designed specially for their use, with the necessary space for a wheelchair, grab rails, a wash basin reachable from the seat and an outward opening door. One such lavatory usable by both sexes is sufficient as the number of chairbound people attending at one time is unlikely to be very great. The licensing authority will probably set a limit to the number permitted to be present at any one performance. For a very full and detailed description of their requirements the reader is recommended to refer to *Designing for the Disabled* by Selwyn Goldsmith, published by the Royal Institute of British Architects.

Deaf aids   Another common form of disability which spoils many people's enjoyment of an entertainment is deafness. A person with poor hearing who benefits from using a hearing aid can be helped. The three systems we shall describe have in common a microphone or microphones which pick up the sound of the performance. These can be the same as those used for the show relay system to dressing rooms and other backstage spaces. The signal is amplified and it is the method of reaching the individual in the audience which differs from then on.

Certain places can be wired to sockets which can have a headset plugged in. The individual earpieces can be provided with volume controls. The great disadvantage of this system is that unless every seat is wired for sound, which is an expensive business, there will be administrative complications at the box office. If the special seats are held back in case a deaf person turns up sales may be lost and if they are not they may all be sold to people who do not need an aid before a deaf person asks for one.

Another method is to have a small radio transmitter with a loop aerial. Receivers and earphones can be hired at the box office. This is the system used in the World Theatre Season at the Aldwych for simultaneous translation. The radio signal can be picked up anywhere in the auditorium without elaborate permanent wiring or trailing temporary flexes. The disadvantages in this case are the expense of the receivers and the problems of maintaining them. A

radio loop may be installed as an intercom for the stage management and it is possible to extend the system on another broadcast
wavelength to include a transmission for radio hearing aids.

The third method is to amplify the signal and put it through an
induction loop. This would consist of ordinary electric cable under
the auditorium carpet or in the floor screed passing backwards and
forwards beneath the seats probably of every other row. Most hearing aids contain an induction coil which will be activated by the
field set up about this wire. The system is cheap to install and has
the advantage that most people will be able to use their own
hearing aid. A few receivers can be kept at the box office for loan or
hire to those who are not so equipped.

In the UK permission to use this or a radio system must be obtained
from the Post Office.

Outlook   The question of taking advantage of the outlook from the site is
one worth discussing in general. The auditorium and stage are
entirely inward-looking spaces sealed from contact with the outside world. The foyers on the other hand may, if the site is a good
one, have opportunities of splendid views over parks or city squares
tempting the architect to introduce vast glazed walls. This can be
successfully done, but care should be taken to see that the audience
is not dazzled by direct sunlight as they emerge from the dim light
of the auditorium. The glare from too bright a foyer also has the
reverse effect of making it more difficult for people to adjust to the
gloom as they enter the auditorium. This matter has been referred
to when discussing artificial lighting, but not all performances
take place after dark and the effects of daylight in foyers should
also be anticipated. At night a large glass wall to the foyer is probably more effective from outside than from inside. Seeing people
moving about from one level to another and the pattern of artificial
lighting within the building can be very attractive and a good
advertisement. From inside a large uninterrupted dark area of
glass can be rather forbidding especially on a wet and stormy
night.

If the outlook is the most important feature of the foyers then it
should be as interesting at night as during the day. When there is
not enough street lighting it might be worthwhile floodlighting
trees or a building nearby. But in any case, even with the finest
view it is not imperative to have a wall of glass to be able to appreciate it and there are many disadvantages of large, badly insulated
glazed areas causing either excessive heat losses or solar gains and
placing a heavy load on the heating and ventilating plant.

Another way of exploiting good views and a sunny aspect is to
provide outside terraces which can be opened up to the foyers.
In Britain we are at the mercy of our weather and the number of
days in the year when this is possible does not encourage us to

invest much money in providing for such facilities.

Entrance   The location of the main public entrance to the theatre is dependent upon site conditions. Needless to say, the position chosen should be a prominent one, easily recognised by strangers making their first visit. There should be a canopy over the entrance to protect those arriving and it is an advantage to extend this to a porte cochère where people may alight from cars, taxis or coaches under cover. All this area should be brightly illuminated and there should be a display of publicity material including posters, photographs, cast lists, etc.

The theatre entrance may have to compete with shop displays and it is particularly important that it should hold its own with its advertising material at all times of day and not just when it is open for performances in the evening. The main entrance doors should not open directly into the foyer or they will let in draughts or street noises every time they are used. There should be a lobby with double swing self-closing doors at either end. Some situations may allow this to be enlarged to form a waiting area or a place for the box office.

Foyers   Inside the foyer the routes to the entrances to the various parts and levels of the auditorium should be clear and easily appreciated without too great a reliance on signposting. There will have to be

No. 18:5   *Nottingham Playhouse at night.*

No. 18:6   *Entrance portico to the Theatre Royal, a familiar landmark in London's Haymarket since 1821.*

notices, but where the routes arise naturally from the layout of the building, results are more satisfactory.

Entrances to auditorium

Means of escape regulations will determine a minimum number of exits from the auditorium and from the point of view of the licensing authority there is no reason why more than one of these for each tier should connect with the foyers. On the other hand the circulation can be freer if several entrances to the auditorium are used. Members of the audience do not wish to find that they have unwittingly chosen an exit which takes them right out of the building before they have had a chance to retrieve their coats from the cloakroom or if all they want is a drink during the interval. Fire separation between alternative means of escape must be maintained but if at the same time a connection with the foyers can be contrived for each escape route better use is made of the building.

The disadvantages of having a lot of entrances to the auditorium are the number of stewards and usherettes needed to check tickets and the possibility of some confusion in the public about which entrance they should choose. This is where clear sign-posting closely related to an equally clear indication on the ticket is important. Unified graphic design here serves a practical purpose though it hardly needs any such justification.

Acoustic separation   All connections between foyer and auditorium should have acoustic treatment in the form of a lobby with doors at each end provided with acoustic sealing strips. Only with these precautions carefully observed can any activity continue in the foyers while a performance is in progress.

Latecomers   The attention of the audience must not be distracted by external noise, which can be kept at bay by careful design and detailing, but their own members can cause worse disturbance by coming late. There was a time when it was alleged that dramatists never put any dialogue or plot that mattered into the first twenty minutes of the play to allow the more ostentatious latecomers time to arrive and settle down. If people are late nowadays they are very often not allowed into the auditorium until the first interval. There are less severe remedies such as providing a special place with a viewing window to the auditorium and a relay through a loudspeaker or installing a closed-circuit television monitor somewhere in the foyer where the show can be watched until there is an opportunity for the transgressor to creep to his seat without disturbing the virtuously punctual.

Public telephones   There should be coin-operated telephones for the public in the foyers. Quieter positions off the main circulation routes should be chosen and it may be considered necessary to provide them with acoustic cowls or separate kiosks.

Cloakrooms   The cloakrooms and lavatories should also be closely related to the visitors' natural route. They must be placed so that queues which may form do not interfere with the flow of people through the building. The ideal situation is for these facilities to be on such a scale that queues do not form at all, but this is very difficult to achieve with reasonable economy. By the very nature of the use of the building there are bound to be short periods of intense demand and the rest of the time relative idleness. This applies to all the front-of-house facilities: cloakrooms, lavatories, bars and refreshment counters. In the case of the cloakroom, for instance, an audience arrives over a period of fifteen to twenty minutes before a performance, but will expect to retrieve its coats and umbrellas within a fraction of this time at the end. Where cloakrooms are attended there is a limit to the number of coats each attendant can deal with in a given time. For example, if it takes six seconds to retrieve and hand out one coat, each attendant can deal with fifty coats in five minutes and it would take ten attendants to cope with 500 coats in that time or five attendants would take ten minutes. These figures are if anything optimistic and many people are not prepared to wait for more than two or three minutes for their coats. In Britain, this is probably why it is rare for more than one third of an audience to part with their outer garments. Another reason is the unreliability of the heating arrangements in many buildings. As standards of heating and ventilation improve, more people will expect to be able to divest themselves of overcoats provided they know they are not going to suffer irritating delays in getting their belongings back. Attended systems can only be efficient if enough staff are employed and this is expensive. Management policy can improve efficiency by, for instance, switching the usherettes to the cloakroom counter at the end of the performance. The alternative is some form of self-service where each individual is responsible for depositing and retrieving his or her own coat.

In clubs and smaller amateur organisations, security may not be very important and it may be quite satisfactory for coats to be left unattended on a hook or hanger. This system has been used on quite a big scale outside the British Isles. A coat hanger is allotted to each seat in the auditorium and carries the same number. Buying a ticket entitles one to a particular seat and a particular coat hanger.

The British, it seems, are less trusting, or possibly less trustworthy, and they are not usually prepared to part with their possessions without some assurance of security. This is normally provided by the attendant, but self-service arrangements can be equally secure. One solution is to provide lockers with keys. These can be coin-operated, as at railway stations, or free. Their disadvantage is that they are expensive and space consuming. Another method which is gaining in popularity is the tethered hanger. This consists of a hanger fixed to a coat rack frame upon which the coat is hung in the usual way. Each hanger has a chain attached to it which is passed through the sleeve of the coat and locked off on a rail in the front of the rack. The special lock is designed to secure an umbrella at the same time. The user withdraws the numbered key and pockets it until he wishes to release his coat. This system is marketed under the name of Paralok, by Lock Systems Ltd.

Lavatories

Lavatories for the public are intensively used for short periods of time during intervals. A minimum number of fittings for an audience of a given size will be laid down in local authority byelaws, but this minimum is seldom enough to avoid people having to wait at peak times.

A more appropriate scale given in British Standard Code of Practice CP3: Chapter VII (1950) 'Recommendations'. Table III (cinemas, concert halls and theatres), is as follows:

Fitments	*for Male public	*for Female public	for Male staff	for Female staff
WCs	1 per 100 up to 400. For over 400, add at the rate of 1 per 250 or part thereof.	2 per 100 up to 200. For over 200, add at the rate of 1 per 100 or part thereof.	1 for 1–15 2 for 16–35	1 for 1–12 2 for 13–25
urinals	1 per 25 in concert halls and theatres. 1 per 50 in cinemas.	—	nil up to 6 1 for 7–20 2 for 21–45	—
lavatory basins	(No specific requirement is listed but generally one basin for each WC or urinal should be provided)		1 for 1–15 2 for 16–35	1 for 1–12 2 for 13–25

* it may be assumed that there will be equal numbers of males and females.

If the foyers and refreshment areas extend through more than one level the lavatories should be distributed so that they are within easy reach of the various parts of the building used by the public. This is usually done by having the main lavatories at the principal foyer level and secondary lavatories at another level which will serve other entrances to the auditorium or the restaurant or refreshment area.

Women's lavatories should include an area designed as a powder room where make-up can be repaired. It will need mirrors and a wide shelf for make-up, hair brushes, etc. Long mirrors should be provided and the lighting designed so that people standing in front of the mirrors are properly illuminated. Chairs or stools and ash-trays will be needed and the provision of tissue dispensers should be considered.

In the women's lavatories the disposal of sanitary towels can cause problems. Staff lavatories can be provided with a single in-cinerator in the wash basin area but this is not acceptable in the public lavatories. There should be means of disposal within each wc compartment. Bins or containers may have to be emptied into a central incinerator or disposal unit by the cleaning staff.

The wash basin area should be provided with towel cabinets and each basin should have a soap dispenser.

The men's lavatories should also be provided with an area equipped with mirrors where hair can be combed and clothes brushed.

Refreshments   The traditional pattern of theatre-going still typical in many places including the West End of London, does not make heavy demands on the refreshment facilities.

The audience arrives in the half-hour before the curtain rises and some will give themselves time to have a drink at the bar. During the interval, or intervals, there are more chances to visit the bar. Sometimes coffee or tea can be served in the auditorium or the foyer and usherettes sell ice-cream and chocolates. After the performance there is nothing more offered and the building is closed as soon as the audience can be got rid of.

The licensing laws are framed to suit this orthodox pattern of use and in England there is usually little difficulty in obtaining a licence for a theatre bar provided it is open only at these very restricted times, that is to say, half an hour before the evening performance and during intervals.

With many new theatres, particularly those run by a resident company, this pattern is no longer typical. The building becomes a social centre, a meeting place where people expect to go at any time of the day. Instead of teas served on trays in the auditorium, there is a permanent coffee bar serving coffee, tea, soft drinks, sandwiches, cakes, biscuits and ice-cream.

Audiences can be lured from their seats if the foyers are attractive enough, if there is enough room to move about and if the source of refreshments is efficient enough. The sale of sweets, nuts, ice-cream and cold drinks is too valuable a source of revenue to be neglected and if customers cannot be persuaded to leave their seats, managements will pursue them into the auditorium.

There is a contrast in the behaviour of theatre-goers and average cinema-goers. Separate performances punctuated by intervals are expected in the live theatre and the audience are accustomed to leaving their seats if for no other reason than to stretch their legs. It is becoming increasingly rare for smoking to be allowed in the auditorium and this supplies another motive for the more addicted to go into the foyers. In the cinema, however, the continuous performance with people coming and going all the time, still lingers on and in Britain it is seldom possible to book a numbered seat. This situation inhibits people from leaving their seats during an 'intermission' for fear that somebody else will come and take possession while they are gone. Even smokers can indulge their habit without moving from their seats in most commercial cinemas in the UK.

Though the pattern is changing slowly, and there is a tendency towards bars serving refreshments in the foyers, most of the sales in cinemas are made by girls carrying trays. This has its effect on the seating layout. Continental seating in long rows does not make it so easy to reach customers in the middle. This is one more factor which increases the difference between an auditorium designed for live performances where the close relation between actor and

No. 18:7   *A bar at Liverpool Playhouse, part of the addition made in 1968.*

audience is crucial and one designed for showing films where most people prefer to be further away from the screen rather than in the front rows.

In the new theatre enterprises there is generally a much greater importance attached to creating an attractive meeting place not restricted solely to those who are actually attending performances. If the public can be persuaded to enter a theatre by the refreshments and amenities it offers, they can more easily be tempted to buy seats for the shows it puts on. This is in itself good business, but the real aim is to make the building an accepted part of the life of the community. The least that is expected is a coffee bar serving simple snacks and most new schemes try to include a restaurant where a more elaborate meal can be served.

The licensing laws in Britain, related as they are to the old pattern of theatre-going, are an obstacle to further development of social activities. Unless a club is formed, which by its definition is exclusive, it is difficult to get permission to serve alcoholic drinks to the public except for the very restricted hours before and during intervals in a performance. It is to be hoped that this anomaly will be cleared up when the promised reforms of the licensing laws are carried out.

Bars   The refreshment areas in the foyers are, like the lavatories, subjected to periods of intense activity. There should be plenty of bar space to cater for the likely number of customers, although how many can be served will depend as much upon the staff available as the actual length of counter.

The location of the coffee bars and other bars within the foyer must relate to the public circulation in such a way that routes to and from the auditorium are not impeded by those taking refreshment. Obvious though this may sound, it is too often found that a bar has been installed apparently as an afterthought in a position where it jams up the circulation to one of the auditorium entry points.

The bars should be easily accessible for an audience emerging from the auditorium and in large multi-tier theatres it may be better policy to have several bars distributed to cover each level or part of the house. The audience will thus be spread more evenly throughout the building.

It is not appropriate here to go into great detail over the fitting out of bars, but there are some fundamental planning considerations that must be borne in mind from the start. For the well-being of both customers and management the bars must work efficiently in those brief periods of intense activity when the bulk of their trade is done. Time-consuming tasks must be avoided; for instance, bottled beer is much quicker to serve than draught beer and this is one of the reasons why it is rare to find the latter in a theatre bar. Each person serving behind the bar should have a till and access to a set of bottles with optic measures. The back of the bar is as important as the counter itself and island bars set in the middle of the foyer for instance, are at once at a disadvantage unless there is some vertical storage unit in the middle. Underneath the counter is bound to be untidy and unless there is some sort of barrier in the middle the back of the other side of the counter will be too obvious to customers. The back of the counter can also be revealed by too much mirror on the wall behind a bar. An island calls for more staff if it is to cover all points of the compass. If it does not it will lead to

frustration for its customers at peak periods of demand. Security
and licensing conditions will require that the alcoholic drinks be
locked up. This can be done in various ways with shutters or grilles
covering the back of the bar or coming down on the counter. Without them, the only alternative may be to stock the bar before opening it and laboriously remove full and partly full bottles to a store
after it closes. Another expedient is to have a mobile bar on
trolleys which can be wheeled back into store and locked up after it
has served its purpose. There will in any case have to be a store
from which to replenish the bars. Security there is particularly
important because spirits and tobacco carry such high excise duty
that the money value of the stock is very great.

The delivery, storage and distribution of supplies to the bars
must be taken into account. Crates of bottles are heavy and it
should be possible to avoid staff having to carry them up and down
stairs.

Each bar should have a small washing-up sink with hot water
and mains drinking water. Some public health authorities may insist on a basin for hand washing in addition to the sink. Serving
cold drinks, soft or alcoholic, is a much quicker process than serving tea or coffee. Instead of just a glass, there is a cup, a saucer, a
spoon and the complication of some preferring with or without
milk and some with or without sugar. The tea or coffee must be at
the right temperature and if it has been kept too long its flavour
deteriorates. However, the demand is there and it would be unwise
for any management to ignore it. From this point of view, the
economic advantage of vending machines is attractive and if the
quality of their products can be made acceptable they will become
more and more common in public places. The process of brewing up
tea or coffee is an exacting one and machines which rely on pow-
dered substitutes do not yet produce results which can be compared
with beverages prepared in the traditional manner. A machine
vending alcoholic drinks on the other hand would be quite simple
mechanically and there is no reason why there should be any
detectable difference from a drink dispensed by hand. Clearly the
objections are legal rather than mechanical.

Bars need storage space for bottles and glasses, cooling shelves,
ice-making machines and it may be worthwhile to have a machine
for washing up glasses. Where tea, coffee and snacks are served, the
equipment needed to do the job efficiently can become elaborate and
the electrical loads considerable. Storage of crockery and cutlery is
needed, display cases and hot cabinets for food begin to fill up the
counter and the washing-up problem is more than can be adequately
dealt with in a small bar sink. In this case there should be another
room opening off the back of the counter where preparation of
simple snacks and washing-up can be done. If communications
within the building permit, it may be possible for this preparation

and washing-up to be done centrally in the restaurant kitchen.

The restaurant   The restaurant has become established as an essential ingredient of most new theatres. Many people like to have a restaurant meal to complete the evening's outing and unless the theatre is right in the centre of the entertainment district of a big city, there will not be much choice of places to go. Even with competition close by, an attractive restaurant forming part of a theatre has advantages over its rivals. From the management point of view it has a regular potential clientèle and from the customers' angle the convenience of being on the spot. The opportunity of exploiting the theatrical connection of the restaurant should not be missed though there are problems involved in deciding how close this connection should be. Running the restaurant and the theatre alongside and in the same building has practical difficulties which must not be ignored. The times of opening can be arranged to coincide as far as possible, but if meals are served after the last performance the management will want to be able to shut up the rest of the building so that staff can go home. Although it may be visually more attractive to make the dining area part of the foyer, the difficulties of running a restaurant which cannot be physically separated from the rest of the building should be realised. It is not sufficient to assume that the foyer can have the dual use of circulation and dining area unless it is very large. Diners will not appreciate being swamped by the interval crowd though they may enjoy being able to see the throng moving about from a vantage point in the restaurant. If there are good views from the site, the restaurant is one of the most suitable places from which to appreciate them.

The policy of the management on running the restaurant will affect its planning and should be decided at an early stage. The usual pattern of use is for some people to have their meal in the hour before the show and others in the hour after it. This is an important limitation and it is not possible to serve and enjoy a very elaborate meal in such a relatively short time. The menu should, therefore, be designed to cope with this kind of demand and other customers not attending a performance, may have to conform to similar limitations. On a bigger scale it may be possible to have separate dining rooms or suites which can be let for private functions.

The question of waiter service or self-service will arise. Smaller restaurants where the main demand is for fairly quick meals before and after a show, are probably better with a cafeteria-type service. The public are now accustomed to this system for meals of a very good standard and there is no reason why it should be considered cheap or second rate. In order to make proper use of the investment in the restaurant, its kitchens and furnishings and to provide full employment for the staff it is desirable to open at lunch time as well as in the evenings. The lunch-time customer will not usually be

No. 18:8   *The old box office at the Royal Opera House, typical of many still in use.*

combining his visit with going to a performance except possibly when there is a matinee. His or her motives will be different and the menu will not necessarily be the same as in the evening. The theatre can gain much in publicity if it can establish its restaurant as a popular rendezvous.

The equipment and planning of the kitchen to serve the restaurant is a subject outside the scope of this book, but there are certain basic planning problems which must be considered in the early stages of a design. Deliveries of supplies will be frequent and there must be space to store them and mechanical aids to distribute them if the kitchen is remote from the unloading point. The disposal of empties, old packing materials and kitchen garbage can be an even greater problem. If the local authority rubbish collection is efficient and frequent there may be no troubles but where there is a visit only once a week and for some reason a week is missed then the garbage may begin to rot and breed flies. One safeguard is to get rid of most waste food, vegetable peelings and materials likely to decay, through a waste disposal unit powerful enough to cope with the load; a domestic type would be useless.

The cooking equipment can be heavy and will use a lot of power. Services in the kitchen will be complicated with probably both gas and electricity required at many different points and the same with

No. 18:9   *The new box office for the Royal Opera House which is appropriate for a large and complicated repertoire of both ballet and opera.*

both hot and cold water supplies and drainage. Ventilation must be efficient and the vitiated air laden with grease and cooking smells must be filtered and carried away where it will not be a nuisance in the building or to any adjoining owners.

The kitchen staff must be provided with a staff room and lavatories and coat storage for both males and females. The catering manager will need an office and a large establishment may need space for more administrative staff. Only a brief outline of the problem can be given here and it is advisable to seek expert advice before the final details are decided.

The box office   The simplest box office is the kind used by most cinemas. The seats are not bookable and the cashier's task is to take money, give change and dispense tickets from an automatic machine. There may be more than one price, but this is the only complication. The one important quality appreciated by both public and management is speed of operation.

Where seats can be reserved and bought in advance, which is the custom for most live performances, the procedure is more complicated. The box office will be selling tickets at several different prices for performances of different plays, recitals, concerts, etc. The staff will have to deal with telephone reservations, postal applications, agency bookings and personal callers. They will also have to sell tickets 'at the door' in the hour before the show begins. This is when the box office staff are under the greatest pressure and for this reason there should be at least two windows, one labelled 'Advance Bookings' and one, 'This Performance', or the equivalents, in all but the tiniest undertakings.

The system of seat sales is that each performance has a seating plan and a book or books of tickets representing each seat. The performance, the date and the prices are marked or printed on each and as the tickets are sold, the seats are marked off the plan. To work efficiently, the box office clerk should have space screened from the public to handle the book of plans easily and select the corresponding book of tickets quickly without being overlooked.

It is this need for readily accessible racks for tickets which led to the orthodox ticket window or guichet. The pigeon holes for the book of tickets are ranged on either side of the opening through which the ticket buyers must stoop and peer. This may be convenient for the staff in the box office but it makes most members of the public feel at a disadvantage. It seems too easy for the clerk to hide, to be evasive, to adopt a defensive position behind a weapon slit. These are, no doubt, irrational suspicions but the fact remains that box offices often have a reputation for rudeness and the guichet appears to foster and amplify bad temper. Even the railways are abandoning it in their new stations.

The alternative is a counter such as is found in a travel agency. It can be open, or if it is exposed to cold draughts in a lobby or too much noise in a foyer it can be glazed in with openings for taking money and handing out tickets and for speaking. One of the reasons for the guichet was to prevent the public leaning over the counter and looking at the clerk's book of plans. These are management records and customers should choose their seats from a prominently displayed seating plan giving a more graphic representation of the auditorium. If it is not protected by glass the counter should be wide enough to prevent anyone leaning over and grabbing and to discourage people from interfering with the work of the box office staff. Where the counter is in a vulnerable position close to the street, thieves may be tempted to try a snatch. Security is then, an important factor but the risk is less when the box office is in the centre of the foyer. The house manager should, in any case, transfer cash to the safe frequently to avoid leaving too much in the till.

The most convenient location for the box office is somewhere near the entrance to the theatre so that it is on the route which visitors must pass. This is desirable when tickets are being sold just before a performance, but is less important for advanced bookings. Some larger organizations have a box office quite remote from the rest of the public areas. Where the policy is to keep the foyers open during the day, and to encourage people to patronize the coffee bar, it may be preferred to site the advance booking office in this area combined with a sales counter for books and magazines. The object is to make the buying of tickets as painless a process as possible.

At times, queues will form at the box office wherever it is sited. As a sign of a demand for seats they are welcome but if their occurrence has not been foreseen in planning the circulation of the public, they can cause bottlenecks and irritation.

The box office operation is essentially one of storage and retrieval of information carried out at present by a rather laborious hand process. This kind of task can be handled much more efficiently by a computer as it is already in the comparable case of airline bookings. Schemes for dealing with theatre tickets in a similar manner have made an appearance and the next decade should see them greatly extended. At the moment, the obstacle to development is the cost of the computer and the wide network of terminal points which would be needed to make it economically justifiable. It would save money by doing the job more efficiently with fewer staff, but the true vindication would only be in increasing seat sales generally by providing more and easier opportunities for the public to buy. The old box office could not be eliminated entirely and there would still be some staff required, for example to sell tickets in the hour before the show. However, the vision of a machine which would project the auditorium plan of any theatre one wished for any particular performance and indicating what seats were available and at what price, is an attractive one. It would then print out tickets for the seats chosen in return for a glimpse of a credit card and store all the information instantaneously. The techniques for all this exist and are indeed commonplace in some applications, but they are too expensive for the theatre at present.

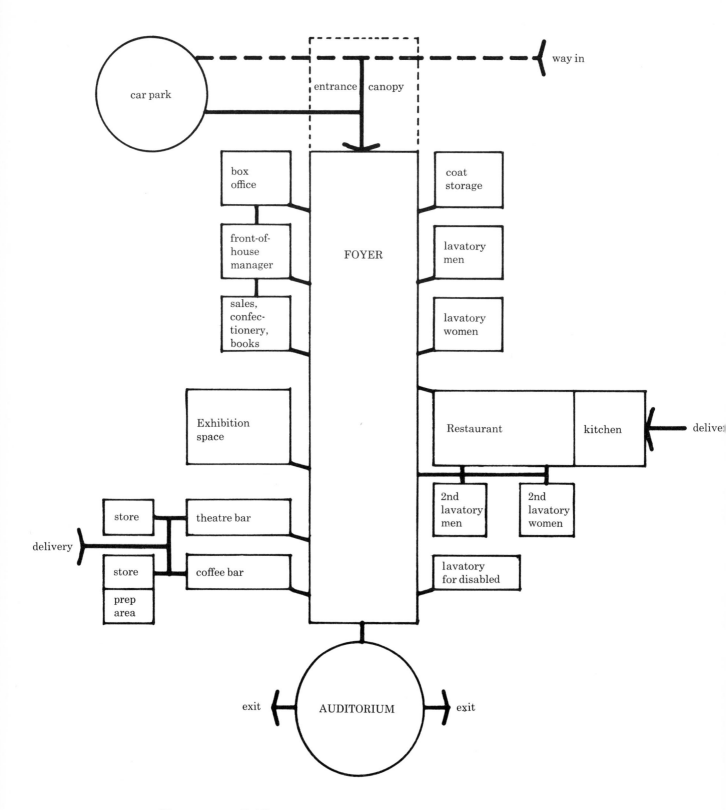

No. 18:10   Public spaces

19   Heating and ventilation

The heating and ventilation of the auditorium and stage is a particularly complicated problem which cannot be dealt with as an afterthought. The design criteria are exacting and the system must be integrated with the main functions of the building. A consulting engineer for the mechanical services should join the design team at an early stage in the development of a scheme.

There are too many examples of ventilation plants which cannot be switched on during a performance because they are too noisy and of ducting running riot and obstructing access to cat walks, lighting positions, etc.

Design factors

Extreme weather conditions for any length of time are rare in the British Isles. For this reason and because most performances take place in the evening, after the heat of the day, air conditioning with complete control of humidity and temperature has seldom been installed in Britain. The heat generated by the members of the audience sitting in an auditorium is enough to balance the fabric heat losses and a good deal of the ventilation loss even in winter conditions. In summer, temperatures can rise quite high and cause discomfort and if the rise is to be limited to anything less than 6 deg. C, cooling will be necessary. Regulations will require an auditorium to be ventilated and it is convenient that the air supply should at the same time provide whatever heating is required. It is then not normally necessary to have any other form of heating such as radiators. Ventilation must be designed to produce the correct air movement and the desired resulting temperature. People are most comfortable when fresh air is blown towards their faces rather than from behind their heads. A certain amount of mild turbulence set up by the incoming air stream gives a feeling of freshness. The dividing line between this and what is called a draught is difficult to define, but draughts must be avoided. Air should reach every part of the auditorium without leaving stagnant zones and the temperature should remain constant over the whole area. The system must operate at a very low noise level.

The auditorium

If the walls or the roof of the auditorium are exposed to the elements without being protected by any other part of the building or a large roof void, the burden on the heating and ventilating plant will be much greater, both in winter and summer. A poorly insulated roof for instance, will absorb solar heat and re-radiate it to the audience below. If the auditorium is well-cushioned by other accommodation around it conditions will probably be tolerable without a cooling system, except for a few of the hottest days in the year. But if the auditorium walls are exposed to the sun with very little protection the audience will often be uncomfortable. The licensing authority will state its ventilation requirements which may differ from one authority to another. The GLC normally requires the supply of air to the auditorium to be not less than 28 m³ per person per hour. If the air is suitably warmed and cleaned this may consist of 75% of fresh air direct from outside mixed with 25% of re-circulated air. If the air is fully conditioned so that relative humidity can be kept from exceeding 55% the supply may be half fresh air and half re-circulated air. The GLC usually ask for 75% of the air input to be extracted mechanically. This leaves 25% to find its own way out and most of this will flow through the proscenium opening to the stage. Of the air which is extracted mechanically the authorities may ask for a proportion to be taken out from the stage, increasing still further the flow from the auditorium. If the air movement is increased too much there is a risk of the curtains and scenery being blown about. The authorities are concerned about the stage fire hazard and they want to make sure that there is no danger of smoke being drawn into the auditorium. If the auditorium has a downward system of ventilation it may be necessary to have emergency controls which will stop the low level extract, and an additional fan extracting from a point above the proscenium opening or from the stage end of the auditorium ceiling, brought into operation by the closing of the safety curtain. It would not switch on before the proscenium opening was sealed off in case it pulled any smoke from the stage into the auditorium.

Stage area

Where the stage is separated from the auditorium, and particularly where there is a fly tower the volume of the stage area is usually far greater than the auditorium, and the walls of the stage area are much less likely to be protected by other parts of the building. The heat gained from people is much less than in the auditorium. The problem on the stage is more often one of heating in the winter than of cooling in the summer. A warm air system can move scenery and curtains about, a radiant system would be obstructed by or would obstruct scenery and radiators and convectors take up space which is needed for all sorts of other stage purposes. A certain amount of heat comes from stage lighting lanterns, but this seldom has much effect as many of the sources of light will be in the auditorium itself. Probably radiators recessed into the walls have the least disadvantages. If the stage is cold when the curtain rises a column of cold air will fall on the people in the front rows of the auditorium much to their discomfort.

Air distribution in the auditorium

The distribution of air in the auditorium can either be with input at a low level and extraction above which reinforces the natural circulation of the hot air upwards, or the input can be at the top with extract from underneath the seats. The upwards system can only be used if the incoming air is at very much the same temperature as the air already in the auditorium. If there is a larger temperature differential this will be felt as a cold draught. In small or narrow theatres an upwards system with the air or some of it brought in at the side walls is possible. The velocity of the side inlets can be higher producing better conditions than inlets in the floor. The downwards system is the only way of introducing cool air into a large auditorium without causing draughts. Downwards air distribution can be by displacement ventilation or jet ventilation. The diagrams illustrate how this system works. The inlets may be in the ceiling or in the side and back walls at high level. The disadvantage of the system is that it is not easy to control air movement and there is a tendency to get stagnant zones. The air movement set up by the system may not be sufficient to counteract the natural convection air currents arising from the audience combined with temperature difference between the walls and the air in the room. These problems are less likely to arise when the jet principle is employed, but this has to be carefully designed to avoid draughts. An apparently fresher and more invigorating atmosphere is produced by this method. The penetrating effect of the jets thoroughly mixes the fresh air input with the air already in the room. It is possible to calculate the angle of distribution and the length of throw of air from the jets. Inlets are usually cylindrical, but linear inlets can also be arranged to produce a similar effect. The throw of an inlet, particularly downwards, is affected by the temperature differential as well as by the velocity and area of opening. The terminal velocity is normally set at 14 m per minute. The installation must be designed to avoid creating draughts at audience level which may happen if groups of jets are allowed to fuse together and then travel too far. Jets must, therefore, be placed in such a way that they do not fuse together before they reach the level of the heads of the seated audience. The system will have to be tested and if adjustments are necessary, as they may well be, the jets must be accessible.

Diagram overleaf.

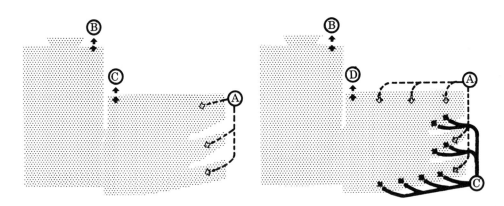

No. 19:1   No. 19:2

Diagrams illustrating displacement ventilation systems based on GLC
requirements

1. *Simple plenum system with one inlet fan and independent stage
    and auditorium extract fans*
A = inlet fan
B = stage extract fan (capacity 40 % of total)
C = auditorium extract fan (capacity 60 % of total)
Total capacity of extracts to equal 75 % of input
Usual order of starting: B, A, C
(Where convenient the stage extract for B and the auditorium extract
for C can be combined into one extract fan common to both)

2. *Downward system with inlet fan and independent stage and
    auditorium extract fans*
A = inlet fan
B = stage extract fan (capacity 40 % of total)
C = auditorium extract fan (capacity 60 % of total)
D = auditorium emergency extract fan (capacity 60 % of total)
Total capacity of extracts to equal 75 % of input
Extract from the auditorium in normal circumstances is by ducts
under the seating. The stage extract discharges directly to the open air.
On lowering the safety curtain or operation of emergency controls,
the normal extract from the auditorium stops and the emergency
auditorium extract fan starts.
Usual order of starting: B, A, C

Note: A single fan may combine the duties of fans C and D; changeover
dampers being arranged in the ductwork so that in normal circumstances
air is extracted from below the seating. In an emergency, this is shut off
and the extract duct above the proscenium arch is opened. Order of
starting would then be: B, A, (C and D).

Air extraction   Air extracted from the auditorium is usually taken through grilles
in the risers formed by the steppings of the rows .
    In sloped floors the extract grilles can be placed under the seats
or incorporated in the standards supporting them.
    A substantial source of heat is the stage lighting and much of it

will be in the auditorium ceiling and side walls. With a downward system the heated air round the lanterns may be carried down to the audience by the input air. In summer this would make conditions worse or where there is cooling it places a heavier load on the refrigeration plant. One way of avoiding this difficulty is to have some extract at high level to take away hot air from around the lights.

Noise levels   In chapter four on acoustics the importance of a very low level of background noise in the auditorium and the stage area was emphasised. There is a certain amount of noise which will penetrate from outside and the audience themselves are not completely silent even at moments of the highest tension, but the most likely source is the ventilation system. For small and medium size theatres the noise criterion of 25 dBA and for larger 20 dBA maximum are total levels and the mechanical ventilation should be designed to be quieter than this. Noise can come from the air itself moving through ducts, nozzles, grilles and diffusers. This depends partly on the design of the outlets and their distance from people's heads, and partly on the velocity of the air. From this point of view velocities should be low.

The other source of air noise is from the fans themselves and depends on their type and power and on their distance from the auditorium and stage. The ventilation plant should be on flexible mountings to prevent vibration being transmitted to the structure as far as possible, but it is both difficult and expensive to reduce the noise criterion to less than 25 dBA by this alone. The plant room and fans should be structurally separated from the auditorium and stage areas. To reduce noise travelling along the ductwork itself sound insulating and absorbent lagging must be applied. The material chosen for this purpose should be something non-combustible like glass wool or mineral wool. Anything burning or smouldering inside ductwork would rapidly distribute smoke to everybody. None of the foamed plastics are at present suitable for this kind of insulation. Even the bonding agent in non-combustible materials may be suspect and if unbonded mineral wool or glassfibre are used there is a danger of air erosion even at low velocities. The sound absorbent can be protected from this by a perforated metal covering. Another effective way to reduce noise transmission along ducting is to introduce lengths of flexible ducting (providing it has a satisfactory fire resistance).

Public areas   The rest of the building does not present any particularly uncommon problems outside the general experience of most heating and ventilation engineers. Conventional methods can be used to heat the public areas depending on their size and how much natural ventilation there is. If the street is noisy outside it may not be desirable to have too many open windows and a mechanical ventilation system will then be needed. It will in any case be difficult to achieve comfortable conditions from purely natural ventilation when there is a crowd of smokers in the foyers and the weather is cold outside. The auditorium has to have a ventilation plant and it is not difficult to find economic justification for enlarging this to provide the foyers with warmed and filtered air. There will have to be independent extracts from lavatories if they have no natural ventilation, and from any area where cooking of any kind is carried out such as in the coffee bar or the restaurant kitchen. More air would be put in than taken out and the surplus would escape through doors thus helping to reduce draughts from outside.

Back-stage areas   Back-stage areas can have simple heating systems such as low-pressure hot water radiators. Only in those rooms where no natural ventilation is possible is it necessary to have mechanical ventilation introduced. In some larger areas radiators may be supplemented by fan convectors. In the workshops blown air is less satisfactory because of the dust problem and an overhead radiant panel system is probably most satisfactory.

20   Economics

A book on theatre planning would not be complete without some general discussion of the economics of theatre building. The word 'economics' is used in an attempt to drain away the passions which can be induced by arguments about cost. The whole questions of costs is often so shrouded in mystery that it is difficult to discover the real truth.

When the cost of a project is announced the figures are usually coloured by political expediency. In a generally puritan country such as Britain, every effort is made to conceal the true cost for fear of righteous outcries against extravagance, but in some other places the citizens are proud to know that no expense has been spared in making their building worthy of their own city or nation.

Cost comparisons   While we need to have some standard of comparison by which to assess theatre costs, quoting sums of money which are alleged to have been expended on a particular building is a very misleading method. It is always difficult to find out what has or has not been included in the calculation. For instance, has the cost of purchasing the site been included or should it be given a notional value? How much equipment has been included and how much furniture and furnishings?

It is apparently indelicate for architects, engineers and other consultants to include their fees though, from the promotor's point of view, these are bound to form a substantial proportion of the total cost.

There are many variables which affect the cost of any kind of building in a stable economy and in an inflationary situation comparisons which are not precisely contemporary, rapidly become meaningless.

Economic factors are, nonetheless, vitally important but to avoid adding to the confusion, figures and amounts in money will not be mentioned in this book. There are economic implications in every aspect of theatre planning from the kind and scope of production it is intended to present to the capital and running cost of labour-saving machinery. Both artistic and economic factors are involved in every decision that has to be made.

At the present time, the clients' original motivation is most likely to be artistic, used in the broad sense to include social and educational purposes. It may to a lesser extent be commercial, but as there are many other investments which will produce much higher and safer returns, commercial motivation is unlikely to be very strong.

Theatres are not physical necessities, like housing, schools or hospitals. When they are built it is not by an Act of Parliament but by an act of faith. Faith that they will contribute to the quality of living. They offer various degrees of participation in a creative process, from appreciation of a professional performance, to taking part in an amateur one.

On one level they provide a leisure activity competing with other forms of entertainment, but on another level it is the opportunity they give people to exercise various creative talents which gives them their particular social value.

The type of building which emerges from the consideration of these artistic and economic factors, will probably come within the categories discussed in chapter one, but these do not exhaust the possible forms a project can take. It may end up in quite a different shape or size from the promoter's original idea. Sometimes artistic ambitions shrink when faced with economic realities, but the opposite process is not uncommon. Small projects intended for example for amateurs or as rehearsal rooms begin to grow as more potential uses and users appear. The expanding brief leads to demands for more space and equipment, and the whole scale of a scheme can alter. The original brief may turn out to be misleading and if such developments have not been anticipated the architect may be in difficulties and the building will suffer.

Theatres are likely to be initiated by enthusiasts whose ideas and methods differ widely. The preparation of the architect's brief for a new building or for the rehabilitation of an old one, is a task with heavy responsibility. Best results are obtained when the architect takes part in the process of assembling the brief. A sponsor operating in the capacity of landlord only, such as a local authority, a development company or a benefactor may delegate the carrying out of the project to a committee, a trust or a theatre board which might consist of councillors, local citizens, or members of a theatre company if one exists in the area. Their task would be to get the project under way and decide on general policy.

A body of this nature is well advised not to involve itself with the detailed artistic policy. For this purpose they should appoint an artistic director, theatre consultant or someone to represent the interests of the prospective user. On the other hand the theatre company management or individual visionary may have very clear ideas on artistic direction, but no adequate organisation to cope with the financial arrangements for carrying out a building.

A cautious sponsor may want some reassurance on the viability of a theatre building. Some kind of social survey may be called for but it should be remembered that theatrical enterprises are not very susceptible to the normal techniques of this kind of investigation. The quality and reputation of both the activity and the building, will profoundly influence the demand. A company with a vigorous policy can stimulate demand in a community where little interest is evident from a survey. The location and ease of access by various means of transport gives an indication of the potential catchment, but no guarantee that the audience will be persuaded to come.

Pilot scheme

Another cautious approach is to have a trial run with a pilot scheme before embarking on a large-scale project. This may be a way to test demand and stimulate and build up the public for theatre, but there are dangers in this approach. A pilot scheme must essentially be cheap, but if it is too obviously make-shift, an uncomfortable audience is not likely to be converted to theatre-going. It should at least have a satisfactory audience to stage relationship. It does not necessarily follow that the success or failure of a small-scale scheme gives any indication of the success or failure of a large-scale one. Each is likely to develop a personality of its own and succeed or fail in its own right.

The quest for cheapness often leads to temporary buildings, but temporary buildings have a habit of becoming very permanent.

Subsidy and self-sufficiency

For very brief periods, social and economic factors have made it possible for the live theatre to pay for itself out of charges for admission. We are just emerging from such a period. In the last century the live theatre was the popular mass public entertainment. People prosperous from the proceeds of the industrial revolution could pay for entertainment and found it in the live theatres and music halls. Their taste was not for highbrow intellectual drama; they responded to unashamed sentiment and broad comedy. Theatres and music halls sprang up all over the British Isles and medium-size towns might easily support five or six. There was no question of subsidy.

This boom was hit by the arrival of the cinema, which grew from a sideshow curiosity at the beginning of this century, to take over as the mass form of entertainment after the first world war. The movies had their heyday between the two great wars, but after 1945 they too yielded first place to television, which is far and away the most widespread and universal purveyor of entertainment that has ever existed. It is difficult to imagine any new medium ever displacing television as the mass popular entertainer.

However, the cinema did not kill the theatre any more than television has killed the cinema or the long-playing record has killed the orchestral concert. In one way each innovation has liberated its predecessor. The sheer mass of output required to feed the voracious appetites of a mass public leads to mediocrity in most of the material. Competition for the attention of the majority only encourages the suppliers of this material to seek for the lowest common denominator of public tastes.

When the live theatre was challenged by films it lost its mass audience, but there remained the people for whom the theatre had a meaning, who took a more discriminating interest in it. The theatre patrons became a minority, largely middle-class and better educated than the average. Plays became more sophisticated. Ibsen, Chekhov and Shaw made people feel and think in a different way and the audience for the drama expected some intellectual stimulation from what it saw and heard. There was a move away from the stereotyped comedy or tragedy with stock characters, into more adventurous ideas both in subjects for plays and in staging. But this change from a mass medium to a more sophisticated minority interest inevitably started the change back to the more normal state of affairs where the performing arts are supported by state patronage rather than box office returns. This process is not yet complete, but it gathers momentum all the time. The West End remains a commercial enterprise, but it subsists on wasting assets. It is possible, at West End prices, for theatres to make a moderate profit on running expenses, but little or nothing can be set aside for rebuilding. The prospects for investment of capital for private gain in the building of new theatres are not attractive. Almost any other investment would produce a better return. However, in terms of the community as a whole, there is a very considerable dividend on investment in new theatres. It may fairly be said that they add to the quality of life and thereby make the area they serve more attractive to other undertakings. They certainly do much to attract tourist trade.

The memory that theatres were once built for profit dies hard and the implications of the new situation have not yet sunk in. Nobody now expects libraries and swimming baths to pay for themselves though their appeal is only to a minority. The need for subsidy is not new and without it the theatre would wither away to a very minor insignificant activity.

The site Usually the first essential for getting a project off the ground is the ground itself. The availability of a site is often the catalyst which triggers off the whole scheme. Even if it is not ideal it may have to be accepted for reasons of political expediency. One has only to look at the comparative plans of existing theatres to see how seldom the site is ideal. If it is too cramped it may not be possible to fulfil the requirements of the client's preliminary briefing. Certain critical dimensions are implied by the kind of theatre it is proposed to build and if these cannot be fitted on the site the programme will either have to be reduced in scale or another site chosen. Some preliminary studies will have to be done to find out what the critical dimensions of a theatre, for a particular purpose, holding a particular number of people, will be. For instance, a medium-size proscenium theatre, initiating its own productions and having workshop facilities on the site, would need an area of about 40 m × 50 m.

Access to the site   An island site is ideal; access from two sides is essential. Regulations will demand means of escape for the audience to two separate thoroughfares and the fire brigade will want to get its engines to all parts of the site. The public requires access for cars, taxis, coaches, buses and in some instances, boats, monorails, hovercraft and other as yet unimagined means of transport. The staff and artists will have their entrance, preferably on another side of the building. Lorries and pantechnicons must get to the stage to unload and collect scenery and properties. Costumes must be delivered to the wardrobe and dressing-room area, raw materials to the workshop, provisions to the restaurant, supplies to the bars, fuel to the heating plant and the rubbish has to be removed. Car parking for visitors somewhere in the vicinity is essential. If the area is not well served by public transport, parking spaces for one car per two persons in the audience may be required. As the main demand for parking for the theatre will be in the evenings it may often be possible to make use of car parks used for other purposes during the day, for instance, for offices and shopping.

The policy for new theatres is often to make them a part of the everyday life of the community, not just an evening entertainment. During the day they become a meeting place serving coffee, snacks and sometimes meals and hold exhibitions and lunchtime entertainments. They can only do this successfully if they are sited in the centre of a busy part of the town. A site outside the town may have a magnificent view and a beautiful setting, but if it can only be reached by car it has little chance of becoming a popular rendezvous at all times of the day.

Large cities often have an entertainment area where theatres are just one of a wide range of diversions offered to the public. There has been a tendency to group the more highbrow activities together in a centre which may earn the description of cultural ghetto if it is remote from the more vulgar entertainments offered by the town. Successful theatres are very likely to have to put up with the restrictions of city sites.

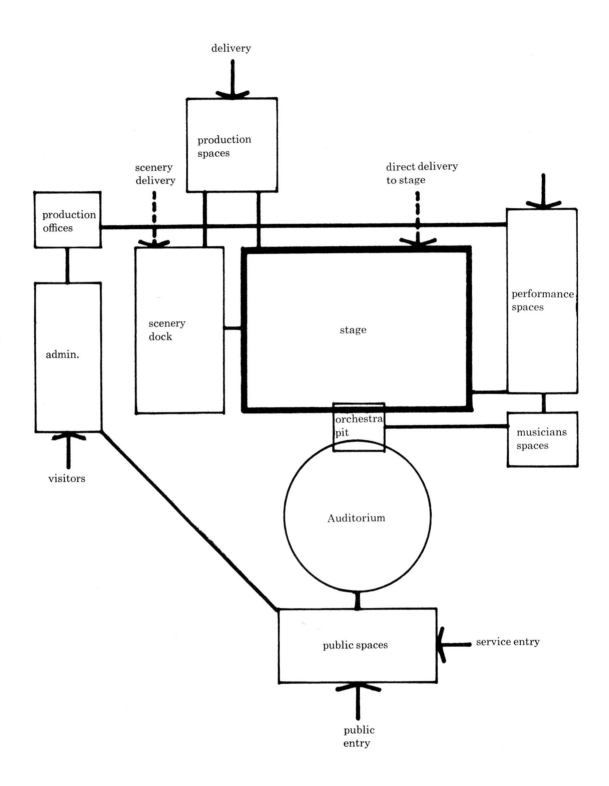

No. 20:1   *Relationship of functions*

Relationship of functions   All the various component parts of the theatre have been described in some detail. The relation between activities and departments is summarised in the diagram opposite.

The economic framework   Once the kind of theatre and the purpose to which it is to be put have been decided and it is known whether drama, opera, ballet or musicals are to be produced there and the scale upon which these are to be mounted and whether it will play in repertory or repertoire and whether it will originate productions and set them up on the premises and the number of seats in the auditorium and the standard of amenity for the audience and the standard of provision of all the elements which go to make up a theatre and have been described in this book, have been decided, then it is possible to make some estimate of how much all this will cost. Usually the largest single expense will be the cost of constructing the building itself, but there are many other costs which must be taken into account.

Capital costs   **The site:**   The site may have to be purchased freehold or leasehold. If it is given or leased at a peppercorn rent this is a form of subsidy equivalent to the market value of the site at the time. Certain works may have to be carried out in order to make it suitable, such as demolitions and diversion of services before construction can begin. Landscaping and the provision of car parks may add further expense.

Building: The building contractor has to be paid as the work proceeds and the client has to arrange for the cash to be available.

The services including heating, ventilating and electrical, the plumbing and drainage will be included as in most building contracts but theatres are very much more complicated than the general run of buildings and a good deal of specialised stage equipment will form part of the contract. Loose equipment and tools for the stage and workshop will usually have to be purchased separately. Built-in furniture, carpets and curtains can be within the main contract or within a separate furniture and furnishings contract.

Loose chairs and tables may still be wanted for the restaurant and coffee bar and the offices will have to be provided with chairs, desks, office equipment, typewriters and office machines. Heavy catering equipment will probably be built-in as part of the main contract, but cooking pots and pans, cutlery, crockery and table linen will still have to be found.

Fees: The complexity of theatre design involves the skill of a wide range of specialists. Professional fees will be a larger proportion of the total cost of the work than for most building projects. Fees will have to be paid for the services of most of the following, according to the complexity of the project:

Solicitors, Land Surveyors, Architects, Quantity Surveyors, Structural Engineers, Heating and Ventilating Engineers, Electrical Engineers, Theatre Consultants for the general stage planning, equipment for stage lighting, for stage sound equipment, Acoustic Consultant, Interior Designers, Graphic Designers, Landscape Architects.

Running costs   The client should prepare a draft budget of the expected running costs of the building. It is very important that this should be done realistically. A large building with sophisticated equipment will be expensive to run, it will need permanent staff with the right training and calibre to look after it efficiently. The lighting and fuel bills will be high; large stages can swallow up a great deal of scenic material. Amateur enterprises should beware of falling into the trap of creating an over-ambitious scheme which they will find a great burden to run with unskilled part-time staff.

Running costs and capital costs are, of course, related. All too often capital costs are cut in a way which has a baleful effect on later running costs. Cheap materials often do not last long and cost a great deal of money to maintain properly or replace. The cost in labour may soon outweigh the saving made in cutting out some mechanical aid. Unfortunately, problems of the moment are more pressing than those which may arise in the future. Short-term savings are too often made in the knowledge that extra running costs will be covered by subsidies or by tax exemptions. The reluctance to invest in the future and the readiness to accept continually rising day-to-day expenses, are symptons of an economic malaise which is not confined to theatre building.

The following is a list of headings under which regular running costs can be classified:

Interest on loan and repayment of mortgage for the purchase of the site.

Ground rent.

Interest on loan, repayment of mortgage, amortisation of capital on the cost of the building.

Rent.

Building maintenance.

There will be a number of maintenance contracts for the regular inspections and servicing of items of equipment such as the boilers and ventilation plant, the lifts, the kitchen equipment, the stage lighting and sound equipment.

Local Authority rates.

Heating and power.

Cleaning.

Insurances.

Accounting and legal fees.

Wages and salaries of permanent staff.

Administration costs including printing, advertising, telephones, office expenses, stationery, postage, etc. Actors', directors' and designers' salaries or fees. Production costs: scenery, lighting, properties, costumes, music and musicians, royalties.

Taxation of profits: very often a theatre company is a registered charity which being non-profit making will not be obliged to pay tax.

Sources of capital finance

There are many possible sources of finance available for the building of theatres and it is most likely that several of them will be tapped in each individual case. They include:
private gifts, legacies and endowments;
loans from banks, building societies, insurance companies, local authorities or private individuals;
grants from local authorities paid for out of local taxation, for instance out of the 'sixpenny rate' (now $2\frac{1}{2}$p) that local authorities in Britain are authorised to levy for the arts;
grants from national sources out of general taxation, for instance the Arts Council's 'Housing the Arts' fund, the Ministry of Education's grants, the University Grants Commission, and the British Film Institute;
charitable trusts and foundations with interest in the arts;
a fund-raising appeal in which the public is asked to contribute towards a fund with private gifts, subscriptions and covenants, the appeal being accompanied by fund-raising activities of many kinds such as garden parties, sweepstakes, dances, dinners and charity performances.

Commerce and industry will sometimes lend support, but tax advantages do not play much part in this in Britain. The whole situation could be changed overnight by new government legislation. For instance, if in Britain the severe restrictions on lotteries were relaxed, the problems of fund-raising might be simplified out of all recognition. If companies were allowed to set off expenditure on the arts against taxation or if there were a substantial increase in the money from central government sources, a more favourable situation would arise.

Continuous sources of income

Once the building opens the continuous sources of revenue can be classified as follows:

1   Sources direct from the activities of the theatre:
box office receipts;
sale of refreshments and bar profits which may be either direct or from concessionaires;
restaurant profits;
sale of programmes and advertising in them by outside firms;

kiosk sales of books, records, etc;

club members' subscriptions;

revenue from transfer of successful productions;

film and television rights;

hiring out of costumes or scenery to outside groups or companies.

2   Indirect sources connected with the particular theatre:
If the theatre is part of a much larger building complex which may include, for instance, shops and offices, the revenue from these may be collected by the theatre. It is more likely that the landlord may offset a reduced rent from the theatre against income from these other sources.

Touring companies using the theatre may themselves be subsidised. There have also been hidden subsidies such as the readiness of actors to accept low wages which did not bear comparison with other occupations. The pay and conditions are showing signs of improvement and this situation may not exist for very much longer.

3   Revenue from sources outside the theatre:
the local authority may choose to support a theatre with a revenue grant taken from the same authorised rate for the support of the arts;

local authority education grants for instance for plays put on in connection with school examinations;

Arts Council revenue grants;

charities and foundations;

commerce and industry;

private gifts and subscriptions;

fund-raising activities.

21   Comparison of theatres

Having examined the practical requirements of the various departments which go to make up a theatre and considered what is expected of the site, it is interesting to see what has actually been done by comparing plans and longitudinal sections to the same scale of a number of theatres, with the basic elements of auditorium, stage, backstage and dressing room accommodation and space for public circulation and amenity, shown in simplified form.

Twenty-five theatres, mostly in England, have been chosen for this analysis. Their differences in shape and scale can clearly be seen in the drawings and more detailed statistics, areas and dimensions, have been set out in the table of comparison of statistics.

The table overleaf gives an approximate percentage of each building devoted to each basic element. These figures are calculated on areas, not volumes, and they can indicate only the quantity of space, not its quality. For instance, under the title of 'other space' foyers and public circulation are included but in multi-tier theatres a large proportion of this space will be taken up with escape stairs and additional circulation. Not only does the scale of the various theatres differ, but there are marked differences in the proportion of space allotted to the various elements. The site areas of the theatres shown range from approximately 650 m² for Wyndhams to over 14,400 m² at Ottawa.

The only common factor is the individual theatregoer in an auditorium seat. Site lines and audibility restrict the maximum dimensions and standards of comfort restrict the number who can be accommodated within the space defined by these dimensions.

	Theatre	Normal use	Date built	Architect	Seating capacity	No. of tiers	Approximate site area at ground level (m²)	Approximate site area per seat (m²)
1	Wyndham's London	Drama	1899	W. G. R. Sprague	765	3	680	0·89
2	Apollo London	Drama	1901	Lewen Sharpe	827	4	777	0·94
3	Shaftesbury London	Drama & Musicals	1911	Bertie Crewe	1 300	3	873	0·67
4	Aldwych London	Drama	1905	W. G. R. Sprague	1 030	3	905	0·88
5	Piccadilly London	Drama & Musicals	1928	Bertie Crewe & E. A. Stone	1 144	3	921	0·80
6	Mermaid* London	Drama	1959	Elidir Davies	498	1	985	2·01
7	Palace London	Musicals (built for opera)	1891	T. E. Collcutt & G. H. Holloway	1 462	4	1 036	0·71
8	Old Vic London	Drama	1818	Rudolf Cabanel	878	3	1 137	1·29
9	Festival* Chichester	Drama	1962	Powell & Moya	1 360	1	1 171	0·86
10	Forum Billingham	Drama	1968	Elder Lester & Partners	637	3	1 304	2·04
11	Thorndike Leatherhead	Drama	1969	Roderick Ham	530	1	1 417	2·67
12	Belgrade Coventry	Drama	1957	Arthur Ling Coventry City Arch.	910	2	1 435	1·54
13	Shakespeare Memorial Stratford	Drama	1932	Scott, Chesterton & Shepherd	1 353	3	1 444	1·34
14	Playhouse Nottingham	Drama	1963	Peter Moro & Partners	756	2	1 537	2·03
15	Crucible* Sheffield	Drama & Studio	1971	Renton Howard Wood Associates	1 018	1	2 090	2·06
16	Royal Opera House Covent Garden London	Opera & Ballet	1858 1964	Sir Edward Barry (upper tiers reconstructed by Peter Moro)	2 110	6	2 638	1·25
17	Coliseum London	Opera	1904	Frank Matcham	2 340	4	3 075	1·31
18	Bayreuth Germany	Opera	1876	Otto Brueckwald (& Richard Wagner)	1 645	3	3 131	1·90
19	Civic Theatre Trier, Germany	Drama	1964	G. Graubner	622	1	3 140	5·03
20	Theatre Royal Drury Lane London	Musicals	1812 1922	Benjamin Wyatt (Auditorium reconstructed by Emblin Walker & Edward Jones)	2 283	4	3 196	1·40
21	New York State Theatre, U.S.A.	Musicals	1964	Philip Johnson	2 729	6	3 577	1·31
22	Civic Theatre Gelsenkirchen Germany	Drama & Opera	1959	Werner Ruhnau Ortwin Rave Max von Hausen	1 059	3	4 385	4·15
23	Helsinki City Th. Finland	Drama & Studio	1967	Timo Penttila	920 (200)	2	6 466	5·76
24	National Opera House, Paris	Opera & Musicals	1874	Charles Garnier	2 150	6	8 770	4·08
25	National Arts Centre Ottawa	Opera Drama & Studio	1969	Affleck, Desbarats, Dimakopoulos, Lebensold, Sise	2 300 (O) 900 (D)	4 2 1	14 420	4·65

*open stage

Approximate allocation of space (per cent)				Auditorium dimensions metres (see key plans & sections in margin)			Proscenium dimensions		Stage dimensions		
Auditorium	Working stage	Total stage area including scene dock, property rooms & all ancillary accommodation	Other space	Width (W1) for a fan shaped auditorium the greater width (W2) is shown in brackets	Horizontal distance from proscenium to back of auditorium (D)	Height above stage of topmost seat (T)	Width (P)	Height above stage (H)	Width (S1) (S2)	Depth (S3) (S4)	Height to grid above floor (G)
37	23	32	31	10 700 (16 800)	18 300	11 900	8 200	7 900	19 200	8 800	14 900
38	23	38	24	13 700	20 400	15 200	9 100	8 800	21 300	8 500	18 300
55	22	27	18	20 700	23 200	12 200	10 100	9 100	21 300	9 700	15 500
34	23	32	34	16 500	22 200	11 000	9 100	7 900	20 100	12 200	17 100
39	24	36	25	17 400	23 800	13 400	9 400	8 500	20 700	12 200	16 500
30	14	16	54	14 900	24 100	5 200			14 900	8 200	
38	21	35	27	15 500 (19 200)	26 800	18 300	10 400	10 400	20 100	14 600	22 900
44	17	43	13	21 600	25 600	9 100	8 500	8 500	18 900	10 400	16 200
60	10	15	25	12 200	24 400	5 800			11 000	12 800	
28	20	32	20	20 700	20 700	7 900	13 400	7 000	21 300	11 900	17 100
23	15	44	33	12 200 (23 500)	17 400	4 600	9 700	4 900	18 900	10 100	14 000
25	13	36	39	14 600 (21 900)	19 800		11 000	5 500	18 300	8 800	12 500
36	18	39	25	18 300 (26 800)	25 900	10 100	9 100	7 000	17 700 36 600	14 000	19 800
24	22	40	36	21 900	20 400	9 100	9 700	6 500	29 000	15 200	18 300
32 10	7	28	30	14 600		4 900			5 500	28	
28	19	47	25	23 200	36 600	16 500	15 200	11 900	27 400	27 100	22 000
29	24	38	33	30 500	32 300	15 200	16 800	11 900	27 400	25 000	21 000
21	21	57	22	15 200 (32 600)	33 000	12 900	12 900	11 600	28 000	23 200	29 600
10	18	78	12	15 800 (30 500)	19 800	3 700	12 200 15 800	7 300 10 400	20 200	16 800	20 700
19	18	48	33	17 100 (23 200)	25 000	15 800	12 800	9 500	24 100	23 800	21 600
21	12	30	49	30 500	40 800	21 300	17 100	15 500	23 200	15 200	29 300
10	21	51	39	22 900	19 800	12 200	11 600 15 800	8 500	23 800	16 800 33 000	24 400
8 4	13 4	55	33	36 000	21 300	9 100	11 600	10 100	32 000 58 000	22 900	23 200
17	11	24	59	23 200	30 500	12 200	15 800	13 700	45 700	26 000	36 300
8 4	10 4 2	42	44	(O) 35 000 (D) 27 400 (37 200)	35 000 20 700	15 200 12 200	18 300 13 700	12 200 7 900	27 400 56 300 24 400 38 000	18 900 35 000 14 600 19 812	28 000 18 900

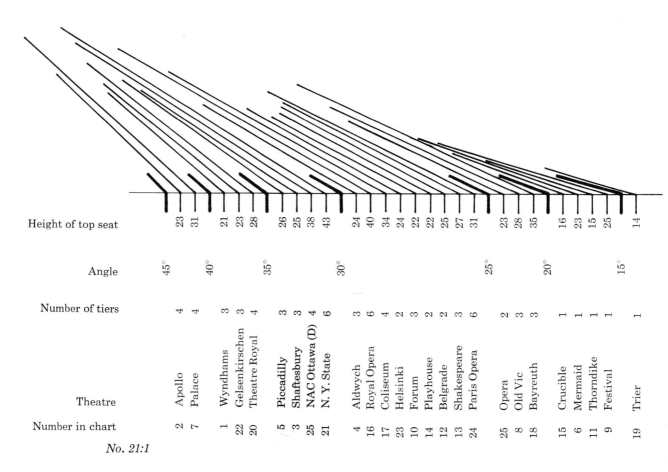

Height of top seat	23	31		21	23	28		26	25	38	43		24	40	34	24	22	22	25	27	31		23	28	35		16	23	15	25		14
Angle	45°		40°			35°					30°										25°				20°				15°			
Number of tiers	4	4		3	3	4		3	3	4	6		3	6	4	2	3	2	2	3	6		2	3	3		1	1	1	1		1
Theatre	Apollo	Palace		Wyndhams	Gelsenkirschen	Theatre Royal		Piccadilly	Shaftesbury	NAC Ottawa (D)	N. Y. State		Aldwych	Royal Opera	Coliseum	Helsinki	Forum	Playhouse	Belgrade	Shakespeare	Paris Opera		Opera	Old Vic	Bayreuth		Crucible	Mermaid	Thorndike	Festival		Trier
Number in chart	2	7		1	22	20		5	3	25	21		4	16	17	23	10	14	12	13	24		25	8	18		15	6	11	9		19

No. 21:1

This diagram shows how the form affects the distance and the angle of sight from the topmost seat to the front of the stage. In the case of proscenium theatres this point has been taken at the curtain line disregarding any forestage.

Each theatre plan and section is numbered to correspond with its number in the tables of comparative data above.

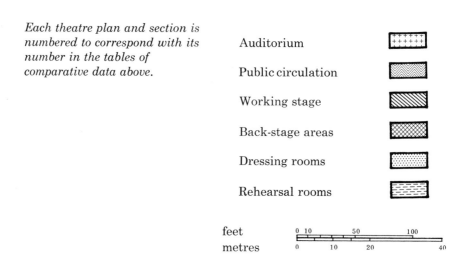

Auditorium

Public circulation

Working stage

Back-stage areas

Dressing rooms

Rehearsal rooms

feet

metres

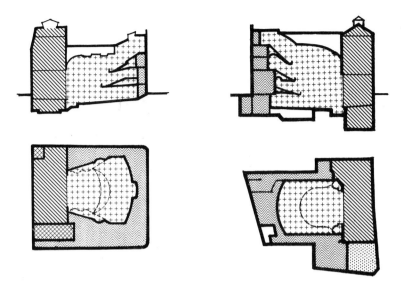

1 *Wyndham's Theatre, London*   **2** *Apollo, London*

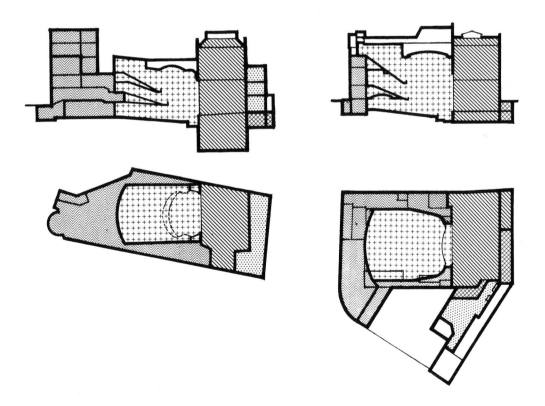

4 *Aldwych, London*   **5** *Piccadilly, London*

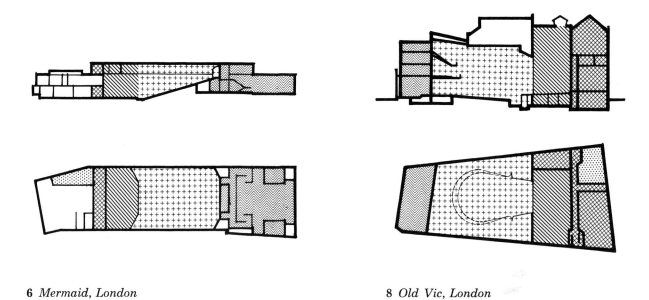

6 *Mermaid, London*

8 *Old Vic, London*

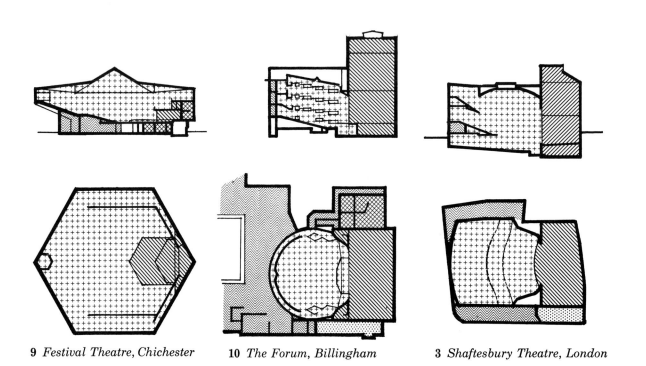

9 *Festival Theatre, Chichester*

10 *The Forum, Billingham*

3 *Shaftesbury Theatre, London*

In the last century, it was acceptable to cram many more people into an auditorium than would be tolerated at the present time. For instance, when the Grand Theatre, Leeds, opened in 1878, it had a seating capacity of 2600 with standing room for a further 200. The same auditorium now seats a maximum of 1558. Recent theatres in Germany and in the United States have sometimes spread the audience so thinly that the characteristic concentrated atmosphere of a closely packed audience is entirely dissipated and it becomes very difficult for live players to make any dramatic contact with the audience.

The floor area per seat in the auditorium does vary from theatre to theatre and from era to era, but still there is more in common between auditoria of similar seating capacity than there is in any other department of the theatre building. Compare for example London's Royal Opera House, Covent Garden, with the National Opera House, Paris.

They each have a traditional horseshoe-shaped auditorium with very similar seating capacities. Not surprisingly, the shape and size of the auditoria are almost identical, but in every other respect the difference in scale of the two buildings is enormous. In Paris, the auditorium is completely submerged in a vast baroque building on the scale of a cathedral rather than a theatre. In fact the plan dimensions correspond remarkably closely with those of Amiens cathedral, including transepts.

While the auditorium floor area per seat does not vary widely, the site area taken up by the auditorium as a whole, depends upon how many tiers there are. The main reason for introducing seating on several levels is to get as many people as possible within seeing and hearing distance of the stage. At the same time it is a method of squeezing more accommodation on to a restricted site. The proportion of site area occupied by the auditorium is seen at its maximum of 55% at the Shaftesbury Theatre, and at its minimum of 10% in the two modern German theatres. In the cases of Ottawa and Helsinki the large auditorium accounts for 8% of the site area, but these buildings contain more than one auditorium.

In terms of providing the maximum number of seats on a small site, the achievement of the architect of the Shaftesbury is remarkable. By ingenious planning the amount of dead space is reduced to an absolute minimum. Like other London West End theatres, the entrance is arranged at approximately front circle level and the space under the circle tier is used for foyers and public spaces. But however cunningly economic the planning, the auditorium can only occupy a greater proportion of the site at the expense of the stage or public areas or both.

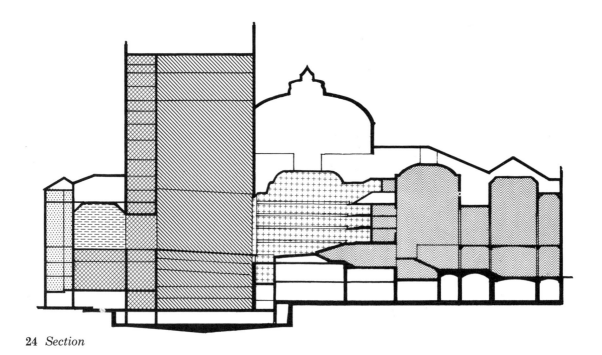

24 *Section*

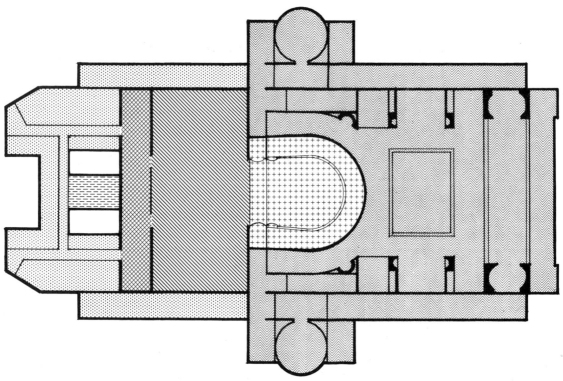

24 *Plan*   *National Opera House, Paris*

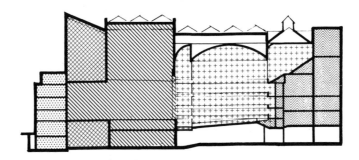

16 *Section*

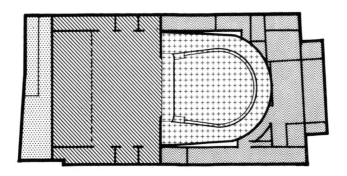

16 *Plan*   *Royal Opera House Covent Garden, London*

The auditorium of the Covent Garden Opera House is about the same size and capacity as that of the Paris Opera but the rest of the building is by comparison on a diminutive scale.

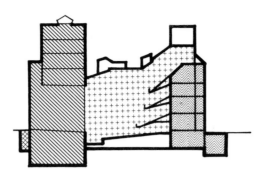

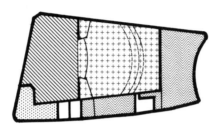

7 *Palace Theatre, London*

Even our largest London theatres, Covent Garden, Drury Lane and the Coliseum do not occupy island sites. One of the few in London which does is the Palace Theatre, built as an opera house and now used for musicals, but the shape and size of the main elements of the theatre were obviously dictated by the tight boundaries of the site.

The problem in London has been to provide an auditorium and enough seats to enable the theatre to pay its way on a site which, because of the high land value, is invariably restricted and frequently of irregular shape.

Unlike most other European nations, Britain has no tradition of civic theatres. Virtually all theatres built up to the time of the second world war were commercial ventures. Since the war the economic situation has changed and most new theatres have a measure of civic or national support even if they cannot be classed as civic theatres in the German sense. The stringent economic curbs remain and many schemes only get under way because there is an old building which it is possible to convert or even because a new one designed for another purpose happens to be available as at Leicester 1963 and Leeds Playhouse 1970.

The horseshoe-shaped auditorium with several tiers facing a proscenium stage was the traditional theatre plan in the nineteenth and early twentieth centuries. For a scenically dominated theatre, sight lines were not very good from many of the seats and it was to satisfy Wagner's requirements for the focus of all seats to be the conductor that the fan-shaped auditorium was introduced at the Bayreuth Opera House in 1876.

Here the stalls are stepped and there are two shallow tiers at the rear, all with excellent sightlines. However, the house was designed not just for opera, but a particular kind of German Grand Opera which, in Wagner's view, was to be a personal experience for

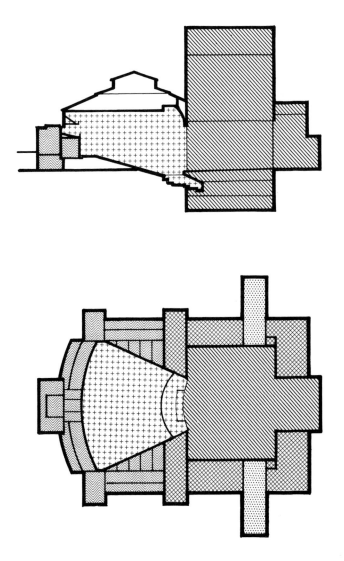

18 *Bayreuth Opera House, West Germany*

each individual present at a performance. The flow of the music drama might be interrupted by a corporate audience response which must therefore be avoided.

The flow of a film can only be interrupted by a mechanical break-down and sight lines being the most important factor, the fan shape was a very suitable shape for a cinema auditorium for which, with the addition of a deep balcony, it became standard. But the Bayreuth influence spread further and the fan shape with deep balconies was used in many theatres whose principal use was for drama, and some of its shortcomings became apparent. A deep gallery tends to divide the audience into two and makes it more difficult for the players to get a unified audience reaction. The diverging side walls give an effect of false perspective which exaggerates the distance from the stage. In an auditorium with boxes or balconies lining the side walls, it is unquestionable that the sight lines from seats in these positions are not so geometrically excellent as those enclosed within a fan. This is the principal argument in favour of the fan form, but the experience of attending a live performance is neither entirely visual nor entirely aural and auditorium shapes are also chosen to improve the sense of audience participation. Bringing spectators round to the side of the auditorium helps to emphasize the acting area as a part of a combined audience and performance space and avoids the directional and distancing effect of a true fan shape. Attempts have been made to get the best of both worlds by placing an essentially fan-shaped seating arrangement within a curved or circular-shaped auditorium.

The search for new forms of expression in the drama has in this century led to a revival of interest in open stage forms. Until quite recently these were only found in universities or small unlicensed premises where experimental work was done. Open forms are now much more common and the qualification 'experimental' should be dropped. The blame for their slow development has sometimes been placed upon fire regulations and while it must be conceded that these have delayed the building of open stages on any large scale it does not follow that the picture-frame theatre was invented for the convenience of the safety curtain. Already by 1880, some twenty years before the first regulations were issued, there were theatres with a picture-frame moulding carried right round the proscenium opening including along the edge of the stage floor. A number of disastrous theatre fires occurred at the end of the last century which led to the widespread adoption of fire regulations and in particular to the familiar and almost universal safety curtain in a proscenium wall. The regulations were framed to meet an *ad hoc* situation which had developed as a natural historical process. Inevitably they tend to perpetuate the situation which they were designed to regulate.

The auditoria of the various theatres have common factors which can be compared wherever they are situated, but when it comes to other departments there is a division on national lines. The contrast between the Royal Opera House, Covent Garden, and the National Opera House in Paris has already been pointed out, but comparison of a British theatre with any of the German theatres, of which those illustrated are typical, will show similar striking differences. In Germany there is an operatic tradition of vast heavily mechanised stages and an industry has grown up to provide them. Whether such elaborate and expensive installations are necessary for the health and survival of the drama is questionable, but at the other extreme the lack of working stage space, wing

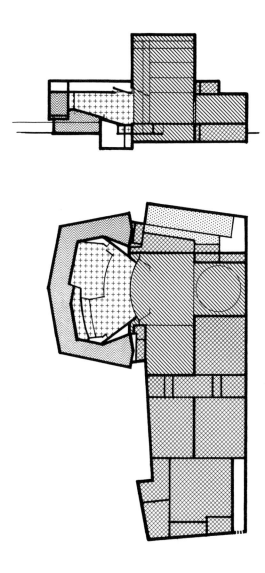

19 *Civic Theatre Trier, West Germany*

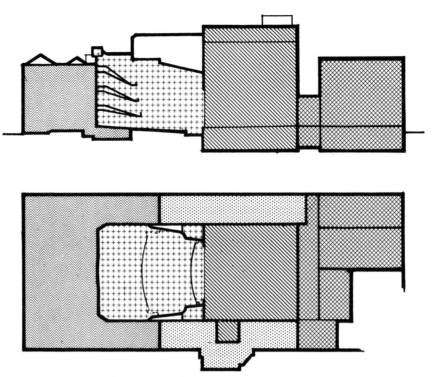

20 *Theatre Royal, Drury Lane, London*

space, scene docks, workshops, storage space, dressing rooms and all ancillary accommodation in most British theatres is a constant handicap and an expensive burden to bear. It is less onerous for West End theatres designed for long runs, than for theatres used for repertory or productions in repertoire, but as this more flexible pattern of use becomes more common, the demand for more space and equipment will become stronger.

The Theatre Royal, Drury Lane, seats 2283 and has an exceptionally large stage space for a London theatre, but compare it with the municipal theatre at Trier which has a seating capacity of 622 and a site almost as large.

The size of the Trier theatre is not exceptional for a small German town; Ingolstadt, which is smaller, has a much larger theatre. Trier is exceptional only in the proportion of the total area devoted to the stage and all backstage accommodation including dressing rooms which amounts to 78%. The figure for this element in the Gelsenkirchen theatre is only 51%, but this is due more to the lavish scale of the public areas than to any lack in the area taken up by the stage.

At the end of the nineteenth century, the Paris Opera House was the grandest example of a type of theatre built in many major cities at the time. Helsinki and Ottawa illustrate the present-day concept of a national theatre. In terms of scale and in the way the

25 *National Arts Centre, Ottawa, Canada*

three separate theatres are united within one building complex, our own National Theatre, now under construction on the South Bank in London, has much in common with Ottawa. For the first time we shall have a building with space and technical equipment on a scale appropriate to the standing of the company which will occupy it.

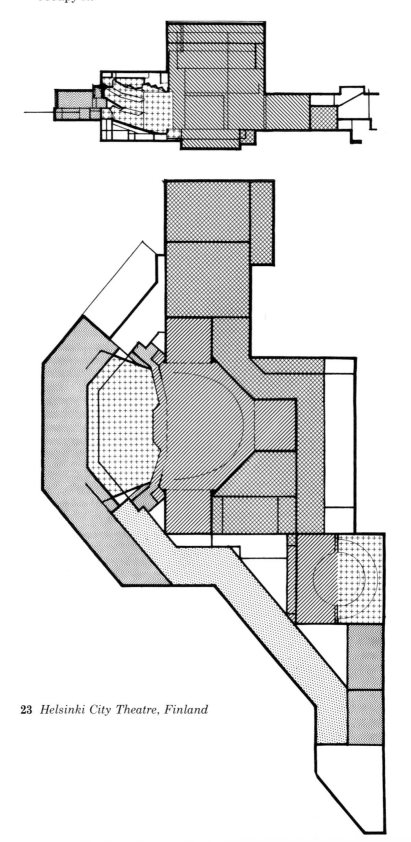

23 *Helsinki City Theatre, Finland*

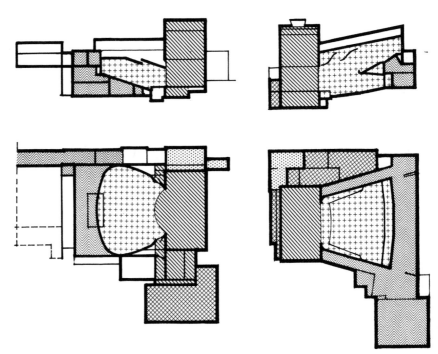

11 *Thorndike Theatre, Leatherhead* 12 *Belgrade Theatre, Coventry*

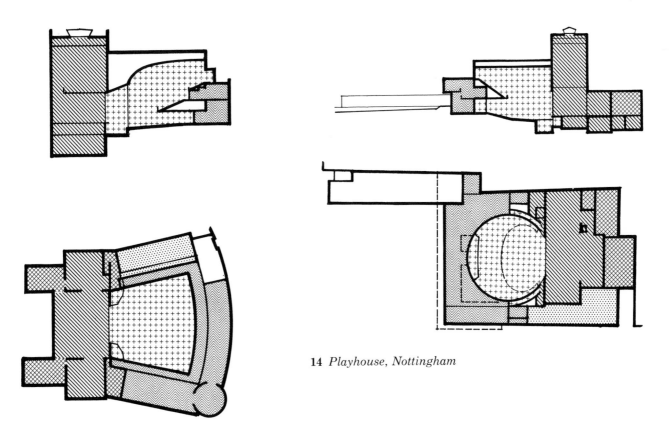

14 *Playhouse, Nottingham*

13 *Shakespeare Memorial Theatre, Stratford-on-Avon, England*

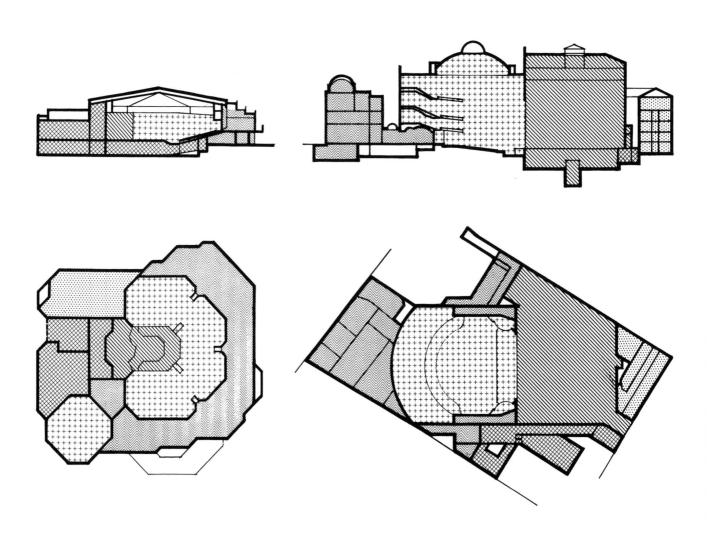

15 *Crucible, Sheffield*   **17** *Coliseum*

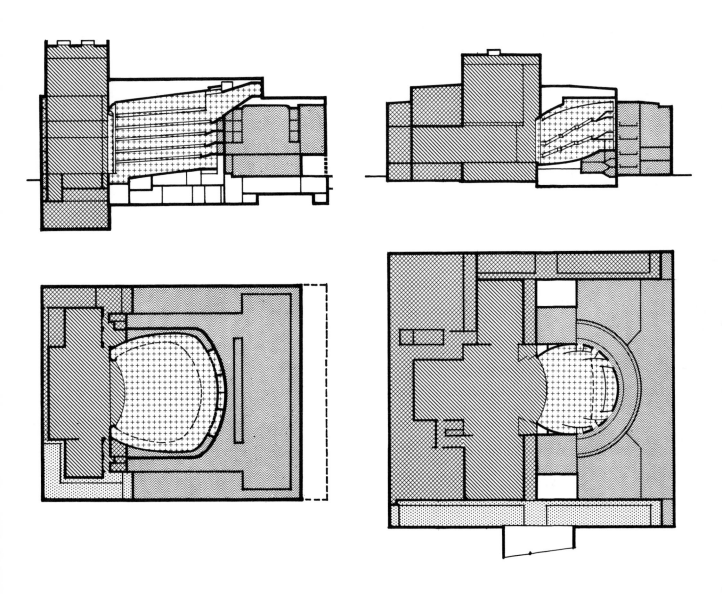

21 *New York State Theatre, USA*   **22** *Civic Theatre, Gelsenkirchen, West Germany*

Glossary of stage terms

This Glossary does not attempt to be exhaustive. A number of American terms have been included which should make it easier to study theatre literature from the United States.

Above *See Upstage.*

Act drop Painted cloth or curtain that may be lowered at the end of each act. *See also Cloth and Drop.*

Acting area Those portions of a stage in which any action of a performance takes place.

Amphitheatre Stepped banks of seating surrounding an arena. Also used to describe one of the tiers of a multi-level auditorium.

Apron The extension of a stage projecting outwards into the auditorium: in certain types of theatre the apron may be quite large. *See also Forestage.*

Arena One of the terms used to describe types of open stage. As it derives from the sand-strewn combat area in a Roman amphitheatre it should be a term for 360° encirclement, but it has been used to describe thrust stages.

Backdrop (Backcloth) *See Drop and Wing set.*

Backing Scenery used behind, and limiting the view of the audience through, an opening (e.g. doorway or window) in a set. *See also Masking.*

Band room Musicians' changing room.

Band shell Movable sound reflector placed behind a group of musicians on a stage or in the open air to improve acoustics.

Bar A tube, pipe or barrel for holding spotlights.

Barre A horizontal rail usually of wood used by ballet dancers when practising.

Barrel Length of metal pipe, suspended on a set of lines, to which scenery may be attached by means of snatch lines instead of being tied directly to the suspension lines. It is a standard part in a unit of the counterweight system.

Batten (lighting batten) Length of metal troughing carrying lamps, suspended above and lighting the acting area.

Batten (scenery batten) Length of rigid material, usually wood, used in scenery construction generally; also a length of timber carrying and stiffening a hanging cloth.

Bastard prompt The prompt side is always on the actor's left. The other side of the stage is called the op side (opposite prompt). If the stage manager's control desk and therefore the prompt corner happens to be on the op side it is called a bastard prompt.

Belay pin *See Pin.*

Below *See Downstage.*

Block *See Loft Block.*

Boat (boat truck) *See Truck.*

Bobbin (sliding bobbin) Cylindrical carrier for the suspension and movement of draw curtains on a horizontal track.

Book-flat Pair of flats hinged together and set like a book upon its edges.

Book-wing Wing constructed and set in a manner similar to a book-flat.

Border Abbreviated drop or pelmet used to mask the line of sight over a setting and to hide the flys, lighting battens, etc. (Sometimes painted to represent overhead foliage, etc.)

Box set Setting comprising a series of canvas flats arranged in a more or less continuous line around the three sides of the acting area away from the audience. Normally used for interior scenes. May be provided with a ceiling piece over.

Brace Piece of wood used diagonally in the frame of a flat to strengthen it.

Brace (extending brace) *See Stage Brace.*

Brace (french brace) *See French Brace.*

Brace-weight Slotted iron weight, normally rectangular, which can be set on the footiron of a brace to hold it in position (in lieu of a stage screw) for speed in setting and striking.

Bracing eye (brace cleat) Small metal plate attached to the frame of a flat, for attachment of a stage brace. Simple screw eyes are also used for this purpose.

Brail (brail line) Line used to pull and retain any piece of hanging scenery or property from the position it would occupy if left hanging free.

Break-up Scene or part of a scene, or a property, constructed to collapse or disintegrate as part of the action of a performance.

Bridge 1. A gallery bridging across the stage or auditorium used for lighting equipment.

2. A lift in the stage floor extending across the stage opening.

Bridle   A short length of cable or chain used to distribute the stress on a barrel at a suspension point.

Built-up-ground   *See Rocks.*

Canvas (canvasing)   The fabric used to form a cloth or to cover a flat, etc.

Call   Warning to be ready for a part of a performance. Once the job of the callboy, now done over the show relay system controlled at a 'call board'.

Carpenter   In touring theatres the resident stage manager is often called the 'stage carpenter'.

Carpet cut   Series of flaps in the stage floor which can be closed upon the downstage edge of a stage cloth to hold it in position.

Ceiling (ceiling piece)   Large canvas covered frame hung on two or three sets of lines and used to close in the top of an interior set.

Ceiling plate   Metal plate with a ring, used in bolting together and flying a ceiling frame.

Cill iron   *See Sill Iron.*

Clearing stick   *See Longarm.*

Cleat   Wooden or metal fitment round which a line may be turned and/or made fast. *See also Flyrail cleat, Throwline cleat, Tie-off-cleat.*

Clew   *See Trip.*

Cloth   Any hanging painted cloth. *See also Cut cloth, Drop, Stage Cloth.*

Collapse   *See Break-up.*

Column   Three-dimensional scenic piece, normally constructed from canvas on a wooden frame or from a lightweight plastic, to represent a structural or decorative column or pier.

Contour curtain   A curtain which is pulled up by cords or cables in swagged folds. The opening can be adjusted by pulling each cord to a different height. *See Festoon.*

Corner plate (corner block)   Small triangular piece of plywood used to reinforce joints in the frames of scenery.

Counterweights (counterweight system)   Mechanical system for flying scenery in which the weight of the pieces of scenery is balanced by adjustable weights in a cradle running up and down in guides in a frame normally at the side of the stage.

Cradle   *See Counterweights.*

Crossover   A passageway behind the stage for actors or technicians to cross from one side to the other.

Cue   The signal for an action by an actor or a technician during a performance. Actors' cues are mostly verbal, but for technicians they may be given verbally over the intercom by the stage manager or visually by a cue light.

Curtain line   The imaginary line across the stage immediately behind the proscenium which marks the position of the house tabs when closed. The term is sometimes used to describe the line of descent of the safety curtain, but this is normally downstage of the true curtain line. *See also Setting line.*

Curtain set   A setting comprising either curtains only or mainly curtains with a small amount of painted scenery in the form of an insert or a set piece. The curtains may be any combination of tabs, surround, legs, borders or gauze cloths.

Curtain track   Rails from which draw tabs are hung and along which the runners or bobbins travel when the curtains are moved; the track may be fixed or flown.

Cut   Any long opening in the floor or a stage. *See also Carpet cut.*

Cut cloth   A cloth which has a part cut out to reveal another cloth set behind; the cut-out portion is often filled with gauze.

Cyclorama   Plain, curved, stretched cloth or rigid structure used as a background to a setting, giving an illusion of infinity. *See also Surround.*

Dead   The predetermined level to which a suspended scenic piece is raised or lowered to take up its correct position in the setting. *See also Trim.*

Dips   Stage dips or dip traps are small traps in the stage containing stage-lighting outlets and electrical cables.

Dock   The scene dock is a store for scenery next to the stage. Scenery is unloaded and taken through the 'dock door' into the stage area.

Door flat   Scenic flat into which a door unit has been fitted.

Door stop   Metal plate screwed to the edge of a flat or other piece to provide positive location for the edge of another flat.

Door unit (insert door & reveal)   Wooden door frame, with practical door, made to fit into a flat.

Dope   *See Priming.*

Double purchase   A system of blocks and suspension ropes which gears the movement of a counterweight to half that of the scenery it is supporting.

Downstage   Portions of a stage nearest the audience. (To move downstage means to move towards the audience; to move below a person or object means to move on the side nearest the audience.)

Draperies (drapes)   Any unspecified fabric hanging in folds as a scene or part of a scene, especially curtaining fabrics such as woollens, velvets, etc. *See also Curtain set.*

Draw tabs (curtains)   Curtains suspended from sliding or rolling carriers running in an overhead track and opened by being drawn to the sides.

Drencher   A perforated sparge pipe which in the event of a fire will spray water on the back of the safety curtain.

Dresser   Personal assistant to a star performer or to someone with an elaborate costume.

Drop   Large sheet of canvas battened at top and bottom, hung on a set of lines. The term is also used sometimes to describe a curtain hung on lines and lowered vertically. *See also Act drop.*

Drop holder   Metal fitting for attaching a drop direct to a suspension line.

False proscenium (show portal)   Arrangement of scenery forming an arch immediately behind the proscenium opening. *See also Teaser and Tormentor.*

Festoon tabs (curtains)   Curtains fixed at the top and raised (opened) by drawing the bottom upwards towards the top and/or sides. *See also Contour Curtain.*

Fire curtain   *See Safety Curtain.*

Fireplace flat   Scenic flat to which a fireplace unit has been fitted.

Fireplace unit   Framework of timber covered with painted canvas, arranged to represent a fireplace and made to fit into a flat.

Fireproofed (flameproofed)   Treated with a flame-inhibiting substance so as to reduce the danger of ignition. (NB Fireproofing does not render a material non-combustible.)

Fit-up   Arrangement of constructional units which can be put together and taken apart in a relatively short time and which can be transported from place to place and set up to form a stage, etc, in premises not equipped for the performance of stage plays.

Fixing iron   Metal plate with a fixed ring (as distinct from a flying iron which has a hinged ring) used for scenery suspension.

Flat   A unit section of flat scenery, in the form of a tall screen of canvas stretched upon a wooden frame. *See also Door flat, Fireplace flat, Window flat, Book-flat, Threefold, French flat.*

Flipper   Small piece of flat scenery hinged to a larger piece of flat scenery.

Floats (footlights)   Row of lamps on front edge of stage at floor level and in front of main (house) curtain, used principally to neutralise shadows cast by overhead lighting.

Flown   Suspended on lines as distinct from standing on the stage floor or hanging from fixed rails, etc.

Fly   Lift above the level of the stage floor by means of sets of lines run from the grid. The term flys is also used as an abbreviation for fly gallery.

Fly gallery (flying gallery)   A gallery extending along a side wall of the stage, some distance above the stage floor, from which ropes used in flying scenery are operated. Also known as a fly floor. The fly galleries are usually referred to collectively as the flys.

Fly rail   Heavy rail along the onstage side of a fly gallery, equipped with cleats to which the ropes can be made fast.

Flys   *See Fly gallery.* Sometimes spelled flies.

Flying iron   Metal plate with a hinged ring used for scenery suspension.

Flyman   Stagehand employed on a fly gallery.

Fly-rail cleat   Metal fitting secured to a fly rail, to which a rope can be easily made fast.

Folding rostrum   *See Rostrum.*

Follow spot   A high-intensity spotlight controlled and directed by an operator used to follow, for example, a performer in a variety act.

Foot-iron   Metal bracket used with a stage screw or braceweight to secure scenery or a stage brace in position. *See also Spring foot-iron.*

Forestage   Portion of the stage floor in front of the curtain line. *See also Apron.*

Frame (paint frame)   Wooden frame to which cloths can be attached for painting in a vertical position.

Framed cloth   Scenic cloth battened all round.

French brace   Triangular frame hinged to the back of a piece of standing scenery and folded flat for storage.

French flat   Arrangement of several flats battened together and flown as one unit on a set of lines.

Front cloth   Sometimes a painted cloth is brought down near to the house curtain for a front scene to be played on the forestage. This front cloth usually masks scene changes behind it.

Front of house (FOH)   Areas of a theatre on the audience side of the proscenium wall or stage area are called FOH.

Gauze (gauze cloth)   Flat curtain of fine mesh mosquito netting or similar fabric, either painted or unpainted, which when lit solely from the front appears to be opaque, but when lit from behind becomes transparent. It is used for a transformation scene or other illusions. A fabric known as 'shark's tooth' is also used for this purpose.

Get in (and out)   The process of delivering and taking scenery and props in and out of a theatre.

Glue size   A preparation used in priming and paint for scenery.

Grave trap   An oblong trap usually downstage centre; originally the 'ghost trap'.

Grid (gridiron)   Framework of steel or wooden beams over the stage used to support the sets of lines employed in flying scenery.

Grid pulley   *See Loft block.*

Ground plan   Plan of a stage on which is marked the position of the scenery in a setting (including borders, hanging pieces and sometimes lighting equipment).

Groundrow   Low topped piece of flat scenery, profiled and painted to represent ground foliage, a bank of earth, a distant mountain range, etc, designed to stand up independently on the stage.

Grummet   Metal fitting resembling a saddle, for attaching a throw-line to a piece of scenery.

Handling ropes   Ropes actually manipulated in flying scenery, as distinct from suspension ropes or cables (counterweight system), also called hauling line. *See also Hemps.*

Hanging iron (hanger iron)   Metal fitting, formed into a square hook at one end, used in flying flats and other framed pieces.

Hanging loft   The space above a stage in which scenery can be flown out of sight of the audience. Also called fly loft or stage loft.

Head block   *See Lead block.*

Hemps   The term is usually employed to signify lines used for flying scenery which are made from vegetable fibre as distinct from the steel wire ropes used in the counterweight system. Hemp lines are hauled up manually and tied off on a cleat or pin on the fly rail. A *hemp house* is a stage equipped with these hand-operated 'hemp sets' and no counterweights. *See Pin-rail system.*

House tabs (curtains)   The main curtains between stage and audience, normally placed immediately behind the proscenium (they may be either draw tabs or festoon tabs, and they may be flown).

Insert door and reveal   *See Door unit.*

Inset   Small scene set within a larger one.

Iron (iron curtain)   *See Safety curtain.*

Jack   *See French brace.*

Jigger   Narrow section set between and hinged to two of the flats forming a threefold so as to allow both of the outer flats to fold painted side inwards on to the centre flat. This section may also be referred to as a tumbler (qv).

Jog   Narrow flat, usually substantially less than half the width of a standard flat, used to form short return to a major surface and thus increase the illusion of solidity. *See also Reveal (thickness).*

Keystone   Small piece of plywood in the wedge shape of an architectural keystone, used to reinforce joints in scenery.

Lantern   Stage lantern or haystack lantern is the term given to the automatic smoke vent over the stage. 'Lanterns' are also stage-lighting units though the recommended word is now Luminaires.

Lash cleat   *See Throw-line cleat.*

Lashline   *See Throw-line.*

Lashline eye   *See Grummet.*

Lead block (head block)   Device comprising three or more sheaves set together either in a line or parallel to each other on a common shaft and attached to the grid directly above the fly rail. The lines from the three or more loft blocks in a set are brought together at the lead block and pass on down to the fly-rail cleat in a hemp set or to the weight cradle in a counterweight set.

Leg   Vertical length of unframed canvas or other fabric used in place of a wing. *See also Curtain set.*

Lift   Section of stage floor that can be raised or lowered or tilted to provide differing levels of acting area, or to enable changes of setting to be made in the stage basement. Also known as a bridge or in N. America as an elevator. *See also Rostrum.*

Lighting batten   *See Batten.*

Limes   Now a front of house position for follow spots.

Lines   *See Set of lines, also Brail, Spot line and Throw-line.*

Loading gallery   Narrow gallery above the fly gallery, used for storing the weights and loading them on the cradles when balancing scenery in the counterweight system.

Locking rail   In a counterweight system the handling rope passes through a rope lock attached to a locking rail which runs the length of the counterweight wall frame.

Loft block (grid pulley)   Sheave in a metal frame bolted to the grid and used to pass a suspension line; there is one block for each line in a set. *See also Set of lines.*

Longarm (clearing stick)   Long piece of wood or other lightweight material fitted with a short crosspiece at the upper end, used for freeing scenery, lines, etc, when accidentally caught up or fouled.

Louvred ceiling   Arrangement of ceiling pieces, each hung on two sets of lines with the downstage edge higher than the upstage edge, so as to form a ceiling with gaps through which light may be projected.

Luminaire   An illuminating engineer's term for a stage-lighting unit or lantern.

Masking (masking piece)   A piece of scenery, not necessarily painted, used to cut off from the view of the spectators any part of the stage space which should not be seen. *See also Backing and Permanent masking.*

Off-stage   Any position on the stage floor out of sight of the audience.

On-stage   Any position on the stage within the acting area.

OP (opposite prompt)   The side of the stage opposite the prompt side: traditionally stage right is actors' right. When the prompt corner, occupied by the prompter, is on this side of the stage, it is sometimes known as a 'bastard prompt'.

Pack   All the pieces required for a particular scene when stacked together in the correct order for setting.

Packing rail   Or 'stacking rail'. A rail, usually of steel tube, projecting from stage or store wall against which flats are stacked.

Paint bridge   A platform or wide cradle the width of the paint frame which can be hauled up and down usually mechanically so that all parts of a cloth can be reached.

Paint frame   The frame to which backcloths, flats, etc, are fixed for painting in a vertical position.

Panorama hinge   A hinge formed by two interlinked rings each attached to a metal plate.

Parallel   *See Rostrum.*

Pass door   A door connecting the front of house with the back-stage area.

Pelmet clip and socket   *See Picture-frame hook and socket.*

Perch   Position above stage level on the stage side of the proscenium wall either side of the opening.

Periaktoi   A triangular-plan-shaped scenic device originating in the classical Greek theatre. Each surface can be painted with a different subject, colour or texture so that revolving periaktoi can change a scene.

Permanent masking   Show portal, or teaser and tormentors, or similar arrangements of masking pieces which remain in place throughout a performance, regardless of scene changes.

Picture-frame hook and socket   Two-piece metal fitting used to hang one unit of scenery, or a stage property, on another unit.

Piece   Any unit of scenery, but more especially a major item.

Pin   Belaying pin, used for making fast hemp lines. *See also Fly-rail cleat.*

Pin hinge   A hinge with removable pin, used so that the two halves may be easily separated.

Pin rail   *See Fly rail.*

Pin-rail system   A system for flying scenery in which the suspension lines are taken over loft blocks and lead blocks and then brought straight down to the pin rail (fly rail); there are no counterweights or other means of sustaining the load of the scenery when the lines are free of the pins (cleats).

Pipe batten   *See Barrel.*

Platform   *See Rostrum.*

Portal   Unit of permanent masking set between the show portal and the backdrop or cyclorama. In America the term is also used to signify the proscenium opening.

Power line   Suspension line in a flying system operated by a motor.

Practical   Capable of being used for its apparent function, as distinct from being merely decorative, e.g. a hinged door, a switch that actually controls a light, etc.

Priming   Mixture of glue size and whiting in solution, used as a primer in scene painting.

Profile   Plywood or other thin material covered with canvas or scrim, used for forming non-straight edges to wings, groundrows etc.

Prompt corner   The stage manager's control point.

Prompt box   The traditional position for the prompter in opera is in a box let into the front of the stage.

Prompt side (PS)   Traditionally stage left, i.e. actors' left, regardless of the position of the prompter.

Properties (props)   Objects, such as furniture, pictures, carpets, flowers, books, implements, weapons, etc. used in a performance.

Proscenium (pros)   The theoretical 'fourth wall' of a stage, comprising the proscenium opening and its surrounding treatments. *See also False proscenium.*

Proscenium doors   Doors on either side of the stage leading on to a forestage in front of the house curtain or act drop.

Proscenium opening (proscenium arch)   The opening through which spectators view the stage.

Pulley   *See Loft block.*

Rail   Horizontal member of the frame of a flat. *See also Fly rail and Toggle rail.*

Rake   A sloped floor of auditorium or stage.

Raking piece   Length of wood tapered for placing under a scenic piece so that it will set level on a raked stage floor.

Ramp   Inclined rostrum, normally sloping up from the stage floor.

Return   The narrower of two flats cleated, hinged or otherwise fixed together at an angle. *See also Jog.*

Reveal (thickness)   Piece of timber or other material attached to the edge of an opening (e.g. a doorway) to give the effect of depth or thickness.

Revolve   Circular table forming a permanent part of the stage floor or standing upon it, upon which scenery can be set for quick changing of scene or for creating various effects. Sometimes the revolve is formed of two or three rings and a centre, capable of independent or simultaneous movement, differing speeds and opposite directions. It can be turned through 360° either manually or by motor.

Rig   Set-up scenery on stage. 'Rigging' is a collective term for the suspension equipment.

Riser   The vertical front of a raised stage where it faces the auditorium is the 'stage riser'.

Rocks   Rostrum of irregular form, to simulate uneven terrain. If not to be stood or walked upon, the piece comprises only a canvas or other lightweight material covering a wooden framework.

Roller   Where there is no flying space over the stage a backdrop can be rolled and is then called a roller or roll drop. Roller safety curtains are permitted in some circumstances.

Rope lock   The handling rope of a counterweight set passes through a 'rope lock' which when locked prevents any further movement.

Rope sheave   *See Loft block.*

Rostrum   Platform placed on the stage floor to create changes of level where required. A large rostrum is usually constructed in sections with loose tops and folding frames, but some small ones are rigid. A sloping rostrum is known as a ramp. *See also Lift.*

Runner   Length of stage flooring that can be drawn off sideways leaving a long narrow opening (cut) through which a cloth or flat may be raised.

Saddle iron   *See Sill iron.*

Safety curtain   Screen or shutter comprising a framework of steel or wrought iron faced with sheet iron and asbestos fabric, mounted immediately behind the proscenium opening and fitted with mechanism for raising it clear of the top of the proscenium arch and with a quick-release device to allow it to descend by gravity in the event of fire on the stage.

Sandbag   Bag of canvas with strap and ring, filled with sand and used for weighting purposes.

Scene pack   A set of flats, etc, which form a particular set.

Scenery paint   Paint composed of glue size and powder colour in water, sometimes with whiting added to give body, used for painting scenery (p.v.a. emulsion paint can also be used for this purpose).

Scrim   Coarse woven hessian, or similar material, used in scenery construction.

Set   Arrangement of scenery units which together represent a single location. The term is also used as a verb to mean to put up or assemble scenery for use (e.g. to set a stage).

Set of lines   Unit group of suspension lines hanging from the grid for the attachment and flying of scenery; there are usually three or four lines in a set. *See also Counterweight system and Pin-rail system.*

Set piece   Built-up unit of scenery, complete in itself, often three-dimensional, and capable of standing free on the stage floor.

Setting line   The imaginary line across the stage, in front of which scenery cannot be hidden by the house curtain. *See also Curtain line.*

Sheave   Grooved wheel (pulley) over which a line may be passed.

Shot-bag   Similar to a sandbag but smaller and filled with lead-shot.

Show portal   *See False proscenium.*

Sill iron (saddle iron)   Narrow strip of metal, often half-round, used to brace the bottom of a door flat across the doorway opening.

Single purchase   A suspension system where there is no gearing of pulleys. The counterweight and its travel will be the same as that of the object which is suspended.

Size   *See Glue size.*

Sky cloth   Unit of scenery used to convey the impression of open sky. *See also Backdrop and Cyclorama.*

Spot block   Pulley fixed to the grid specially for a spot line.

Spot line   Single suspension line specially rigged from the grid to fly a piece of scenery or stage property which cannot be handled by the regular lines.

Spring foot-iron   Form of spring hinge screwed to the bottom of a piece of scenery or a french brace, for securing to the floor, self-closing out of the way when not in use.

Stacking rail   *See Packing rail.*

Stage brace   Adjustable device, comprising two lengths of wood sliding one along the other and held fast by clamps used to prop scenery from behind. *See also French brace.*

Stage cloth   Large piece of canvas, used to cover the stage floor, often painted to represent paving, etc.

Stage left   Actors' left. *See Prompt side.*

Stage right   Actors' right. *See Opposite prompt.*

Stage screw   Large tapered wood screw with a ring handle, used to secure a foot-iron to the stage floor.

Star (star trap)   *See Trap.*

Steps (treads)   Light portable stairway, normally in unit sections for easy handling.

Stile   Side or upright member in the frame of a flat.

Strike   Take apart and remove from the acting area a set of scenery after it has been used, usually at the end of an act.

Surround (curtains)   Set of legs (ordinary pleated curtains) hung from a curved or angled bar to form the sides and background to an acting area. *See also Curtain set.*

Swag   Looped-up curtain, border or leg.

Swivel arm   Device for suspending a leg so that the angle of the leg in relation to the proscenium can be varied.

Tableau curtains (tabs)   Either the house tabs or similar curtains which can be opened to reveal a scene. *See Draw tabs, Festoon tabs, House tabs, also Curtain set.*

Tail   The length of flex from a stage lighting unit.

Teaser   Border hung between the tormentors, just behind the proscenium opening. *See also Permanent masking.*

Thickness   *See Reveal.*

Threefold   An arrangement of three flats hinged together.

Throw-line   Length of cord attached by a grummet to a piece of scenery and used to secure the piece to an adjacent piece.

Throw-line cleat   Metal fitting attached to a flat or other piece, round which the throw-line is passed when securing adjacent pieces together.

Thunder sheet   A sheet of metal usually steel, suspended somewhere on the stage area. When it is shaken it gives a sound effect of thunder.

Tie-off cleat   Metal fitting around which a throw-line is made fast.

Toggle rail   Movable horizontal member in the frame of a flat, between the top rail and the bottom rail.

Top batten clip   *See Drop holder.*

Tormentor   Substantial wing, not necessarily painted, placed immediately behind the proscenium opening, to mask the offstage edges of the setting, etc. *See also Permanent masking.*

Track (curtain track)   Rails from which curtains are hung and along which they may move.

Trap   An opening in the stage floor. Special-purpose traps are grave traps, dip traps, star traps.

Treads   *See Steps.*

Tree   Set piece representing a tree trunk, with or without foliage.

Trim   Level off a piece of suspended scenery at the right height for use during a performance.

Trim chain   Short length of chain used in attaching the top batten of a cloth to a barrel.

Trip   Raise the bottom of a drop or other piece of suspended scenery, using an auxiliary set of lines, so as to make it occupy a space approximately half its height; tripping is resorted to on stages where there is not sufficient height above the stage floor to get the unit out of sight by taking it straight up with one set of lines only.

Truck   Low trolley, either running in tracks or free-moving, on which scenery, etc, can be mounted for horizontal linear movements of settings.

Tumbler   Batten or roller fixed to the bottom edge of a cloth, about which the cloth can be rolled upwards when not in use.

Twofold   *See Book-flat.*

Upstage   The portions of the stage furthest from the audience. (To move upstage means to move away from the audience; to move above a person or object means to move on the side furthest from the audience.)

Velarium   Ceiling cloth, not stretched or battened out, but hanging as a canopy.

Vomitory   An entrance through a block of seating as distinct from through the surrounding wall.

Wagon   *See Truck.*

Winch   Mechanism, either hand-operated or motorized, for opening and closing curtains, etc.

Window flat   Scenic flat into which a window unit has been fitted.

Window unit   Window frame with sashes made to fit into a flat.

Wing   Two or three flats hinged together and used at the side of the stage to mask off-stage space.

Wings   Off-stage spaces to left and right of the acting area.

Wing set (backcloth-and-wing set)   Setting comprising back-cloth (or cyclorama) and pairs of wings with borders above. Sometimes cut cloths are used in the place of wings and borders (e.g. for a woodland scene).

Theatres illustrated	Architects	Theatre consultants
Gulbenkian Centre, Hull	Peter Moro and Partners	Theatre Projects Consultants Ltd (lighting and sound)
The Crucible Theatre, Leicester	Renton, Howard, Wood Associates	Theatre Projects Consultants Ltd
The Phoenix, Leicester	City of Leicester Architects' Department	
The Nottingham Playhouse	Peter Moro and Partners	
The Coliseum, London	Frank Matcham, modernized by Martin Card	
The Thorndike Theatre, Leatherhead	Roderick Ham	Theatre Projects Consultants Ltd (lighting and sound)
The Royal Opera House, Covent Garden	Sir Edward M. Barry, amphitheatre modernized by Peter Moro and Partners	
The Piccadilly Theatre, London	Bertie Crewe	
Wyvern Theatre, Swindon	Casson, Conder & Partners	Theatre Projects Consultants Ltd
Theatre Royal, York	Modernized Patrick Gwynne	
Theatre Royal, London	John Nash	
Liverpool Playhouse	Hall, O'Donaghue & Wilson	

Photograph number, copyright (c) and photographer (p)

2:4 c Colin Westwood

2:7, 11:5, 12:4 c Theatre Projects Consultants Ltd

2:18, 2:20, 9:15, 10:2,3,4, 11:9, 13:1, 18:6 c by courtesy of TABS, published by Rank Strand Electric, p R. W. Sheppard (2:18, 2:20, 9:15, 10:2,3, 11:9), p Graphotos Studios (11:9b), p John Waterman

(10:4) 2:19, 7:5, 12:1, 15:6, 17:1, 17:6, 17:8,

18:5, 18:7, c Architectural Press, p John Isaacs (2:19), p W. J. Toomey (7:5, 18:7), C. J. Arthur (12:1, 17:1, 17:6, 17:8)

5:1, 9:8, 9:9, 9:14, 9:16, 9:17 c Hall Stage Equipment Ltd

9:6, 18:2, 18:3 c John Donat

9:25 c Mole-Richardson (Stage & Studio Engineering) Ltd

10:1 both parts from Diderot, p TABS library

10:5 c Group Three Photography Ltd

11:6, 12:5, 12:6 c Frank Page Studios

11:7 c British Insulated Callender's Cables Ltd

11:8 c Birmingham Repertory Theatre, p Willoughby Gullachsen

12:2 c Stage Sound (London) Ltd, p Group Three Photography

18:1, 18:4 c Concrete Quarterly, p Richard Einzig

18:8,9 c Reg Wilson photography

Bibliography

A.B.T.T. Information Sheet No 5 Safety Check Lists for Theatre Managements

Aloi, R. **Architetture per lo Spettacolo** Milan 1958 *Hoepli*

Aloi, R. **Teatri e Auditori Theatres and Auditoriums** Milan 1972 *Hoepli*

Baur-Heinhold, Margarete **Baroque Theatre** 1967 *Thames & Hudson* **(first German edition 1966)**

Bellman, Willard F. **Lighting the Stage** San Francisco 1967 *Chandler Publishing Company*

Bentham, Frederick **The Art of Stage Lighting** London 1969 *Pitman*

Bentham, Frederick **New Theatres in Britain** London 1970 *Rank Strand Electric Ltd.*

Burris-Meyer, H. & E. C. Cole **Theatres and Auditoriums (2nd edition)** New York 1964 *Reinhold* London *Chapman & Hall*

Burris-Meyer & Mallory **Sound Reproduction in the Theatre** New York 1965 Theatres Arts Books

Elsom, John **Theatre outside London** London 1971 *Macmillan*

Gascoigne, Bamber **World Theatre** London 1968 *Ebury Press*

Gillette, A. S. **Stage Scenery its construction and rigging**

Giteau, Cecile **Dictionnaire des Arts du Spectacle** Paris *Dunod*

Graubner, Gerhard **Theater-Aufgabe und Planung** Munich 1968 *Callway*

Greater London Council **Places of Public Entertainment Technical Regulations** Publication 378 London 1971 *G.L.C.*

Greater London Council **Play Safe — A guide to standards in halls used for occasional stage presentations.** London 1968 *G.L.C.*

Hartnoll, Phyllis (Editor) **Oxford Companion to the Theatre (3rd edition)** London 1967 *Oxford University Press*

Home Office **Manual of Safety Requirements in Theatres and Places of Public Entertainment** London 1935 *H.M. Stationery Office*

Joseph, Stephen **Theatre in the Round** London 1967 *Barrie & Rockliff*

Joseph, Stephen **The Story of the Playhouse in England** London 1963 *Barrie & Rockliff*

Joseph, Stephen **New Theatre Forms** London 1968 *Pitman*

Les Lieux du Spectacle **L'Architecture d'Aujourd'hui No. 152** October–November 1970

Marshall, Norman **The Other Theatre** London 1947 *John Lehman*

McCandless, Stanley **A method of lighting the stage** New York 1958 *Theatre Arts Books*

Mielziner, Jo **The Shapes of our Theatre** New York *Potter*

Mullin, Donald C. **The Development of the Playhouse** Berkeley and Los Angeles 1970 *University of California Press*

Nicoll, Alardyce **The Development of Theatre** London 1958 *Harrap*

Parkin, P. H. and Humphreys, H. R. **Acoustics, Noise & Buildings (2nd edition)** London 1963 *Faber & Faber*

Pilbrow, Richard **Stage Lighting** London 1970 *Studio Vista*

Schubert, Hannelore **The Modern Theatre** London 1971 *Pall Mall Press* **(first German edition 1971)**

Silverman, Maxwell & Bowman, Ned. A. **Contemporary Theatre Architecture** (includes extensive bibliography) 1965 *New York Public Library*

Southern, Richard **The Georgian Playhouse** 1948 *Pleiades Books Ltd*

Southern, Richard **The Open Stage** London 1953 *Faber & Faber*

Southern, Richard **The Seven Ages of the Theatre** London 1962 *Faber & Faber*

Southern, Richard **Proscenium and Sight Lines** London *Faber & Faber*

Sweeting, Elizabeth **Theatre Administration** London 1969 *Pitman*

'Tabs' Publications **Stage Planning 1971** London *Rank Strand Electric Ltd*

The American Theatre Planning Board Inc. **Theatre Check List** Middletown, Connecticut 1969 *Wesleyan University Press*

The Arts Council of Great Britain **The Theatre today in England and Wales** London 1970 *The Arts Council of Great Britain*

Warre, Michael **Designing and Making Scenery** London 1967 *Studio Vista*

Periodicals **A.B.T.T. Newsletter** *Association of British Theatre Technicians* London

Acta Scaenographica Praha 2, Vinohradská 2.

Buhnentechnische Rundschau Berlin

Tabs Quarterly *edited by Frederick Bentham* London *Rank Strand Electric Ltd., 29 King Street, London, WC2*

Theatre Crafts Rodale Press Inc. Emmaus, Pa. U.S.A.

Theatre Design and Technology *Journal of the U.S. Institute of Theatre Technology, New York.*

Index